——————————— One Teacher in Ten:
Gay and Lesbian Educators Tell Their Stories_____

One Teacher in 10

Gay and Lesbian Educators Tell Their Stories

Kevin Jennings

editor

Boston ♦ Alyson Publications, Inc.

Typeset and printed in the United States of America.

A trade paperback original from Alyson Publications, Inc.,
40 Plympton Street, Boston, Massachusetts 02118.
Distributed in England by GMP Publishers,
P.O. Box 247, London N6 4BW, England.

First edition: September 1994

5   4   3   2   1

ISBN 1-55583-263-6

LIBRARY OF CONGRESS CATALOGING-IN-PUBLICATION DATA

One teacher in 10 : gay and lesbian educators tell their stories /
    Kevin Jennings, editor. — 1st ed.
          p.   cm.
    Includes bibliographical references.
    ISBN 1-55583-263-6 : $9.95
    1. Gay teachers—United States—Biography.   2. Lesbian teachers-
-United States—Biography.   I. Jennings, Kevin, 1963–   .
    II. Title: One teacher in ten.
LB2844.1.G39O64   1994
371.'008'664—dc20   94-13204
                                                                        CIP

For
Pam Shime,
who flew across a continent to help me come out to my students,
&
for
John DiCarlo,
my real brother

IN MEMORIAM

Christopher Dunstan
Karl Laubenstein
Paul Marx

Colleagues, Mentors, Teachers, Friends,
killed by an epidemic of bigotry, greed, and political indifference.

"Tell yourself: none of this ever had to happen, and then go
make it stop, with whatever breath you have left.
Grief is a sword, or it is nothing."
—PAUL MONETTE

Contents

Acknowledgments

his is always the most anxiety-provoking part of a book for me. The help of innumerable people made this collection possible, and there is not space to thank them all here. Apologies go out to anyone omitted.

The first and most obvious place to begin is with Alyson Publications. Thanks go to Sasha Alyson for his support of the project from inception to completion; to Karen Barber, for her indefatigable attention to detail and warm personal support; and to Adrien Saks and Lynne Fletcher for their help.

Numerous organizations and individuals helped with outreach to make this anthology as broad and varied as it is. Among those who deserve special recognition are: Kathy Sorrells of the Pacific Northwest Association of Independent Schools; Melanie Dana, editor of the Gay, Lesbian, and Straight Teachers Network (GLSTN) newsletter; Wendy Leighton; Jan Smith; David Bruton; Tony Prince; the Lesbian Teachers Network; and GLAAD-LA.

The time to edit this anthology was afforded by a Joseph Klingenstein Fellowship at Columbia University's Teachers College for the 1993–94 academic year. I am grateful to the Klingenstein Fund (John Klingenstein, president) and Concord Academy (Tom Wilcox, head, and Joanne Hoffman, associate head), who together funded my fellowship. Pearl Kane, director of the Klingenstein Center, has been consistently supportive, and I also feel deeply indebted to the interim Klingenstein directors, James Van Amburg of the Dwight-Englewood School, and Veronica McCaffrey of the Convent of the Sacred Heart, whose personal and professional support remains a great source of inspiration to me.

My deepest thanks go out to my New York family, my fellow 1993–94 Klingenstein Fellows. Their enthusiasm, love, and support came at a time when it was deeply needed, and I have been truly blessed to be a part of this group. In alphabetical order, they are: Pat

Barnes; Lynn Bennediktson; Ann Emerson; Maureen Walsh Heffernan; Deborah Henry; Ed Kim; Alec Lee; Bob Riddle; Tom Stege; Charlie Tierney; and Jim Valhouli. I have to especially thank Pat Barnes, who was endlessly supportive and turned out to be pretty cool for a straight guy from Cleveland, and the entire Stege family — Tom, Susie, Erin, and Pyper — who adopted me, fed me dinner (even though I was always late), and generally made me feel like a million bucks. You would never know they were from Texas.

Numerous other friends helped to support me through a difficult and lengthy process. Among those who were there when I needed them most were, in alphabetical order: Ellen Abdow and Laurie Lindop; James Appleby; Devin Beringer; Nan Dunham and John White; Jeff Dupre; Stefan Dursch; Lee Fearnside; David Gorman; Kathy Henderson; Cynthia Katz; Wendy and Peter Kiritsy; Mark Melchior; Miriam Messinger; Arthur and Deborah Parlin; Jody and Bill Prinzvalli; Morgan Robinson; Chris Rowe; Jennifer Shannon; Amy Spencer and Richard Colton; and Michael Malone Starr. As usual, I wouldn't have been able to do any of this without the love and support of Bob Parlin.

Finally, the writers who have contributed their work are the whole reason this book exists in the first place. I thank them for their patience throughout the editing process, their courage in being willing to share their stories, and their leadership in creating a world where homophobia will be a thing of the past. Our schools are blessed to have them. Readers should be aware that, except when names are in quotations, all the names and locations mentioned in this book are real.

I was especially moved by the efforts of two contributors, Pat McCart and Gary Dowd, who wrote their essays while seriously ill. I honor the memory of these two fine educators, both of whom died in January 1994, shortly after sending me their final drafts.

Preface

*I*n the fall of 1988 I was called by the editor of a special issue of *Independent School* magazine, the premier professional journal for private schools in the U.S., which would focus on homophobia. He asked me to write an article about being an openly gay teacher. I was only twenty-four at the time, thought of myself as a beginning teacher and a relative nobody, and was therefore prompted to ask the Kerriganesque question: "Why me?" "Because you're the only one I know of," he replied.

Times have changed.

I knew times had changed when I spoke with Sasha Alyson about the idea for this book in December 1992. Having been a founder of GLSTN (the Gay, Lesbian, and Straight Teachers Network), I had seen firsthand the rise of homophobia as an issue that schools were, at last, beginning to address. In three years after its founding, GLSTN had grown to twelve hundred members and had sponsored conferences that drew hundreds of teachers, both gay and straight, who were tackling homophobia head-on in their schools. The number of "out" teachers in the group rose from a handful to hundreds in those few short years. Symbolizing the changes that were under way was the fact that William Weld, the governor of my adopted home state of Massachusetts, had honored GLSTN with a special gubernatorial proclamation in 1993 for its "outstanding contributions to quality education." Weld had even created a special Governor's Commission on Gay and Lesbian Youth to investigate homophobia issues, and the work of this Commission led to Massachusetts becoming the first state in history to ban discrimination against public school students on the basis of sexual orientation. At last, gay and lesbian educators seemed to be moving out of the shadow of bigotry into a light that revealed the depth of our invaluable contribution to American education.

But editing this book showed me that times had changed even more than I thought. I feared that these kinds of changes were limited to traditionally liberal states like Massachusetts and urban centers such as New York and Los Angeles. Being determined to put together a collection that reflected more than those realities, I worried about whether or not I would be able to find enough contributors to have any geographic balance in the book. I went out of my way in my "call for submissions" to reassure people that they did not have to be "out" to contribute, fearing that otherwise I wouldn't be able to muster enough essays to make a book.

What I discovered was that the revolution among gay and lesbian teachers has spread far beyond the places it is "supposed" to happen. Out lesbians in Ohio, openly gay men from Nebraska, even a "lemon" from Australia, all responded to my tentative call for submissions. With each story I received, my own sense of pride grew. I was thrilled to be one of those brave, determined, and committed folks who are America's gay and lesbian teachers. I found myself getting choked up when I read pieces, moved at times to tears by the heroism of the writers and the changes they were making in the lives of their students. I thought back to my first teaching job, where I was told to remove my earring or get fired, and didn't feel that fighting back was even an option. I couldn't wait to get the book to press, so that other lesbian and gay teachers, who perhaps felt as alone and isolated as I had then, would know that they were not alone, that they could fight back and win. I couldn't wait to show people how much times had truly changed.

Yet, in other ways, I was reminded that some members of the gay and lesbian community are not as free as others, even if times were changing. Three institutionalized barriers — regionalism, sexism, and racism — became painfully evident as I put this collection together. In my native South, few teachers were willing to contribute, even anonymously, so heavy is the hand of homophobia in the Land of Dixie. I was inspired by the three out Southern teachers who did contribute (two from my original home state of North Carolina), but was aware that their limited number spoke volumes about how unsafe their counterparts still feel.

Similarly, it became quickly apparent that women felt much more at risk than men in sharing their stories. The final collection is over sixty percent male, even though education is a female-dominated field. Furthermore, of the women who contributed, one-third felt the need to use pseudonyms for themselves or their hometowns, while only one man did so. Clearly, male privilege continues to exist.

Finally, my inability to bring greater cultural diversity to the collection was a tremendous disappointment. Over and over, gay and lesbian teachers of color expressed their tremendous anxiety over contributing to the book. In the process, they educated me on how homophobia, racism, and sexism can intersect in an individual's life in truly powerful and destructive ways. At one point, seven of the potential contributors, or approximately twenty percent, were people of color. But, as the deadline drew near, the bulk of those individuals felt compelled to withdraw, some for personal reasons but, more often than not, out of fear of the consequences of publishing their stories, even under assumed names. As a community, we have a long way to go before all of our members feel equally safe in leaving the closet behind.

Nevertheless, I believe the publication of this collection marks the beginning of the destruction of one of the most well-fortified closets in our community. For centuries, dominant groups in society have used the "they're after your kids" myth to marginalize subdominant groups. The stories change but the pattern is always the same. In nineteenth-century Russia, Jews were supposedly after Christian children to use their blood in the Passover Seder, a convenient fiction which was used to justify pogroms by the Christian majority; in early-twentieth-century America, the need to protect the sanctity of young white females was used as a pretext for the lynching of twelve hundred black men between 1900 and 1940; and today, the far Right ignores statistics that show heterosexual men (not gay men, not straight women, not lesbians) are the disproportionate majority of child sexual abusers, to proclaim that gay and lesbian people (gay teachers in particular) are motivated only by a desire to commit abuse. As long as we remain silent and allow our enemies to define us, we will never be free. Only through telling our stories can we shatter the myths and expose the lies that allow bigots to portray us as a threatening "other."

This collection shows gay and lesbian teachers in a truer light, as individuals triumphing over ignorance and oppression to lead their students into a future where people will truly be judged on the content of their character. In so doing, gay and lesbian teachers remain true to our nation's ideal of equal opportunity for all, and stand fast against those who would drag us back into a miasma of prejudice and fear for the benefit of their own narrow political agenda. As my fundamentalist father said so often in his sermons, "the truth shall set you free," and a simple truth was reinforced for me by the editing of this collection: A school with an openly lesbian or gay teacher is a better school. It is a school where truth prevails over lies; it is a school where isolated students at last have a place to turn for support; it is a school where our nation's rhetoric about equality moves one step closer to becoming a reality. As gay and lesbian teachers win our freedom, we help to free our students, our colleagues, and our communities of the burden of bigotry which has, for too long, taught some members of families to hate their own sisters, brothers, mothers, and fathers. We are the true upholders of "family values." I am proud to be associated with the thirty-five contributors who have generously shared their stories to make *One Teacher in Ten* a reality. I invite you to share in their memories, their journeys, their struggles, and their victories.

—Kevin Jennings
New York City
April 1994

NOTE: All individual and place names cited in this work are real, except in those cases where quotation marks indicate the use of a pseudonym.

Prologue

A Letter to Jerry

————David Ellison

Eighth-Grade Teacher
"Becket Middle School"
"San Francisco, California" ———————————

In addition to teaching, I write a column in The Argus, *a local paper. In my column, I write open letters to parents, teachers, students, politicians — to anyone, real or imaginary, as long as the person relates somehow to education. I try to raise the important issues about education that often get overlooked. The letter below is based on my own experiences as a young teacher in Texas.*

Dear Jerry,

I've tried to forget about you, how I let you down, leaving you utterly alone. But the gift you gave me — a clay statue of an Aztec king — still haunts me, denouncing me from atop my bookshelf, even as I write you this letter.

At the time, the statue seemed an appropriate Christmas gift for me, your high school Spanish teacher. Now I realize that nothing then was as it first appeared.

For example, nearly everyone considered you the most fortunate, enviable kid on campus. You were, after all, captain of our school's state champion football team. You excelled in all your classes too, especially mine.

Nonetheless, behind your easy success and your captivating smile, Jerry, you hid a dark secret: you were gay.

You never told me, of course, at least not with words. Yet, in many other not-so-subtle ways, you revealed your desperate longing for acceptance, for companionship.

I recall the day you first sought me out. It was after I had admonished a classmate for jokingly insulting another with the epithet "Faggot!"

"Pardon me," I chastised. "That is very offensive, even in fun. It's just as bad as any racial slur — expressing prejudice against people who are different. I won't tolerate it in my class."

At the end of the period, you lingered, Jerry, to tell me I was the first teacher you'd met who had ever defended homosexuals. After that, you stopped by often during lunch to chat, your questions becoming ever more personal. Was I married? Was I presently dating anyone? You seemed pleased when, distracted, munching on my sandwich, I shook my head.

At Christmas you timidly presented me with the statue. "I really like your class ... and you, Mr. Ellison." Then you grasped me in a clumsy hug.

I was flattered. But I still didn't get it. Perhaps I was too young, too naive. Or maybe I just didn't want to comprehend.

One evening a few weeks later, you came running up to me at a varsity basketball game. You insisted eagerly that I sit next to you in the bleachers. When I introduced you to the attractive woman at my side, though, you were stunned. You stared at me wide-eyed, shaking your head in disbelief and betrayal. Then, after muttering a choked "Pleased to meet you, miss," you fled the gym. At that awkward moment, I finally understood.

Jerry, I wish I had followed you, or reached out to you at some other time. I should have broached the taboo subject, assured you that you were not evil or weird and, above all, that you were not alone. But I was afraid. What teacher wouldn't be in a small, Catholic, homophobic high school in Texas?

I tried to laugh off the incident, to convince myself that I had misinterpreted your behavior. You made it easy for me. You retreated obediently back into your murky closet, and never approached me again. Indeed, you even went on to become prom king!

But your gift, the Aztec king on my shelf, still whispers otherwise, Jerry. And he reminds me bitterly that, in the end, I didn't deserve him.

Part One:

Memories

"The struggle of man against power is the struggle of memory against forgetting."

—Milan Kundera

I Remember

Kevin Jennings

History Teacher
Concord Academy
Concord, Massachusetts

I remember Mr. Hooker (his real name!), my seventh-grade gym teacher at Southwest Junior High School in Clemmons, North Carolina, in 1976. Quite simply, he scared the hell out of me. Whereas his co-teacher, Mr. Mercer, was all smiles and encouragement, Mr. Hooker seemed to have a smoldering rage burning inside him, and I tried to steer as clear of him as possible. He made gym class an ordeal.

This was a shame, because, as the youngest of four athletic boys, I loved sports, and was one of the better students in P.E. But there were even greater problems with gym class than dealing with Mr. Hooker. The locker room was a source of tremendous anxiety, as I was terrified that my eyes would linger a little too long on the male bodies around me, to which I was increasingly (and disturbingly) drawn. I wasn't yet ready to admit what that meant to myself, much less to anyone else.

Sometime in the winter we did a unit on wrestling. The stimulation of this particular sport was just a little too much for me, and I began to approach class with dread, as I feared for my ability to keep my feelings successfully hidden from my largely fundamentalist class-mates. One in particular, Gary, was the most distracting of all. With feathered blond hair parted in the middle (this *was* the eve of the disco era, after all) and a budding musculature that seemed to predestine him for the pages of *International Male*, Gary entranced me, even though I hated him and, more importantly, myself, for his doing so. I could barely take my eyes off him.

I was fighting just this internal battle on the day we began our wrestling unit, as Mr. Hooker droned on and on about the sport's scoring system. Try as I might, I just couldn't seem to look away from Gary, who was blissfully absorbed in Mr. Hooker's lecture. Mr. Hooker, however, seemed more attuned to where my eyes were focused. He stopped in midsentence, fixed his gaze on me, and said very slowly and clearly, "Stop looking at his legs."

As my classmates slowly turned to look at me amidst the dead silence of the wrestling room, I felt as if a stake had been driven through my heart. A few moments of silence passed, and Mr. Hooker then went back to his lecture.

I never went back to being the person I was before that moment. I never played on an organized school team again from that day forward, even though playing sports was (and is) a source of great joy for me. I never again felt like I belonged at school. I never forgot Mr. Hooker.

————
————

I remember Mr. Korn (not his real name), my ninth-grade geometry teacher at Mt. Tabor High School in Winston-Salem, North Carolina. I hated math, but I loved geometry. I loved geometry because I loved Mr. Korn. I loved Mr. Korn because he noticed me. One time, I had been out of class with the flu for a week. Fearing the effect on my grades, I had dragged myself back, even though I still wasn't feeling well. No one else much noticed my absence or my return, so I was feeling pretty sorry for myself by the time I went to Geometry. When he called the roll, Mr. Korn customarily stayed next to the overhead projector and rarely looked up. On this day, however, when he got to my name and I croaked, "Here," Mr. Korn looked up with a smile. "Kevin Jennings is back," he said, and then went back to calling the roll. In those few seconds, he let me know that I mattered to him. I would have walked off a plank if he'd asked me to.

While the other kids acknowledged Mr. Korn as a gifted and inspiring teacher, they also mocked him behind his back. Slightly effeminate and conspicuously unmarried, Mr. Korn was a "faggot." His being labeled that didn't bother me; it intrigued me. At Mt. Tabor High School, the only person who seemed to get called "faggot" as often as Mr. Korn was a sophomore named Kevin Jennings. Unlike Mr. Korn, I was not given the courtesy of having it done behind my back. Haunted by Mr. Hooker's "outing" in seventh grade, I was taunted daily in the hallways, in the locker room, in classes before the teacher called the roll, even during class. Whenever I volunteered to answer a question or write on the board, a slightly audible murmur from my classmates would arise. "Faggot," I would hear. I learned not to volunteer or raise my hand.

In Mr. Korn's class, it was different. While most teachers looked the other way in the face of this verbal onslaught, Mr. Korn made his class an oasis of safety. No one dared harass me there, perhaps because they feared Mr. Korn himself would take offense at the epithet. I was protected there, and Mr. Korn encouraged my participation. I found myself excelling in math, a feat never duplicated before or since in my academic career, as I would eventually go on to flunk pre-calculus senior year and took no more math in college. I excelled because I mattered, and was valued, and was safe, all conditions created by Mr. Korn.

One day in the spring of freshman year, I simply couldn't take my peers' harassment anymore. I fled my homeroom, where the lack of a teacher-directed lesson left plenty of space for verbal targeting, and fled to the library. I asked the librarian to go and get Mr. Korn, to tell him that I desperately needed his help. He came a few moments later, clearly concerned. I poured out the story of my harassment, fighting hard not to cry so I wouldn't look like a "faggot." Mr. Korn listened sympathetically, comforted me, and promised to speak with some of my other teachers about putting a stop to this. Grateful, I looked up at him and asked, "Do you have any children, Mr. Korn?"

Startled, he replied, "No. What makes you ask that?"

"Because I think you'd make a great dad. I think you should have children, Mr. Korn."

He laughed. "I don't think that will be happening, Kevin." And, with a smile, he was on his way.

I know now that Mr. Korn must have been gay. And I know that this was what I was asking when I queried after his children. What I was truly asking for, however, was not information about his sexual orientation. I was asking for information about me. I was asking him to tell me that I was going to be all right, that I was going to grow up and be gay and be okay. I was asking him to show me something I had never seen before in North Carolina: a gay man who was happy with himself.

In 1978, in the land of Jesse Helms, I was simply asking too much. Mr. Korn could never have told me what I needed to hear. He told me what he could. And that got me through freshman year.

———
———

I remember John, one of my history students at my first teaching job at the Moses Brown School in Providence, Rhode Island, in 1985. On the surface, John had everything going for him. A varsity soccer player, he was a gregarious, handsome boy with many friends and a bevy of girls who followed his every move. He hid his needy side well from his peers, but shared it with me. John's parents were working-class people of Portuguese descent, who had little connection with their prep school–educated son. His sisters had long ago moved out of the house, and John desperately needed an adult presence in his life. He wanted and needed a man who could serve as his role model. Early on in my days at Moses Brown, he latched on to me as just such a role model, and I was happy to take the time to help him. I felt like I was doing for him what Mr. Korn had done for me all those years ago.

All, however, was not well in my first teaching job. Fresh out of college, where I had been an openly gay activist, I found life at the Moses Brown School a bit of a shock to my system. My Harvard credentials had gotten me the job, but on my first day, I was quickly informed that the rules would be different for gay teachers in Providence than they were for gay students in Cambridge.

The headmaster took me aside after our first faculty meeting, a look of concern on his face. He said, "I'd like to talk with you about that piece of metal in your left ear." I had gotten an earring that summer, but, not being sure how I wanted to deal with being gay in the high school setting, it was my left ear that I had pierced, remembering the dictum "Left is right and right is wrong," to throw off any suspicions that this was a statement about my sexual orientation. It soon became clear that I had failed to throw this particular bloodhound off my scent. "If you're going to wear that tomorrow on the first day of classes," he continued, "don't bother coming in." Stunned and cowed, I took it out that night at home. I noted, a year later, that no such fuss was made when a colleague well known to be straight had the same ear pierced.

The whole experience of working at Moses Brown was difficult. Having grown used to freedom at Harvard, I couldn't adjust to the closet in Providence, a small city where you frequently run into students and parents in the course of daily life outside the school. The attitudes that my first encounter with the headmaster evinced hardly disappeared as time wore on. In one faculty meeting, an advisor encouraged the faculty to stop students from harassing a boy they had nicknamed "Veg," short for vegetable, because of his phlegmatic demeanor. "Better a veg than a fruit," the head quipped in response.

The classroom, by contrast, was an oasis for me. Filled with first-year enthusiasm, I eschewed our uninspiring texts and instead sought new ways to engage my students. I found primary documents, invented games designed to show how colonialism worked in Africa ("Wheel of Misfortune," I think I called it), and worked to get every student involved in discussion. I tried to remember the lesson Mr. Korn had taught me: if a student knows he or she matters to you, he or she will excel in your class.

These students were my lifeline. They loved my class, they loved my subject, they loved me. Feeling unloved by my colleagues (only two of whom, one a gay man mentioned on the dedication page of this book, ever invited me to a social occasion), their affirmation was crucial. Older teachers were scandalized by my teaching methods and my emphasis on topics such as African-American and women's history, and it was only the fact that my students loved this material so much that enabled me to fight off the pressure to conform to the school's norms. These kids deserve better than the run-of-the-mill textbook garbage, I told myself, and I hung in there.

John, in particular, was a source of pride for me. Underachieving in the rest of his classes, he shone in mine. Around the school he often took the time to run up to me to say hello and to share the important events of his day. Having been the youngest in my family, I got a kick out of playing older brother to John. I knew that I made him feel like he mattered and that, in turn, made me feel like my work mattered, even though I was earning only twelve thousand dollars and the disdain of my colleagues for doing it.

In the fall of my second year, I was assigned to coach the JV soccer team — even though I had never played soccer in my life. I was careful not to divulge this to the kids, never playing in practice with them, and relying on my motivational techniques to get me by. Surprisingly, this worked, and we ended up with a winning record. Although dangerously close to being exposed as an impostor, I accepted the congratulations of the athletic director (who never seemed to realize that my name wasn't Keith) and the varsity players like John, who came to our games when they could and seemed to think I knew what I was doing.

At one game, John and some of his varsity buddies were perched on the embankment behind the field, just within earshot as I coached. John's friends must not have realized they were within hearing distance, as they proceeded to initiate a debate over my sexual identity. "He's a fag," one of them said with certainty. John hotly defended me against this "slander," undoubtedly motivated by his affection for me. The debate wore on as I stood frozen, terrified to look around. Finally, John brought it to a conclusion with what he thought was the definitive statement. "He can't be gay," John said, "he's too *cool* to be gay. I know. He's my advisor."

I knew for a moment how Mr. Korn must have felt in 1978, at Mt. Tabor High School, in Winston-Salem, North Carolina. I desperately wanted to be able to say that I *was* gay, and that you could be "cool" *and* gay, that the person John admired and wanted to grow up to be like was *gay* and that this didn't change anything. But I couldn't. By the end of that year, I could no longer tolerate the tension this created, so I left the Moses Brown School.

After some perfunctory attempts to stay in touch, John and I drifted out of contact. I heard a rumor years later that he had developed a serious substance abuse problem in college, and was in fact a major supplier of drugs for his dorm. I felt guilty; even though I knew I was not directly to blame, I found it hard to forgive myself for leaving John. And I have found it impossible to forgive the Moses Brown School for making leaving the only option I could pursue and retain my sense of self.

––––––

I remember Brewster, a sophomore boy who I came to know in 1987, my first year of teaching at Concord Academy, in Concord, Massachusetts. Brewster was a charming but troubled kid. His grades didn't match up with his potential, his attendance could be irregular, and he often seemed a little out of it. He was clearly using some substance regularly, and was not very happy with himself. But I didn't have a clue as to why — at least not at first.

I had come to Concord from Moses Brown in search of a place where I could be more open about who I was. I wore a ring that symbolized my commitment to my partner, and students like Brewster started asking me what it meant. Confused, I went to the head to ask how I should respond. "Tell them it's a gift from someone you love," he said. Incredulous, I replied, "Do you say *your* wedding ring is a 'gift from someone you love'?" I answered Brewster's question about my ring honestly. To my surprise, he and the other students who asked didn't turn away from me, unlike my peers who had turned away from Mr. Korn in 1978. They didn't seem to care much at all about my being gay.

Toward the end of my first year, during the spring of 1988, Brewster appeared in my office in the tow of one of my advisees, a wonderful young woman to whom I had been "out" for a long time. "Brewster has something he needs to talk with you about," she intoned ominously. Brewster squirmed at the prospect of telling, and we sat silently for a short while. On a hunch, I suddenly asked, "What's his name?" Brewster's eyes widened briefly, and then out spilled a story about his involvement with an older man he had met in Boston. I listened, sympathized, and offered advice. He left my office with a smile on his face that I would see every time I saw him on the campus for the next two years, until he graduated.

I was thrilled to be able to do for Brewster what I had wanted Mr. Korn to do for me ten years before. But the conversation also left me troubled. I had been playing a variation on the "don't ask, don't tell" game with my students. If they asked, I told, but otherwise my sexual identity was not a fit topic for discussion. I grew uncomfortable with the message this was sending, with the air of secrecy and shame and scandal that my quasi silence implied. I decided I needed to come out in a more forthright and honest fashion, and made plans to do so the fall of 1988, my second year at Concord.

The venue I chose was chapel. Three times a week, the entire school gathers in the school's nonsectarian chapel, to hear a talk by a senior or a faculty member on a topic of their choosing. It is the central ritual of school life, and a forum wherein personal sharing is commonplace. I decided to come out here, and signed up to give my chapel on October 11, 1988 — the first-ever National Coming-Out Day, and the anniversary of the 1987 March on Washington for Lesbian and Gay Rights, which had been a turning point in my life. It seemed like the right way to commemorate the event and, more importantly, the right way to let students like Brewster know that they should feel no shame over being gay.

I met with my head early upon returning that fall to discuss my plans with him. He reacted with alarm, fearing that such a public statement would frighten off potential applicants and alumni donations to the school. He asked me to postpone the talk while we "worked things out," and I reluctantly agreed to do so as a sign of respect for his goodwill. In the meantime, my intentions had become a surreptitious topic of fierce debate among the faculty and eventually the students. Everyone seemed to know that I was planning to come out, and that whether or not the school would support me was hanging in the balance. It had turned into a litmus test about how the institution viewed gay people. The import of my postponement was duly noted, and I worried about the message this was sending.

None of this was helped by the fact that I was twenty-four and in the midst of a performance review that would determine whether or not I would be offered a permanent position at the school. I had no role models. I didn't know a single openly gay teacher at that time, and had no sources of support from other gay people at the school. In fact, an older, closeted teacher had come to meet with me at the head's request, and had reacted with horror at my plans. My resolve began to falter. Over lunch one day with some straight colleagues, I poured out my confusion, and confessed that I was thinking of canceling my chapel talk. One of them looked at me and said slowly, "If you do, you will never be able to look at yourself in the mirror again. No job is worth that." I decided then that I had to go forward, no matter what the consequences might be.

On November 10, 1988, I rose to the pulpit of the Concord Academy chapel, my talk in my hands, sweat drenching my button-down shirt and soaking through to my blue blazer. My best friend had flown overnight from California to be there. A former teacher at the school named Karl Laubenstein, a gay man who had always wished to come out but had never been able to do so, came almost directly from the hospital to support me, leaning on a cane, as his recent bout of AIDS-related pneumocystis made it hard for him to walk very far. But, most importantly, Brewster had found me in the dining hall right before chapel, had stuck by my side as I walked across campus, and had then perched himself in the front row. We hadn't discussed the whole controversy around this chapel. We hadn't even talked about what I was planning to say. But he knew, and I could tell from the look in his eyes how much my decision to go forward meant to him. I knew I had done the right thing.

Fifteen minutes later, I dismissed the students, having told them about my struggle with being gay when I was their age, a struggle that led to serious substance abuse problems and attempted suicide before I finally learned to love myself as a gay man. The reaction had seemed to be positive, and when I signaled for them to leave, I felt things had gone reasonably well. I didn't expect what happened next. Kids literally leapt up from their pews and rushed the pulpit, surrounding me and hugging me, many of them crying as they tried to thank me for what I had done. I was overwhelmed, and spent a good chunk of my first class embracing them. When I realized I was fifteen minutes late for U.S. History, I ran across the campus to my classroom and burst in, out of breath, to find the board covered with graffiti. I temporarily blanked out, so sure was I that they had written homophobic epithets across the slate. When my vision returned, I read what they had actually written. "We love you, Kevin, and we're so proud of you," it read. Each student had signed the board. Embarrassed and speechless, I simply erased the board, turned, and said, "Okay, let's talk about the Erie Canal." They smiled and opened their books to the right page.

Brewster's problems didn't go away overnight. He struggled with substance abuse and probably got grades below what he should have gotten throughout his time at Concord. But he knew that it was okay to be gay and that he had a place to turn for support, and this enabled him to make it through high school in one piece. In 1990 he graduated from Concord, and went off to college. Except for a few phone calls, I heard little from him, and lost track of him as the years went by.

———————

I remember April 3, 1993, when I went to Club Cafe, a gay restaurant in Boston, for the annual awards dinner of the Coalition for Lesbian and Gay Civil Rights. An organization I had helped found, GLSTN (the Gay, Lesbian, and Straight Teachers Network), was being honored that night, and I had come to accept the award on our behalf. I sat with some friends, my back to the center of the room, and soon got engaged in conversation. From behind me, I heard a familiar voice. "Care for a drink, sir?"

I turned and it was Brewster. Shocked, we were both speechless for a moment, before we hugged each other and caught up. He was now twenty-two, taking time off from college, and living with his boyfriend. His smile showed that he had found his way to a happy adulthood. In that moment, I remembered why I had gone into teaching in the first place.

Spontaneously, I dedicated the award that night to Brewster, who stood mortified in the back of the room while I talked about our relationship. The key moment came when I recalled my own experience with closeted gay teachers in high school (Mr. Korn was *hardly* the only one), and how that had influenced me to come out as a teacher myself. "I'll be damned," I said, "if I will remain closeted and help teach another generation of young gay and lesbian people to hate themselves." Despite all of the struggles I had been through at my school, seeing Brewster that night made it all worthwhile.

The last time I saw Brewster was at the 1993 Boston Gay Pride March. He was standing on the side with his boyfriend as GLSTN marched past. He called my name and I broke away briefly to hug him and say hello. As I stood amidst the sunshine on the beautiful June day, I looked at Brewster, and I thought: You made it. I made it. We, as gay students and gay teachers, are going to make it, no matter how many obstacles and barriers stand in the way of our liberation.

———

I remember when I didn't think I could do any of this. And I am happy that that feeling of hopelessness is now only a memory.

Skeleton Key

——————Hope E. Burwell

English Teacher
North Tama High School
Traer, Iowa

I live in the country, nestled among the hills and fields stretching between Iowa's cities; where I can watch deer browsing on the hayfield at evening; where I must stop my car in the lane so thirty-seven wild turkey may pass on their morning trek to breakfast; where my girlfriend, Sandy, and I work a 640-acre family farm. When I went back to college in 1985 (not so much tired of farming as hungry for company and the sense of affecting the world), I went to round out a bachelor's degree with the course work necessary to certify myself to teach in secondary school. I intended to teach in the country, in one of those red brick buildings that, except for the feed mill, is the tallest one in the town. I intended to open a few insular minds.

Iowa's rural schools keep the steady beat of local life pumping. The seasons here are marked not by solstices, but by school calendars, which darken parks and swimming pools, lighting athletic fields, band rooms, drama stages. Parents know and care about what teachers do, and think, and are. They may see the inside of the gymnasium far more often than the insides of our classrooms, but they know what's going on there, in their school.

So, when it came time to interview for teaching jobs, I knew two things: I'd teach in a fishbowl; and having been an out, farming, politically active lesbian for more than ten years, I wouldn't land a job anywhere near home. I got out an Iowa highways map and a compass I hadn't used since tenth-grade Geometry. Setting the point of the compass down in the heart of our farm, I began to draw concentric circles around us: twenty miles in radius, thirty, forty, fifty. I'd be willing to drive sixty miles one way, I decided, if it would give me some experience in the classroom, some effect on the world, and not force me to leave the farm or my girlfriend. I applied to every school district with a secondary job opening in that sixty-mile radius, and hunkered down to wait.

In the meantime, Sandy's father, principal of a nearby elementary school, said very shyly one afternoon, "What will you say in the interview, about your, uh, living situation?"

"As little as possible," I answered. "I'm walking into those interviews with a four-point grade average and letters of recommendation that glow in your hands. I'll dazzle 'em with pedagogical theory."

He looked somberly back. "All that won't mean a thing if you seem suspicious."

"Suspicious," I laughed. "What's suspicious about a thirty-year-old back-to-the-lander wanting to be a schoolteacher in her middle age?"

"A woman," he said levelly, trying hard to make me see sense as he saw it, "unmarried and attached in some mysterious way to a farm, is suspicious. You can acknowledge ten years of farm labor on your resume because it's honorable-enough work. But they're going to want to know with whom you've been doing it."

"It's none of their business," I countered angrily. "It's against the law to ask if I'm married."

"Hope," he said, his forty-odd years of principalship rising authoritatively in his voice, "it's time you thought up a good lie or two."

Every nerve in my body tingled resistance. "I don't want to live on lies," I groaned. "In silence for a year or two maybe, but not on lies."

He shook his head. "There won't be silence. Not if you don't tell them something from the very beginning that will prevent their asking anything else." He looked across the oak table his daughter had made the first year she'd worked the farm alone. "How would a woman your age, born and raised in the city, come to spend her twenties on a farm?"

I sighed and then smiled naughtily at his daughter. "Fell in love with a farmer."

He winced visibly and I stopped being a brat. "Married a farmer," I corrected myself.

"Okay," he shook his head. "But you don't want to tell them you're married and have to live with a missing husband. How'd you end up with that husband's farm?"

"He died," I groaned. "Farm accident."

The old principal nodded his head slowly, testing out the credibility of the story. "What kind?"

"No way," I groaned again. "I'm not getting into this, a million invented details I'll have to keep straight."

"Exactly," Sandy said very quietly, as depressed with the need for the lie as I, "so the answer to how he died has to be something they won't ask questions about."

———

I turned down the first job offer because the "extra duties" included coaching a cheerleading squad. I didn't get the second job because, when they told me I'd need to choose between cheerleading and pompoms, I said, "I don't approve of teenage girls wiggling their asses on a basketball court." I didn't get the third job, teaching developmental reading and Native American literature in a school populated largely by members of the Mesquakie tribe, because they found an equally qualified Hawaiian and, I had to agree, a nonwhite teacher was more desirable than I. By the fourth interview, the quiet lie barely rankled.

"You live in, let's see, Dundee — that must be sixty miles from here, isn't it?" he queried.

"Almost seventy-five. But it'll be a beautiful commute. Good roads. Time every morning to think about what I'm going to do."

"So, you plan to stay in Dundee?"

"Yes, sir. It's hard to move a 640-acre farm."

"Oh, you're married to a farmer."

"Was." Pregnant pause. Make him feel his own prying.

"Your husband, uh...?"

"Committed suicide."

"Ah. Yes. I'm sorry. And journalism: you're willing to sponsor the newspaper, or perhaps advise the yearbook staff?"

———

A quiet lie, no embellishments, like a skeleton key. It unlocked a number of doors, not least of them the heavy fire door on the red brick building at the top of the hill in Traer, Iowa. Like most Iowa schools, it was a very good one, with a competent, deeply entrenched faculty, a solid curriculum, very little social vision, and a sore need for an idealist in the English department. That quiet lie unlocked the door to Room 311, where a superintendent and a principal who hired me for my credentials left me alone to do what I thought fit; to structure my own curriculum, to write my own rationales, to choose the texts and the contents my students and I would discuss. And maybe, most important, that quiet lie unlocked the barriers many of my students would have built around themselves had they known I was a lesbian.

It was difficult enough, believe me, for them to accept a strong, independent, liberal, unmarried woman, who drove more than an hour every morning to appear before them, her knuckles gouged and scabbed over with farmwork, the hands that tousled their hair calloused against their cheeks. Insecure and sexist, my male students resented having before them living proof that a woman could, even in physical labor, be their equal. Insecure and sexist, my female students resented having before them someone refusing to play the femininity game: no skirts, no heels, no makeup, and somehow still likable. It took at least a semester for them all to get used to me, and I wondered, often, on that long drive home in the evening, whether that would ever have happened if I hadn't told the lie.

Sandy and her father, rural Iowans all their lives, had been right about the silencing effect of that suicide. No one ever asked me about the dead husband, though they made up their own lies about it. In the hallways, at their lockers, or in the teachers' lounge before anyone realized I had entered, I learned all the gory details: what the man had looked like, how old he'd been, how he'd blown his brains out in the bathroom leaving poor Ms. Burwell to find him, to clean up the mess. I pretended not to hear. They pretended not to wonder, and left me holding a skeleton key weighing heavily in my palm.

———————

I'd come among them intending to open a few insular minds. When I started teaching in Traer there was one nonwhite student in a K–12 building of six hundred students. I asked her one September day as she worked in the back of my room, creating a bulletin board in Greek and Latin, if the two toddlers at home were also Asian. "No," she said quietly, a little puzzled by the word *Asian*. "They're normal."

———————

In November I reluctantly followed my students down to the school gymnasium for an assembly. I'd much rather have stayed behind in a silent classroom, luxuriated in an hour of uninterrupted time to check yearbook copy or read student journals. But, obediently, I shepherded an unstraying flock to a gym smelling of adolescent anxiety and aging varnish.

Half a dozen potbellied veterans holding the flags of their wars and wearing American Legion hats paraded the flag up and down the length of the gym in front of six hundred kids, ages five through seventeen, who had never known war, much less want or struggle. The kids listened dutifully to their principal make a speech of loyalty and support, applauded politely when the superintendent introduced the president of the American Legion local, and listened attentively to her.

Suddenly I stopped stifling yawns, straightened my back, and listened as that gray-haired woman told a gymnasium full of kids that their country was great and their constitution two hundred years old because theirs was a Christian government. "It was the grace of God and Jesus marching with the Allies that stopped the Germans in World War II," she said. "It was Jesus flying with those bomber pilots that put an end to the war in the Pacific."

I looked at my colleagues. None of them blinked, stared, seemed the least startled. The principal and the superintendent who had hired me sat behind the speaker, smiling benignly as the woman went on and on. Row after row of aluminum bleachers rattled with people standing to pledge allegiance to the flag of a Christian country. I stayed seated. A colleague on one side jostled my arm. A student on the other stared down in disbelief, and then, anxious, put her hand over her heart and looked reverently at the flag.

On the way back to my classroom, I changed lesson plans and substituted a class discussion on patriotism, on the concepts of choice and judgment in a free citizenry. I would start by asking them to think, to open a dictionary, and to write for a few minutes on the meaning of the phrase "to pledge allegiance."

They had just settled into the task when the office-to-classroom speaker in my room crackled to life. "Please come to the superintendent's office," a female voice said in a tone normally reserved for children. I talked back. "I have a class this period. The assembly upset the schedule, remember? I don't have a prep period today." It felt silly talking to a dark hole in the wall. "I'll be down at the end of the day."

The box died and a minute later came back to life again. This time a stern male voice penetrated my classroom. "...In my office, now." I looked around at my students. I'd seen this look on their faces half a dozen times; they knew when one of their own was in trouble. I smiled weakly. "Please, go on writing and thinking about what it means to pledge allegiance to something. We'll talk about all this tomorrow."

I walked briskly down the silent hallways and echoing stairwells, breathing purposefully, wondering if the ACLU would handle this suit, and if they worked for free. In the newly carpeted office, behind an enormous slab of walnut desktop, sat a silent superintendent looking as if he'd been betrayed. Across from him, their backs to me, were an aged principal and an angry Legionnaire. The Legionnaire rose as I entered, his face scarlet with fury. I half expected him to spit at my feet, but he passed, closed the door behind him.

I stood, waiting. The principal, a man who had told me three times in as many months that I was a remarkably talented first-year teacher, asked me quietly to sit, and we three made a triangle. The man behind the desk tapped his fountain pen absently on the felt blotter and looked at me, pained. "You stayed seated during the Pledge of Allegiance?"

"Yes," I said.

The old principal used his most grandfatherly voice. "We can't have that. We have an obligation to educate patriots. We—"

"I have no obligation to educate patriots," I said quietly.

The superintendent started. "You don't believe it's part of your duty to teach democratic actions?"

"Yes," I said. "Democratic actions include staying seated during the Pledge of Allegiance."

"Now, now," the principal said. "You're not in college anymore. You're a teacher now. You set an example. You have to be conscious of that. We don't want these kids to follow the example you set today, do we?"

"If they're conscientiously driven to do so, we do," I said, looking at him, my heart pounding so loudly in my ears that the secretary's typing in the other room was drowned.

The superintendent's feet hit the Plexiglas beneath his chair with a clap. He leaned forward, pointing at me, threatening. "This is a conservative town. These kids respect their flag. Those veterans fought for it. You've embarrassed me and insulted some of the most prominent men in the town. It'll stop, and you'll apologize."

Following the principal's lead, I tried to keep my temper. I looked long at the superintendent, and shortly at the older man before speaking. "No," I said, "I won't apologize. You should apologize. What you allowed to happen in that gym today is illegal. Public schools are supposed to be free of religious worship." I kept speaking as the superintendent tried to interrupt. "That woman led a prayer in the gymnasium. She did it after insulting anyone in the room who isn't

Christian. The Supreme Court has named that an illegal act. And you allowed it. I don't owe anyone an apology."

He burst from his chair, storming. "This isn't some place where you can hold any radical belief you have and not be noticed. This is a small town and you are a small-town teacher. The community expects patriotism, and you'll give it to them when you're teaching for us."

"Yes," I said, standing. "I will. I'll teach them the term 'free country' means they have the right to voice an opinion or refuse to pledge allegiance—"

He cut me off. "No!" he shouted. "You will not teach them they may refuse to pledge allegiance. Not in my sch—"

"Yes!" I yelled back. "I will. You paid three thousand dollars two weeks ago to put your teachers through an in-service on developing thinking skills in their students. I will do that. I will help them develop thinking skills by teaching them to ask questions, not to make blind pledges to a government. I will teach them to think deeply and to follow their consciences, not what some authority figure tells them to do."

"You," said the principal, for the first time, angry, "are about to get yourself into trouble."

"No," I said, turning toward the door, placing a hand on the knob, and looking back over my shoulder at my employers, "you are. I did, today, in that gym, what the constitution you had us there celebrating allows me to do. I stayed seated. I have the right to do that. And, if you fire me for using that right, you will being teaching our students about fascism."

I didn't realize, until I saw the secretaries' faces in the reception room, how loud my voice must have been. They stared, open-mouthed, hands motionless over their typewriters. I didn't realize how angry I was until I heard my own breathing in the silent corridor, until I felt the heat in my face.

I cried all the way home in the car, angry and frustrated, wondering how I would tell my family I'd been fired. I bought my first pack of cigarettes in a year, rented a long movie, and drank Scotch, smoked cigarettes, and vegetated until I could fall asleep.

The next morning, as I put the period on the end of a quotation on the board, a noise behind me made me turn. In the doorway stood the principal and the superintendent, who spoke. "We'd like to forget yesterday afternoon," he said. "A disagreement among colleagues, period."

My knees buckled. I leaned against the chalk tray to keep myself up. Smiling weakly, I nodded, "Okay."

They turned away. I signed the eighteenth-century quote and was surprised to see the principal still in the doorway, reading, when I turned again. He read it once, and again, and, shaking his head slowly, walked out of the room. "Patriotism is the last refuge for fools and scoundrels." I read it aloud, nodded, and smiled. There were great arguments in Room 311 that day.

———

By my third year in that little Iowa school, my classroom library had become a very carefully sculpted work of art. I'd frequented book sales, library clean-out days, Goodwill stores, leafing through the books sections for titles and authors that would fit.

Not just anything would have done. I was making a library that meticulously reflected the population of the U.S.: 52 percent of the books must be by or about women; 48 percent by or about men; 11 percent by or about black people; 17 percent by or about Jews; 10 percent by or about gay and lesbian people; 1 percent by or about differently abled people. The ratios and proportions went on, carefully.

I never assigned a common book to read, but they had a common assignment. "In the course of the semester you may read whatever you like, but your reading must reflect the population of this country." The students fidgeted when told they had to read about people of color, and they rebelled when told they had to read about gay or handicapped people. And when they rebelled, I got nervous. I'd sit down behind my desk, so they could not see me dance off the hot coals under my feet. I'd look at them, pull a stern mask down over my fear, and speak with a tone of authority salvaged from the wreckage of my fears. "You will do it. There is a world full of people outside of this town, and you must find a way to get to know them. So, you'll read. In some small way, you'll begin to see that being who we are doesn't mean we are better; it may not even mean we are different. If you object to a particular book you select, put it back on the shelf and choose another. But, remember, to get a C, your reading must reflect the population of this country, and this library will make that fairly easy, because it reflects the same population."

Being children, my students rarely took their objections from the room. But on rare occasions they'd pack them up and take them home. At the supper table, when Dad was in a particular foul mood, or Mom more rabid than usual about the pro-choicer who shared her cubical at the office, they'd spill out the gory details of their new English class.

"Do you know, Mom, that in order to get an A in English this semester I gotta read two books about Jews, one about niggers, and one about queers?"

The principal appeared in my doorway at least once a semester to report a parent complaining about the reading requirements. I'd swallow hard and listen to the sound of my heartbeat growing faster and louder, envisioning a call before the school board that seemed to grow more conservative with each election.

"Yes," I'd say to him. "I suspected it would upset that student. That's too bad, I'd guess she needs the diversity in this library more than anyone else in the class."

He'd nod sadly. "I know, but we can't force her. Let her skip the books about black people and lesbians."

"Okay," I'd sigh, frustrated, trying not to think about this one student but about the other twenty sampling a world differently colored and textured than their own.

"I still think," he'd always say before leaving, "that, if you'd get rid of the queer books, we could fight these bigots."

Every time he said it I was glad I had taken Sandy's father's advice and told that quiet lie. They let me among them because they thought I was one of them. Being a lesbian would have made me "Other," and I have no doubt they would not have allowed me to push their boundaries as often and as hard as I did had they known.

The skeleton key had unlocked a number of doors. But it probably locked just as many. I never made a close friend on that faculty, though there were many people I liked and admired. I simply couldn't bear the moment when I would have to admit the lie, so instead I held my distance. And, of course, there were gay and lesbian kids deprived of a role model because I'd lied about my identity. In the end, that lie cost me my secondary teaching career.

Late one afternoon, the superintendent who had hired me, who had come to my defense on a half dozen occasions when parents or fellow teachers thought I was pushing the envelope too hard, called me to his office. On his desk lay a copy of a magazine in which I had recently published an essay. The biographical note attached to the essay said, among other things, that I taught at North Tama High School in Traer, Iowa. Paperclipped to the magazine was a typed, unsigned note.

"Have a seat, Hope," he said, oddly subdued. Silently, he slid the magazine across his desk to me and I read the note. "Are you aware that Hope Burwell is a lesbian?"

I could hear his wristwatch ticking. After several pregnant seconds I looked up. "Do you want me to respond to this?"

"Yes," he said, his voice almost a plea. I liked this man. We'd had our differences, but I'd grown to care very much for him, and to respect the way he dealt with faculty, gave them free rein, let them explore their profession and their potentials.

"Gary," I said finally, "if I admit to this I'm going to martyr my career to a cause; if I deny it, I'm going to become part of the homophobia that makes the accusation dangerous in the first place. I refuse to respond. The ball is in your court."

We listened to his watch tick off the seconds. Finally he smiled very weakly. "You have a yearbook to advise, I believe."

Several weeks later he offered me a contract for the next academic year, but I couldn't sign it. I couldn't make another human being professionally uncomfortable carrying my secret. I couldn't sustain my own righteous indignation about other kinds of hypocrisy in the face of someone who knew my lie. So, I walked out of that high school and turned the key on my secondary teaching career. I went back to graduate school and earned two master's degrees. In my first college-level teaching job interview I came out to a committee of four startled faces, all of them politically correct enough to feel proud of themselves for hiring an out lesbian.

I miss teaching high school the way amputees are said to miss a limb, a ghostly ache that accompanies me some days. But the quiet lie doesn't thunder through my dreams anymore.

Wanda and the Wastebasket

Arthur Lipkin

English Teacher
Cambridge Rindge and Latin High School
*Cambridge, Massachusetts*_____

I remember those old school wastebaskets — stolid, dull green metal ones at the side of the teacher's desk. In grammar school we had to ask permission to throw something away in them; in high school, we approached at our own discretion. In the first three chapters of my story, such a wastebasket figures as a bit player, but in the fourth, it is duly featured in a supporting role.

I

In 1959–1960, my seventh- and eighth-grade years, school was the center of my life. It was the arena in which I could assure myself, often with the help of heavily perfumed, rouged, and bosomed Irish-American spinster teachers, that I was one of the fairest-haired boys in the world, despite polite inferences that I was somewhat handicapped by being Jewish. I was proud of my religion and needed positive assurances for other reasons: I was not skilled on the playground, nor was I a budding lothario like most of my male friends. On the contrary, rather than modeling myself *on* Ricky Nelson, I would have preferred to mold myself *onto* Ricky Nelson. I could never admit such desires, however, even to my private self.

Instead I could be a star student and teachers' pet, editor of the school newspaper, occasional leading man, conveyor of teachers' notes (even to the principal's office), and operator of both the duplicating machine and the movie projector.

My decision to become a teacher had its origin in that singular place where I could be a Jew and a sissy and not only survive but thrive. That was unthinkable for me on the street from which I once ran, stanching a bloodied nose with my white sailor hat and trailing my little red wagon. Above all, I could excel in academics. In the early grades I got gold stars, flower seals, and animal ink stamps on my tests, and later, I got into the fast lane to the honors track. In school, I could even use my brain to avoid a fight. One day I told a bully who wanted to beat me up that I conceded the fight to him and dared him to a contest involving history questions. He was so nonplused he let me walk away. One may think my ploy could just as easily have inspired him to kill me, but timing is everything and one had to be there.

The Longfellow School provided a benign refuge for me from the frightening tangle of male combat and most organized sports. The New England climate and the absence of a gymnasium made the usual athletic contests impossible. But my salvation was not complete; there was always recess. And many times, wastebasketball. First, I emptied the basket of paper, pencil shavings, milk cartons, cellophane cookie wrappers, and the warm, sweet-scented milk that had dribbled down and seeped around wads of hardened old gum. Would that my light tattoo on the dented metal had charmed it for my ordeal to come.

The basket was placed on a desk in a wooden base that propped it at an angle for the game. Everyone counted off by twos, forming long lines for the shooting. Girls and boys both composed the teams and the blackboard was marked for scorekeeping. No one expected the girls to do well. Their shots frequently careened off and were caught by the more agile boys. The boys, on the other hand, were terrific — all but a handful who couldn't score a basket. I don't remember now who the others were, but I was one. I would have had better luck by just focusing on the wastebasket opening, but I couldn't risk that. I had to keep an eye on my audience and gauge from their grimaces whether my form was manly enough. So style won out over skill and I never got it in.

One failure is particularly memorable. I may have been distracted by Ursula, a German immigrant whose precocity frightened me. (One day she was sent home for wearing a tasseled blouse that left her midriff bare.) My throw bounced so wildly that it shot out the open second-floor window. Before anyone else could react, Lenny, a short muscular boy, hopped to a crouch on the windowsill and jumped from the building.

A few of the others ran to peer after him. Not me. I couldn't have survived seeing him in pieces. At that moment, Miss Bateman, who had been out of the room during the whole episode, returned to ask what all the commotion was about. Our answer stilled her twitchy narrow mouth for the first time. Just then, the door opened and Lenny came back into the room, glowing like a hero, clutching the ball in his nail-bitten hands. A light sweat glistened on his broad forehead. He flipped the ball to fat Eddy Boukawiecz and sat down.

He probably wanted to impress Ursula. Lenny struck me as a little crazy, like another boy who lived in the three-decker behind the one where we rented. He bared his buttocks to me once and said "fucking" from the third grade on. These were the kind of boys toward whom I threw sidelong glances when we got to the high school, where there was a gymnasium. And a locker room.

II

In my sophomore year at what was then Cambridge High and Latin School, my quest for best-little-boy status was at full throttle. I filled my class schedule and had only one study period a week, for which I had to sit at the back of Miss Supple's Italian I class and keep quiet. That was a challenge, because the only other study pupil was my friend Liz. Big-limbed, with joyous brown eyes, Liz was the brilliant daughter of Viennese refugees. She had the best sense of humor; that is, she liked my bad puns. Miss Supple's goofy teaching style, vacant stares, and Minnie Mouse feet often brought us to hysterics.

Liz was obsessed with Elizabeth Taylor and had a dramatic flair of her own. I was less starstruck, though a bare-chested movie magazine picture of Richard Chamberlain still lingers in my cortex. We were both in the Drama Club. As with so many other proto-gay boys, it was the center of my extracurricular life. I played stodgy character bits a la Tony Randall, wry humor (Feste the clown), and a few serious parts like Shylock. Insofar as I was repressed, ironic, and Jewish, I was typecast in all my roles.

Our drama club advisor was a chain-smoking hemophiliac, Mr. Border. He was moody and demanding and was the best high school director in the state. We all feared and adored him and were only occasionally critical of his arbitrary snits. We knew he was gay; he had a wistful Italian sometime-lover, who visited our rehearsals when he wasn't in New York, trying to make it off-Broadway. But Mr. Border's homosexuality was never openly named; its character was only expressed in meaningful looks and double entendre.

Liz and I cracked him up with our ad-libs and shtick. We wanted so much for him to approve of our work and to like us. I wouldn't let myself think too much about his sexuality, but I felt uneasy whenever he touched me.

Every afternoon when we weren't rehearsing, Liz and I went over to her family's apartment in a yellow brick building on Harvard Street to do homework together. Dizzy from our math, we joked and horsed around. Once Liz was reading a book called *Mention My Name in Mombassa,* so we improvised skits using the title. I was Patrick Henry rising in the House of Burgesses: "I know not what course others may take, but as for me ... mention my name in Mombassa."

Another time we cavorted in the living room to Rimsky-Korsakov and worked ourselves into an uncharacteristic (at least for me) erotic warmth. I waited for Liz to make a move, but she did not. I lay on the rug in a semifetal position and expected I don't know what. That was it for me heterosexually in 1962 — vague unease, moments of anticipation, and passivity.

It was a little different for me homosexually. A boy I met at summer camp when I was fourteen played with me a few times on randy masturbatory sleep-overs at his house. We acted always as if these activities never happened. I persuaded myself that the urges that precipitated such lapses would pass. Perhaps Liz would help.

And the wastebasket? For that we must go back to the Italian class. The bell had just rung and the students herded toward the door. Liz went by Miss Supple's desk with a wad of crumpled paper. Instead of throwing it away straight on, she pivoted to make an across-the-chest reverse hook shot. Her newish shoes slid out from under her on the polished tile and she fell with a squeal on her broad backside. I cackled at the sight of Liz's reddening face and Miss Supple, in her loose pumps, clattered over to her.

"Who pushed you?" she asked and turned, with a glower, toward me.

"No one. I slipped," Liz finally said, hauling herself up from the floor. I felt a little guilty for laughing. But I always laughed with Liz and the others in our drama club clique. I needed to lose myself among them in that drafty old theater, to have some respite from the demon that mocked me.

It was almost twenty years later that I did push Liz. My initiative brought the old scene from her living room floor to its conclusion. Still a virgin at thirty-four and desperate for intimacy in my life, I turned to my dear friend for love. She gave it and, with it, gave me permission to be a gay man. Mention her name in Mombassa. She is a generous soul.

III

But I've jumped ahead. I must go back some. Two months after graduating from college I was back in my old high school, working for an English department head who had been my teacher. She was Irish-American and full-figured like the avatars of my grammar school years; I was her best boy, who'd returned without having had a prodigal day in his life.

The suppression of my sexuality was still holding. An undiagnosed nervous collapse in my junior year at Harvard had shaken, but not destroyed, my delusion that what I knew about "those people" did not apply to me. The breakdown happened when I fell secretly in love with my roommate, a thin, red-haired, straight boy from New Jersey, and was not able to face what my silent passion meant.

I took my position in front of four classrooms full of students most of whom were only four years younger than I. I jumped fervidly into the reedy marsh of responsibility, into lesson plans, textual analysis, paper correction, and staff development. Within a few years, I was president of the PTA. (Reprise: Arthur as Daddy in the eighth-grade play.)

My contributions to the school were prodigious, but I know now that much of my activity was the result of sublimation and avoidance. I am certain that thousands of repressed gay and lesbian teachers all over the world give more of themselves to their jobs than is healthy. All those Miss Jean Brodies and Mr. Chipses — not to mention Sister Sinceres and Brother Beloveds!

During my first week of teaching, the department head asked me to substitute in her Advanced Placement English class. They were reading *The Return of the Native*. I was jittery and self-conscious conducting the class, so it wasn't long before I blew my cover. Going on about social outcasts, I made reference to Hester Prynne, the ostracized adulteress in *The Scarlet Letter*, who was condemned to wear a scarlet "A" on her clothing as punishment for her sin. Except, I referred to her as "the doomed woman in *The Red Badge of Courage.*" Would any straight man have transformed the bright red stigma of a sexual transgressor into a badge of courage? I got so flustered that minutes later, in midgesticulation, I knocked my foot against the wastebasket. It slammed into the desk. "Oh, excuse me!" I said ... to the wastebasket.

IV

Thirteen years later, in 1981, I had just come out to my family, friends, and a few other teachers. I went to the Boston Gay Pride Parade in my first spring as a gay man. Marching down Tremont Street, I passed by the Park Street Church where there was a TV camera set up on the sidewalk. No one appeared to be operating it. We marched on past the State House and into the Common, crowded with exultant gays and lesbians. What a banquet for me! These were my people — all these men who looked like the boys I went to high school with, both drama-club types and those who might chase a basketball out a second-floor window.

Some friends had planned an afternoon picnic, but rain forced us inside their attic apartment for hummus and feta, and bottles of wine. The fellowship of gay men, the thought of which had for years made me ill, was now my haven.

In our jovial vinous haze, someone suggested putting on the television to see how the march was covered. When the six o'clock news came on, we saw masses of gays, lesbians, and bisexuals teeming through downtown with banners, children, and attitude. An overhead shot of thousands, like so many jujubees, provoked one of my friends to tease, "Oh, there's Arthur."

Everyone else joined in a chorus. "There he is. I see him."

"I see his khaki shorts."

Even I laughed. But just at that moment, there I was — center screen — staring bemusedly out at the millions of home viewers for what seemed like minutes. All the joshing turned to wild whoops. My disbelief became resignation. The others suggested scenarios for the following Monday at school; mine was that since nobody watches the news on Saturday night, there would be nary a ripple.

I was wrong. Before school had even begun, I heard a voice from the other end of the corridor, "Saw you on TV, Mr. Lipkin!" It was a colleague (though I regret dignifying him with the term) with whom I had many differences, professional and political, a man, "Mr. X," who was to become my homophobic nemesis over the following years.

But no matter at that moment. I had intended to come out more generally to other faculty and to some students. My appearance on Channel 5 had merely abbreviated what could have been months of work.

I assumed that the word would spread rapidly among the students. But there was no reaction from them. Perhaps they were the ones who didn't watch the news on weekends or maybe they didn't recognize me in my khaki shorts. Whatever the reason, I endured occasional insults only from adults. Or should I say, "intended insults"? One staff member scratched out Baryshnikov's name from a poster in the Teachers' Resource Center and wrote in my name under his image. I found it hard not to be flattered.

Another time, someone wrote "and Lipkin" under "Ladies" on the women teachers' bathroom door, an entrance inaccessible to students. These were only minor annoyances, however. I had been hardened by years of political conflict, particularly with a small group of reactionary teachers and public figures. I had started my career during the Vietnam War and my opposition made me a "Communist." When I criticized the boys' swim coach for sending his team outside to beat up college students protesting the invasion of Cambodia, I was told by one teacher to put my desk out on the street with "them," where it belonged. Later I was condemned for supporting black students' demands for an Afro-American History course, among other "excesses." I had begun, in 1968, as a sissy Jew and became a Communist and a nigger-lover within three years. I was prepped, by 1981, to be a full-fledged faggot.

More serious incidents occurred over time. First, in 1982, several of my students told me that Mr. X had said "something bad" about me. They were loyal to him and would not repeat the apparent slur. Months later, another student confided, "Mr. X said you're gay and why would I want to be in your class?"

When I informed the principal, he was indignant on my behalf. He said he would ask X's department head to issue a warning. X came to my room the next day and complained that I had not confronted him "man to man." I had to hide my surprise at his granting me male status.

In 1987, two years before the passage of our state's gay rights law, a favorite freshman came to me with an odd question. Jimmy was a disadvantaged African-American kid in a class with whom I had discussed my sexual identity. (As usual the students had brought the issue up. They often ask questions, especially if a teacher is unmarried and includes gayness in discussions about difference. I asked them if their questions were respectful and they said yes, even if some weren't sure. After our good conversation, I overheard one holdout insisting I had said I was gay to test them. Denial is not restricted to gay people.)

Jimmy approached me during a study hall. Was I going to fight Mr. X, he wanted to know. I guessed what had prompted the question and he told me the story with little prodding: He was not X's student, but had been in his classroom that morning, hanging with a friend. A boy at the back of the room began to take off his sweatpants, revealing a pair of gym shorts he had on underneath. Mr. X shouted, "If you take your pants off for Lipkin, he'll give you an A!"

Jimmy had challenged X, "Why are you dissin' Mr. Lipkin? He's cool." X muttered something. He hadn't expected that response.

I am still struck by Jimmy's courage. I know that my being out to his class helped him speak up and made him comfortable telling his story to the principal.

When I met with the principal at the end of the day, I told him I would stay home until gay teachers could be assured a safe workplace. He may have been surprised at my vehemence, but he didn't challenge my leaving. We both expected the matter to be resolved quickly.

I was at home for four weeks. It took that long to arrange a hearing in the superintendent's office. I had rejected an informal meeting with the principal, since this was not the first offense (though even that fact was contested, as there was no written record of X's inappropriate comments to students about me). My principal only vaguely remembered my complaints, and X's department head, a self-styled liberal, had no recollection of reprimanding him. Their collective amnesia was inexplicable. Might it have had something to do with the political strength of X's family in Cambridge?

At the hearing, I had to wait in an anteroom with the teachers' union president while the issue was discussed among the superintendent, the attorneys, and X. Since he was threatened with disciplinary action, X was represented by a union lawyer; I had to hire my own attorney because I was bringing the complaint. The fact that I was trying to defend my moral character and professional standing meant nothing to the union, whose leadership had never supported progressive activism. On the contrary, X himself was an elected union representative at our school.

And yet, we prevailed. Despite Jimmy's not showing up (fifteen-year-old heroes have limits), X admitted making the remark. He was required to write a letter of apology and a reprimand was to be placed in his file. The superintendent agreed to our demand for anti-homophobia teacher trainings. He also issued anti-harassment guidelines for the department, including provisions for homophobic harassment.

I also lodged a complaint with the Massachusetts Teachers Association's Committee on Professional Ethics. After a formal session, at which he did not bother to appear, X was reprimanded by our state union. Two lawyers, his own and one provided by the local, had represented him.

A few people faulted me for overreacting. Several closeted teachers were resentful. One asked, "Why can't you just let go of this? This isn't the Holocaust. What do you expect from X?"

I regretted only the disruption I caused my students. Though I had sent daily lesson plans and even recorded lectures, they suffered somewhat. But I knew I had to take a strong stand. I welcomed public attention, especially in the gay press. Even without a gay rights law, gay and lesbian teachers didn't have to accept abuse. My students learned something from that, too.

In spite of these episodes, being an openly gay teacher was not all conflict and crisis. Those eight years were marked by many sweet moments, thank goodness, and one of the sweetest occurred early on. Its central figure was Wanda, a voluble African-American basketball star, nicknamed Wo, who was a sophomore in my basic English class. Wo had a round face and a loping stride. Her intelligence qualified her to be in a more advanced class, but she wouldn't hear of it. Wanting to challenge such working-class kids intellectually, I never followed the prescribed curriculum of dumbed-down biography, left over Victoriana, and business letter writing. I had them reading *Born on the Fourth of July*, watching *She's Gotta Have It*, and writing about these books and movies and their own lives.

I wasn't out yet to Wo's class. But one morning as I began to take attendance there was a perceptible buzz among the students. In the cacophony I picked out with my teacher's ear, "Who's gonna ask?"

"You ask. I ain't doin' it."

"Wait for Wo, she'll do it."

I had a sense of what "the big question" was. The night before, I had gone to a panel discussion at the Harvard Graduate School of Education called "Gay Teachers as Role Models." A rare event at the Ed School at that time, it was an opportunity to represent those few of us public school teachers who were out. Brian, a Spanish teacher and friend, presented himself on the panel as a good-humored, caring, and brave role model, who had counseled struggling kids for years. He had also helped me accept my gay identity. I made a few comments from the audience and, afterwards, Brian and I were interviewed by the *Harvard Crimson*, the college newspaper.

The next morning at school, I found that someone had made photocopies of the *Crimson* article and put one anonymously in every staff mailbox. So, if there was disquiet in my sophomore class, it might have been spurred by the phantom Xerox.

I began to teach, and within minutes, Wo entered the room. I stopped in midsentence. She gave me her late note and I sat back on the front edge of the desk. "Well," I said. "Wo is here now. Just what was it you wanted her to ask me?"

The students were galvanized. They whispered and fidgeted and pushed Wo toward the front of the room, prompting her with gestures and fragments of speech.

"Do it..."

"Come on ... You said..."

Wo began. "Uh, Mr. Lipkin. Uh ... Mr. Lipkin ... there was this ... uh, this article..."

Poor Wo had never been so hesitant before. She drew closer to the side of the desk. Suddenly she dropped down, plopping her rear end into the wastebasket. It would have been graceful, but for her distressed expression. She tried to smile and began to rock nervously back and forth.

"Are you referring to an article about me?" I asked, to shorten her ordeal.

"Yes," she replied.

Sympathetic as I was, I could not resist a dig. "I didn't know my students read the *Harvard Crimson* regularly."

"It was on a teacher's desk," she offered. "It said that you..." She could not go on and stopped rocking.

"I was at a discussion last night at Harvard," I said. "It was a panel about gay teachers." My palms began to sweat and my breathing was heightened. It was always like that. Though I welcomed the chance to *be* out to my students, it was never easy to *come* out to them. I wanted to maintain my effectiveness with them. I wanted them to like me. I didn't relish reprising my Shylock speech from so many years before, replacing "Jew" in "Hath not a Jew hands" with "gay." And yet this was what it had to be. It made me tremble every time, for all my practice. And it should have. It was important.

Wo extracted herself from the wastebasket during our talk about what my being gay meant to me and them. I tried to be as truthful and matter-of-fact as I could be, drawing the line only at my own erotic practices. They asked if I had a boyfriend and I told them Ron's name as easily as I would have told them I had a girlfriend named Sally.

From that day on, we had an honest, funny, and warm classroom, just like the one we'd had before. Wo continued to shine on the basketball court and, as much as ever, in her studies. When she left Cambridge, she had an athletic scholarship to college. Happily, she dropped in at the high school to say hello once or twice during the next four years.

Then I saw Wo again. It was summertime and I was with my spouse, Bob, for a few days in Provincetown. There was Wo on Commercial Street, arm-in-arm with her girlfriend. We were both ecstatic to see each other there. I don't think I'd ever hugged her so hard. We introduced our partners and caught up on news. She may not have had her career together — she should have studied harder — but she sure looked like someone who loved well. I kissed them and saw them off down the street toward the Pied Piper dance club.

As Bob and I continued toward the East End, I reminded him of the story I'd told him about the sophomore who sat in the wastebasket. "That was Wo," I said.

Later, over scampi adriatico, I offered thanks for Wo and all the others like her. And today I bless all those teachers who make gay kids' lives possible. If there are any adults or young people who need a boost to get going or to keep going, I suggest rocking in an old green metal wastebasket. It can do one a world of good.

Teaching with the Heart

Ron Ritchart

Math Department Chair
Graland Country Day School
Denver, Colorado

The note slipped silently from my hand to a prominent spot on his desk. There it lay, conspicuous in its smallness, a strategically placed sheet of ruled yellow notepaper carefully folded once, then once again, and once more to provide that degree of secrecy so important to a fourth-grader. I was running away from home, and I wanted someone to know. I wanted someone to care.

In my best cursive, I informed Mr. McHenry of both my plan and my sense of alienation. At nine years old, I didn't know I was gay, but I did know that there didn't seem to be a place for me, not in my family, not in school, not in a small Indiana town. The sense of separateness, of isolation I was feeling sparked my visions — visions of being accepted, of finding my true home, of starting over.

These visions had prompted the plan to run away. It was an ill-formed plan, lacking any true focus or design and relying wholly on magic. I wanted something that couldn't be explained or written down on that sheet of paper. I wanted something that I didn't know how to articulate, some location that I couldn't quite imagine. I wanted to be included, to feel that I belonged. I didn't want to feel different. In running away, I was not headed for any specific destination, yet I was in search of a place, my place.

I hoped that Mr. McHenry would somehow understand what I was looking for even if I couldn't define it. From the first day of summer school, I had enjoyed reading class. Not because it was interesting or fun, or that I even liked reading. In fact, the class was a remedial one and filled with students like myself who were standouts for our lack of involvement with books. Still, I felt a certain connection with this, my first male teacher, a connection that was more important than the content of any subject. And so, I dutifully read the passages from the SRA reading kit, filled in my worksheets, and recorded my progress to please him.

It was the connection between teacher and student that was most important in motivating my learning that summer. Sometimes as teachers, we may forget how important that connection is to our students. In our search for better lessons, teaching techniques, and materials, we can lose sight of the fact that our students want most of all to be recognized for who they are and the special gifts they bring. Students may perform for us out of a sense of duty, respect, fear, or reward, but such performances pale when compared to one that originates from a sense of love, belonging, and acceptance.

Leaving the classroom that summer morning, I walked aimlessly along the streets of unfamiliar neighborhoods, through cornfields, and along the dry creekbeds of my rural town. My mind teemed with thoughts of despair, fear, and expectation — despair at my isolation; fear at the possibility that my note had not been found or, worse, that it had been read and rejected or ridiculed; expectation that something might happen, that I might change or be changed.

I returned home that day without a sense of peace or joy, without a sense of belonging, and without even being missed. In a house full of people, no one had noticed my absence. No one asked where I had been or inquired after my health — physical or mental. My isolation had not diminished but increased.

And then the phone rang. "It's your teacher," my mother called. "This is the third time he's called." I picked up the phone with a sense of both apprehension and joy as I wedged myself between my parents' bed and nightstand. I had never had a phone conversation with a teacher before. The experience didn't feel wholly real, but the emotions did. Today, more than twenty years later, I can't remember his words, but I can still feel his caring and how important it was that day. He had read my note and was concerned. I could talk to him. He wanted me to be in his class next year. His caring was an insulator against my feelings of isolation. The conversation was a strengthening of my connection with both my teacher and the world. To someone I was important. I counted. I belonged.

Mr. McHenry and I did not have any long talks together following my attempt at running away, just a short conversation in which his caring and concern were reiterated. I never spent time with him one-on-one or saw him outside of school. I did not stay after school or seek any special attention. I didn't need that. I needed his smile, his "hello," and just knowing he was there. When summer school ended in July, I looked forward to being a fifth-grader in his class come fall.

Mr. McHenry was the first teacher who made school real and vital for me, not for intellectual reasons but for personal ones. We sat in rows, read from basal readers, and practiced math facts, just like in every other classroom; but for the first time, there was a palpable sense of community, caring, and connection. Towering above us all at a height of over six feet, he talked *to* us rather than *at* us, making us each feel valued and important. Slowly, the pale green walls of the classroom began to open up and gradually lose their oppressiveness.

I did not become a great student that year, however — far from it. The particularly arcane and obtuse nature of school learning and its disconnection from real life were to remain a mystery to me for years to come. I still did not enjoy or excel at reading, or any other subject for that matter, but knowing that Mr. McHenry cared, that I could talk to him if I needed someone to listen, made all the difference. I remember my experience in his class warmly — not because of exciting lessons, inspired oratory, or clever wit but because of his presence.

The opportunity to make a difference, to connect with a student the way Mr. McHenry connected with me, helped shape my decision to become a teacher. He was the first role model of a teacher with which I could identify. Later in my schooling, I was fortunate enough to have several other teachers who taught me that learning could be an exciting and rewarding experience not confined within the pages of a textbook. I have had many excellent mentors that have taught me how to engage the mind in meaningful learning much more effectively than the mode of transmitting information modeled in my elementary years. However, Mr. McHenry remains my best model of the importance of engaging the heart as well as the mind in learning. Without this connection, both learning and teaching are empty experiences.

I never saw Mr. McHenry after that fifth-grade year. He left the school and may have left our rural community and even teaching altogether. I don't know. I never had a chance to tell him how much his phone call in the summer of 1968 meant to me and what a difference it has made in my life. He never knew that I was to become an elementary teacher. I think of Mr. McHenry often. Whenever I have the opportunity to help a student who is struggling, to let them know that I care, I think of him and am reminded that a simple act of caring can rescue a person and make all the difference. A difference of which we might never be aware. I think of him whenever my teaching gets stale, when I feel myself just going through the motions. Then I remember what is most important, what Mr. McHenry taught me, to teach with the heart.

"It's the Teachers! The Teachers Are Coming Out!"

———— Pat McCart

Principal
Saint Paul Academy & Summit School
Saint Paul, Minnesota _____

I was fifty-three, a secondary school principal. Outside the gay community, I was out to my immediate family, a few close straight friends, and a few trusted people at work. I was out to, and had the support of, my boss. I had worked patiently and quietly to get sexual orientation included in the school's nondiscrimination policy. I had a Names Project poster in my office. I thought I was out enough.

It was the fall of 1988. One of my advisees was to give the year's first senior speech to the student body. She had chosen the topic of homophobia and at the end planned to say that her mother was a lesbian, and to tell how proud she was of all the risks her mother had taken, and all the work she had done to confront prejudice and bigotry. This student had been my advisee for three years. I knew her mother was a lesbian but the student and I had never talked about it. She hadn't told a soul in the school. When the time came to practice the speech in the empty auditorium, she realized she wouldn't be able to say, "My mother is a lesbian." She came into my office crying, devastated that she couldn't say it. She was afraid of what others might think, say, do ... afraid of the homophobia that might be lurking under all those good manners.

Well, there I sat on my own, personal road to Damascus. I was the school adult responsible for the bright, young woman who wanted so much to make a public statement. I was the adult responsible for the group she was afraid to tell about her mother. And I was a lesbian.

I was struck by two things. One, I had never related my lack of public openness about my sexual orientation to my authenticity as a teacher and a role model. I had mistakenly thought that part of my success was due to how well I kept the two issues separate. And two, that by not being fully, publicly identified as a lesbian, I was maintaining my comfort at the expense of the young — the very group I had spent my adult life working for and with. My fear, my privatization helped keep the fear, misinformation, prejudice, and homophobia alive among these adolescents, whether they were straight or gay. I was not out enough.

The following February I took part in the Equity Institute's Project Empowerment Workshop for Gay and Lesbian Teachers. It was the first time I identified myself as a lesbian to people I didn't know well. Many of us continued to meet monthly. We decided to make a statement at the 1989 gay pride rally. This was heady stuff. Most of us had never been to the rally, much less marched in it or identified ourselves as lesbian and gay teachers! We were nervous and tentative behind our banner (which said, "Gay and Lesbian Teachers") until we reached the first corner. The crowd started clapping and shouting, "It's the teachers! The teachers are coming out!" When it was our time to appear onstage, the group had symbolic brown paper bags over their heads as I spoke a few words on behalf of gay and lesbian educators. I borrowed the title of my advisee's senior speech, "It's a Secret," and spoke the following words:

> We are probably the most deeply closeted group in the gay community. You all know THE BIG RULE for Being Out: "It's okay as long as you DON'T FLAUNT IT." For us there is a different rule: "It's not okay. You are not fit to teach children. You are fired!"
>
> Being so deep in the cloakroom is not healthy for us as individuals, but by far the most damaging effect of the "NO GAY OR LESBIAN TEACHERS ALLOWED" rule is how it perpetuates stereotyping, bigotry, and fear by controlling the perceptions of the young. For the vicious cycle of prejudice and bigotry to be broken, all young people, no matter what their affectional preference — or even if they don't know what that means — need to know adult lesbians and gays who are whole, healthy, happy, courageous, and respected by their communities! And they need to know this about their teachers who are gay or lesbian. We must have the courage to risk if the system is to change. It has been twenty years since the Stonewall Rebellion, when

we began to take back our pride and stand up to bigotry and discrimination...

For the sake of all of us — but especially for the young — help us bring the spirit of Stonewall into the schools. And it is in that spirit and on behalf of all gay and lesbian teachers who can't come out yet, that I say:

> My name is Pat McCart.
> I am a high school principal.
> And I am proud to be a lesbian!

The next day our picture was on the front page of the *Minnesota Daily*. I thought, "This is out enough!"

In the spring of 1990 I was asked to testify at the Saint Paul City Council's hearing on including sexual orientation in the human rights ordinance. At the end of the faculty meeting that afternoon before the hearing, I told the faculty what I was going to do and that I was going to do it as an openly identified lesbian. My coming out to them may have been the only time in twelve years as their principal that I had their complete attention! It was hard news for a few to hear because of their religious beliefs or a feeling that it was wrong to publicize such matters, but I received much support and was thanked for trusting and respecting them enough to come out directly to them. This was really out enough.

But no. In the beginning of September 1990, the first week of my long-anticipated four-month sabbatical, I was asked to be part of an article the *Star Tribune* planned on coming out. I called my boss, hoping he would say something that would give me permission to say no. Instead he said he was not interested in promoting hypocrisy, and that he trusted my judgment. From the ninety-minute interview came one and a half inches of copy. Good, I could hide in the story, I thought, but then I remembered that I had said yes to being in the photograph. Only three of us showed up for it. I had expected a group to hide in. That was really scary: feelings of terror, vulnerability, like being skinned alive and put on display. I understood the indigenous people to whom taking a picture of a person robs the person of her soul. I walked out of the building, hyperventilating. I forgot where my car was. I took a few steps and stopped. "Oh, shit!" I thought. "What will the people at Blake think?" Worrying about our rival across town put things back in perspective for me. I could laugh at myself. I could breathe. I found my car. The article, complete with an incredibly large photograph, was the lead of the Variety section in the September 23, 1990, Sunday *Star Tribune.*

Some members of the school community were upset at what seemed to them to be my flaunting of my private life, or that they hadn't been told before it appeared in the paper. And there was my photograph so unavoidably identified as the principal of the upper school at Saint Paul Academy and Summit School. It meant many of the school community would feel the stings of homophobia in a personal way: co-workers, neighbors, friends at other schools asking about *"their* lesbian principal." But the vast majority of the community was supportive, if not of the "lifestyle" then of the human-rights issues involved. The school addressed the issues openly with the students and parents. Parents seemed to feel positive about the manner in which the school had handled "Pat's article."

Looking back, I was fortunate to have been in a school community that was committed to struggling openly and respectfully with tough issues; fortunate that the usual "silent majority" had been so worried about what might happen to me that they spoke up about their support for human rights, diversity, and the school's nondiscrimination policy. The abstract had become very concrete.

One day early in the spring of 1991, after I had announced my plan to "graduate" at the end of my twelve years as principal, a group of students dropped by my office to hang out and chat about what I was going to do next. It was really to find out what was behind my decision to leave. I assured them that I hadn't been fired or pressured to leave because of my coming out in the *Tribune.* I would never go under those circumstances. Relieved, they started talking about who the next principal might be, and having to "train" someone new, when one of them said, "You know, Dr. McCart, the kids are really sorry you're leaving. We were getting in to having an 'out' principal!"

I thought back to two and a half years before and remembered the school had not felt safe for my advisee to talk openly about how proud she was of her lesbian mother. It might be different now.

Riding the Horse

Social Studies and Music Student Teacher (1970)
Bookser High School
Santa Clara, California

A friend of mine recently asked why I chose to become a teacher of children with visual disabilities. To my own surprise, I quipped without hesitation: "Because no blind person has ever called me a faggot."

Though the reasons for my entering the field of special education were and continue to be quite complex, until that moment I had not been completely aware of how large a part homophobia had played in my career decisions.

I was born during the "McCarthy era" — a conservative time, a time when difference of any sort was held suspect. On the floor of the U.S. Senate, a brash young Joseph McCarthy sternly warned of the evils perpetrated on society by the multitudes of Communists and homosexuals in government. Having recognized same-sex attractions quite early in my life, I knew almost instinctively to cloak my desires in silence.

I suppose my journey on the path toward teaching began in child-hood: a period in my life filled with extreme outer turmoil and inner pain, a time when I felt different from family and peers alike in a number of ways. As a young child I wanted to become a teacher, and by my senior year of high school I had pictured myself standing before a classroom of eager students like my hero, Leonard Bernstein, who throughout the 1950s gave a series of performance-lectures as part of his "Young People's Concerts" for the *Omnibus* television program. I watched this dynamic, creative, talented, handsome (and as I would learn many years later, queer) Jewish mensch displaying his unique pedagogic style blending insight and humor, with more than a pinch of theatrics, inspiring a new generation of "serious" music lovers. A seed was planted during those early broadcasts, and though I was as yet uncertain of the subject, I went off to college in 1965 with the intention of becoming a teacher.

I left my parents' home in the San Fernando Valley of Los Angeles to attend San Jose State University some 450 miles north, in the lowermost city on the San Francisco Bay. A sense of anxious anticipation filled me as I checked into my dormitory room. I unpacked and headed for the cafeteria. When I returned, I found all my belongings — my clothes, books, radio, violin, personal items, everything — randomly strewn in the hallway. Apparently my roommate, Ralph, had arrived while I was at dinner. When I asked what had happened, he angrily informed me that he threw my things out because, as he put it, "I ain't rooming with no guy who has a pink shirt and a violin." I was speechless, tears filling my eyes. I blurted out some halfhearted defense, noting that I didn't own a pink shirt, and if I had, what did that and my playing a violin signify? Ralph shouted, his intent quite clear this time: "I'm not rooming with a fag."

Feeling extremely dejected and embarrassed, I talked to the resident advisor, who got me reassigned to another room, across the hall from my tormentor. I crawled into bed that evening, my idealism and hopes for a productive and happy college career seriously compromised (though, I was to learn, not yet dead). And, as it turned out (this incident with Ralph aside) my undergraduate years in San Jose were some of the most exciting and rewarding of my life.

The mid- to late sixties was an era of tumultuous social change, and fortunately for me, the Bay Area was one of its epicenters. I and many of my classmates organized "teach-ins" and demonstrations against U.S. involvement in Vietnam; we spoke out against racism on campus; and we facilitated ecology workshops. I also volunteered four hours a week tutoring English at an off-campus language center for newly arriving immigrants from Mexico.

I graduated with a bachelor's degree in June 1969, just two weeks prior to the momentous Stonewall Riots in New York, though it took eight months for that news to reach me. By that time I was halfway through my fifth year at San Jose State in the School of Education, earning my teacher certification, where much of the excitement and joy of learning I had experienced in my undergraduate years came to an end.

What sick, diabolical, twisted mind devised this most inhuman of all torments inflicted on innocent, idealistic grad students ... the dreaded, sleep-inducing, mind-rotting, helllllp-it's-coming-to-get-me phenomenon known as "education courses"?

Poor naive little me was actually looking forward to taking some of the courses. Typical, however, was the Audio-Visual Materials course, where the only skill I gained was preparing color ditto sheets. To this day I still couldn't thread a film projector if my life depended on it, and overhead projectors remain a source of frustration. The most compelling experience I had was student teaching. When the time came, I was assigned to a civics class in a high school on San Jose's west side.

Though I was actually anxious, I was also excited. I treated the assignment as my first real job. I walked in, bedecked in my new and freshly ironed "professional" outfit, and introduced myself to the co-operating teacher. Following a few brief words, he informed me of the agenda for the next twelve weeks. After I observed the class for about a week, I would then run the class. He said he would pop in once or twice a week to offer suggestions and be on hand when I needed him.

I entered my apartment after my second day to a ringing telephone. My college supervisor called to notify me that my "cooperating teacher" felt the arrangement wasn't working and didn't want me to return.

In my total bewilderment, I audibly gasped for air. Catching my breath, I mumbled, "I don't understand — what are you saying? What is there not to work?"

My supervisor calmly and sensitively explained that I had done nothing to bring this about, but rather (here her voice lowered gently), "Sometimes personalities just don't mesh."

"Is it because I'm Jewish?" I blurted out.

She assured me it was not. When I pressed her further, she reluctantly said that the teacher was "uncomfortable with your alternative lifestyle, which he said he picked up from your mannerisms, and he doesn't want you influencing his students." Then it hit me full force: the teacher didn't want me to return because he perceived that I was gay.

She reassured me that my next assignment would be positive. In fact, she had already spoken to other teachers who were eager for me to teach their classes. I hung up the phone feeling terribly shaken, seeing my dream of teaching vanishing before me.

The following day, shell-shocked and extremely self-conscious, I headed out with a fellow ed school student to a high school in Santa

Clara to teach two classes: senior American Problems and freshman choir. Though only twenty miles south of San Francisco, Santa Clara in 1970 was a conservative, mainly white, suburban "bedroom" community. As we drove into the parking lot of the single-level brick building, an old truism ran through my head temporarily rising over the din of my fear: "You've got to climb right back on the horse after being thrown."

I met my cooperating teachers; we talked briefly and discussed my role. Following a short observation period, I would take over sole teaching responsibilities for the senior American Problems class, and would co-conduct the choir.

My cooperating teachers were quite different from one another in style and temperament. The music teacher was all business, outlining the parameters of my duties which included rehearsing the choir in the piece "Autumn Leaves," which they would perform under my direction in ten weeks at the annual spring Parents Night open house. (By the look of it, this certainly wasn't going to be a "Young People's Concert," but then I certainly wasn't a Leonard Bernstein.)

The American Problems teacher welcomed me with a firm handshake and a booming "Glad to meet ya." As I was quick to learn, he only taught a couple of social studies classes; basically, he was the football and basketball coach.

He brought me up to date on what the class had been doing. Most of the material, taken directly from a standard textbook, involved contemporary social issues: teen pregnancy, drugs, pollution, crime. Each week the students were expected to read and discuss one chapter from the book, and were tested on Fridays. I suppose he perceived a trace of concern on my face.

"I want to tell you from the outset," he said eagerly, "that I want you to feel free to teach the way that makes the most sense to you. You don't have to continue my format." I brightened, telling him that I was looking forward to working with him and the class.

I left school the first day feeling that, though my horse was trotting on shaky and uncharted terrain, at least I was sitting upright in the saddle.

My observation period was essentially uneventful in the choir — aside from some occasional periods of rowdiness and some commotion in the back of the tenor section, the students were generally attentive.

I found out quite early, however, that the Problems class was well named. Throughout my observation week, a group of young men seated in the back of the room, decked out in their blazing school sports jackets, huddled as the teacher faced the blackboard. They, in turn, looked my way, mouthing under their breath, "Faggot," "Pansy."

The day before I was to take over the class, my cooperating teacher informed me that four of the male students had requested a transfer to another class, which he granted. He told me not to take this personally. "I am their coach," he continued, "and I think they are more angry at me for turning over the class than they are at you." Though I was somewhat shaken by his announcement, I was actually relieved, no longer having to deal with these students' hostility.

Meanwhile, I was busy getting the choir in shape for our command performance. The commotion in the back of the tenor section, however, seemed to increase with each passing day. Though my cooperating teacher chose to ignore it, I was saddened to watch three of the boys poking and harassing "John," a smaller boy, with homophobic epithets.

Thoughts of my own school days resounded in my head. Turning the choir back to the teacher, I took the three perpetrators aside and explained to them that their actions were disrupting rehearsals. I then asked for their help in re-establishing order. They seemed fairly cooperative, and but for a few brief lapses, left John unmolested during class time — though I witnessed them continuing their torment in the hallways. On numerous occasions they surrounded John, mocking him to the point of tears. I spoke with my cooperating teacher and to the head guidance counselor, both of whom advised against interference.

"If we intervene," warned the guidance counselor, "they will only get angry and increase their harassment. John has to learn to stand up for himself."

Though my heart was breaking for this student, I understood my limited role and tried to take a backseat, hoping the situation would work itself out. But, of course, it did not.

The day following a presentation I gave to the choir on the historical roots of rock music, John approached me, eyes aglow, waving a brightly colored record album. "You played one of my favorite songs yesterday in class," he said excitedly. "I brought this record for you to hear some other great songs." I thanked him for lending me the album and for his consideration, and promised to listen to the music that evening at home.

I returned the record to him on the following day. That afternoon, I learned that the three boys had chased John, grabbed his record, and smashed it against a brick wall. He came to choir rehearsal, eyes downcast, barely mouthing the words to the songs.

I followed my heart this time. On my way home, I bought a replacement record. I met John the next day before class and asked if he minded taking a walk with me. We walked around the outdoor track.

"John," I began rather tentatively, "I asked you to take a walk with me because there's something I want to talk to you about." The expression on his face showed confusion. "A few days ago you did something really nice. You shared a record album with me. I heard that yesterday someone broke your record." He looked down toward his feet. "I want to say how terribly sorry I am that happened to you. And in some way I feel responsible."

"Oh no," he screamed out. "It wasn't your fault."

"I guess I know that," I continued. "But anyway, I want you to have this." I handed him the album.

With disbelief, he took the gift and quickly ripped off the paper wrapping. With a quivering lower lip he simply said, "Thank you, Mr. Blumenfeld. Thank you very much." We walked silently back to class.

The following week, I conducted the choir at the open house, the students (including the three boys) appearing as veritable angels in their crimson choir robes. To my pleasant surprise, the audience gave us a standing ovation, with flashbulbs temporarily blinding us. John introduced me to his parents during the reception after the concert. We chatted for a brief moment, then before turning away, his mother grabbed me in a warm embrace, whispering, "Thank you," in my ear.

My American Problems class ended on a similarly upbeat note. A bit to my surprise, my cooperating teacher gave me a glowing evaluation. "Our styles are completely different," he began. "But I learned much from your creativity this semester. Obviously, the topics were more than 'textbook' issues to you," an ironic reference to my dispensing with the classroom text. "I enjoyed the experience, and I know the students did as well."

With my student teaching duties completed, I joined a therapy group in the college counseling center, which helped me handle my sexual identity in a constructive way. Though I still wished to be a teacher, I was hesitant to return to a public high school. I could now begin to examine the nagging question: "What do you want to do with your life?" The answer came to me quite unexpectedly.

While traveling across Scandinavia on vacation in 1972, my retinas detached (due to a previously undetected congenital defect), and I found myself in a Danish hospital. Lying in bed following a series of operations — not permitted to move, eyes securely bandaged for nearly two months — I had plenty of time for reflection, and I decided to enter the field of special education.

With my vision restored, I moved to Massachusetts in 1973 to return to college and to even more education classes, earning dual master's degrees in special education. I then taught for seven years in a residential school for children with visual and other disabilities, with the joy that comes from being myself. I felt an immediate connection to my students. After a short time, I found other "out" teachers, and we formed an informal lunchtime support group. My supervisor invited me to co-author the school's Sex Education and Family Life Curriculum, in which we included age-appropriate discussions of the varieties of sexual expression, including homosexuality.

Over the years, as I supervised a number of student teachers, I never forgot my own experiences and one essential point I gleaned from my Educational Psychology professor back in San Jose — a point that has crystallized for me the intent of true and meaningful learning. My professor explained that the term "education" is derived from two Latin roots: "e," meaning "out of," and "decare," meaning "to lead" or "to draw." "Education," he said, "is the process of drawing knowledge out of the student, which he or she already knows, and not putting or depositing information into what some teachers perceive as the student's waiting and docile mind."

"It is your job," he continued, "to excite, to motivate, to develop or enhance in the student a quest for learning." He said the authentic teacher provides students with the all-too-rare opportunity to learn what is meaningful for them to develop as functioning, growing, self-actualizing human beings.

Even at the lowest points of my student teaching days, I retained a passion for teaching by holding my sights fixed on these words. In retrospect, I understand that this was the incentive keeping my valiant steed on course, finally lifting me across the finish line.

No Regrets

English Teacher
Roosevelt High School
*Los Angeles, California*_____

I first met Danny in my seventh year of teaching. I had been trying to facilitate a lesbian and gay on-campus counseling program called Project 10 at our school for about three years, but had met with only limited success.

Roosevelt, where I taught, is about 98 percent Hispanic. In fact, it is about 98 percent Mexican. The students who go there were mostly born in Mexico, or had parents who were. It is a working-class, inner-city, mostly Catholic neighborhood, representing all types of inner-city problems — everything from drugs and gangs to teenage pregnancy and abusive families. There is little variety in the students' economic and cultural backgrounds, and they tend to be extremely conformist. With those conditions, it is extremely difficult for a gay or lesbian student to take those first few steps toward accepting his or her sexuality.

I used to meet before school with another HIV-positive gay male teacher. We used the time to gossip, talk about treatment issues, and philosophize over the state of our lives. One day my friend told me about a student who had been "flitting about the classroom." He wanted to become an actor. He was interested in the arts. It was a stereotype, but we thought he might be gay. His name was Danny.

We talked about Danny a few mornings. It was clear he was having trouble with school. Poor performance and absenteeism combined to make him a classic "at risk" student. We decided that he might be just the kind of kid who could benefit from Project 10. It seemed safer for me to ask, since he didn't really know me and wasn't in one of my classes.

The next day, I showed up at my friend's classroom during the correct period. I carried my clipboard to seem more official. I asked if

65 —

a certain Danny was in his class, and if I couldn't speak to him for a few minutes. As planned, my friend said yes.

Danny and I found a quiet place outside and I went into a long explanation of IMPACT — a federally funded schoolwide counseling program addressing a multitude of issues, but specifically aimed at reducing drug and alcohol abuse. I listed some of the various groups under the IMPACT umbrella until I ended up talking about Project 10. I felt nervous, but acted very serious and professional. I had done this a couple of times before but without success.

I explained how Project 10 was designed for lesbian, gay, and bisexual students, and for those who weren't sure of their sexuality. (Personally, I don't see how it's possible to go through puberty without becoming sure of your sexuality, but it's a safe place for some kids to put themselves.) Then came The Question: do you think you would be interested in this?

Danny looked quite surprised. I could see on his face that he wanted to know how I knew. I could also see some relief. He said he was interested.

I had talked to students before, however, and they hadn't had the fortitude to show up for a meeting. That was the real test. Danny showed up.

My cofacilitator, Tina, went through our usual talk with him. It's not that difficult. Once you've established a safe space for a kid to be lesbian or gay, the student will often open up. We just showed that we were as boring and normal (almost) as most other people, and that in Project 10 we could talk about it without fear of other people finding out. It was something he had never experienced before. There were only three students involved at that point, which actually felt like a lot, even though Roosevelt High has more than four thousand students.

Our first meetings were a little slow. We had a hard time getting anything really rolling. I didn't feel entirely trusted. One student decided that she wasn't gay and stopped coming. One of the others seemed to have bigger problems than his sexuality.

Around Halloween Tina and I were talking in the group about our plans. I said I was planning to go to Santa Monica Boulevard to watch the "parade," which I briefly explained.

On Halloween in West Hollywood, about two miles of the main street closes down for a giant party of Halloween costumes. You see everything from the best drag to the worst drag to the wildest concept pieces, but there is so much more. It is an annual function of lesbian and gay life. It is a celebration of ourselves and our fantasies.

Suddenly Danny said, "Take me along!"

I thought about it and decided, "Why not?" We made plans and waited for the day.

But I also wanted Danny to see more of gay and lesbian life than the parade. We made plans to meet with a large group of my friends before the parade at one of their homes. This gave Danny the opportunity to meet gay people who would not be in costume. It also gave him a chance to meet some gay people closer to his age.

On Halloween I was terrified about meeting Danny's parents. I was afraid they would think I was some kind of pervert, so I had him meet me in front of his house at a set time. I drove by and picked him up. I found out that his parents were hardly overprotective: they were letting their son stay out as late as he wanted with a total stranger. That made me feel more relaxed for myself, if not for him.

For me there is one thing that is absolutely clear about a counseling relationship: it cannot ever involve any sex. I had made that clear to Danny early on, and he knew that tonight was a date between two friends. I think there is no better way to destroy a young person's trust than to suddenly confuse things with the issue of sex. The person being counseled has to trust that you do not have a hidden agenda. But we did talk about sex — specifically, safer sex, and the importance of never making exceptions.

I took Danny to dinner at a nice gay cafe. We made quite an entrance with Danny looking all of fifteen and I looking all of thirty-one. About 80 percent of the eyes focused on me — evil, vicious, nasty eyes — while the remaining 20 percent focused on Danny — sweet, inviting, nice eyes. I could imagine what they all were assuming. It gave me the opportunity to explain many difficult aspects of gay life to Danny. At times we even switched to Spanish so I could explain why certain men kept looking at him and the different ways he could handle it. Overall, the dinner was a great success as well as a real (and necessary) education for Danny.

After dinner we met my friends. It was a group of about eight. They represented a good range of ordinary-looking people so I could show Danny that most of us are only normal, even rather boring. Danny got the chance to talk to all of my friends individually and he behaved himself remarkably, in a very subdued, adult way. Then we set off to see the parade. He was home by two a.m.

Project 10 started to fall apart after that, but Danny and I did a lot of telephone counseling. He continued to have an attendance problem, and his teachers told me he was in danger of failing his classes. Project 10 had at least gotten him to come to school on Wednesdays, but now that wasn't even guaranteed. I did what I could to motivate him, but how do you convince someone to come to an environment that will not accept you for who you are? He wanted to drop out already, in tenth grade. He talked of continuation school. I couldn't decide if this was a good idea for him or not.

Danny told me of other gay students he had met at Roosevelt High, but they were unwilling to take the risk and come forward to speak with me. I didn't know them from the sea of faces that swept by me every day in the overcrowded hallways, but they always knew who I was and were able to find me — even if they never did.

At the end of the semester Danny told me he had been kicked out of Roosevelt because of his attendance record. I never bothered to verify the story. He decided to go to continuation school. I encouraged him to register there, but the problem was, school had no special place for Danny. Tina and I did our best to keep him motivated, but all his life he had been told he didn't belong. There was not much I could do than watch the disaster grow. Still, within the context of his eventual dropping-out, we discovered one great truth: Danny was gay, and Danny was okay about being gay. He just wasn't okay about school.

It was also around this time that I began to have my own problems. An administrator, after years of barely acknowledging my existence, started going after me because of petty protocol on running a classroom. I had a severely difficult class and I had had to really push some of the students to get them in line. They complained to this man, and he began what became a long, extravagant paper war. I felt very much wronged by this so I took up my end of the battle. I can't help but suspect that a great deal of homophobia was behind his attack on me. Administrators are getting too wise to call a teacher "faggot" or do something else so blatantly homophobic. Instead, insidious harassment of this type is used to mask their homophobia, so that no one (perhaps even themselves) would believe that bigotry underlies their actions.

To further complicate things, I was at the time hospitalized with my first bout of anemia. I finally became so sick that I missed over a month of school. In the meantime, I lost track of Danny, except for what I heard from friends, who bumped into him occasionally. Eventually I had to quit teaching.

Aside from the great physical strain, I just could no longer deal with the continual disappointment that comes with working in an inner-city high school. The students at Roosevelt read about as well as the third-graders over in the "better" part of town. The parents are mostly uninvolved. The administration, with a few valiant exceptions, generally doesn't care. Supplies are never where or when you need them. One can only take so much.

Despite the frustrations involved, I always felt it made sense for me to be there for my students, and I always tried to do my best at that. Kids want to learn, but they get sidetracked by so many things in an unsympathetic environment. How can you learn when your father's an alcoholic and may come home at any time and beat you? It's not possible. I did what I could for those students. To as many as I could, I taught a little bit of English. For a few like Danny, I taught the most important lesson of all: you are a person of worth, regardless of what society tells you. I don't regret teaching. Not at all.

Part Two:

Journeys

"The journey of a thousand miles begins
with a single step."

—MAO

I Have Come Here to Die

—————— B. Michael Hunter
Teacher and Advisor
New York City Public Schools
New York, New York _____

On April 11, 1991, my first day on the job at Norman Thomas High School in New York City, Yarius, a student in my College Accounting course, asked me: "Why are *you* teaching?" His question probed for more than the introduction I offered the entire class: I went to public elementary school in East Harlem, graduated from Brooklyn Technical High School, had an undergraduate degree in accounting, a law degree, spent five years selling computers for IBM, and, after taking a year and a half off to travel the world, had decided to pursue my lifelong desire to teach. I purposely gave a broad sketch of my life, leaving out details of my love interests or political views. I interpreted Yarius's question in two ways: first, "If you have so much going for you, why are you 'just' a teacher?"; and second, "We students don't deserve teachers who want to teach."

"Why am I 'just' a teacher?" I did not want to be challenged so early. I have always wanted to teach, to dance, to act in the theater, and to write. But these were things that "faggots" did. And I was not a faggot. So I chose careers that were strong, tough, and highly principled, like accounting, law, and computer sales, professions you might identify with your father. In fact, people relied on me and I was very comfortable in the role of provider. In turn, I was rewarded with a career and incredible security. I wanted to be a respectable man in a respected profession.

Since childhood I have longed to teach, but every message I received reinforced the notion that respectable men did not become teachers. If men taught at all, men became professors, and only as a second career. If they taught high school, they became principals. So my real desire to teach grades four, five, and six was dwarfed by these capricious standards and my fear of parents accusing me of sexual abuse or statutory rape because I hugged some young boy.

"We don't deserve teachers who want to teach?" I was unnerved because Yarius's question conveyed the sentiment of the system: public school students were not entitled to "the best." Norman Thomas High School, built in the 1970s, had sound physical facilities. The school possessed several computer labs and state-of-the-art audiovisual equipment, and teachers had access to photocopy machines. Major drawbacks included a lack of teachers' aides, basic supplies, maps, magazines, workbooks, and full class sets of current textbooks. In my College Accounting course, a special class for advanced seniors, all of the students had new books. But in every other class I taught, because of my status as a "new jack" faculty, my students were left with incomplete sets of current textbooks, no workbooks, or complete sets of earlier editions. In my naivete, I let a class of mine take home a set of twenty-year-old texts and workbooks. When word got out to the school administration, I honestly felt my job was in jeopardy. Using the computer labs to type up some of my lessons was also a mistake. I later found out that I needed permission *and* proper supervision (either the chairman of the department or one of the two paras assigned to the labs) to do so.

My biggest *faux pas* was returning a telephone call in the general office. While I was in mid-dial, the vice-principal for administration walked over, put her hand on the switch hook, and recited the rules and regulations on telephone usage. I know I looked at her as if she were a madwoman. The fact that she was a middle-aged white woman who probably taught students my age fifteen years ago contributed to why she felt she could address me in such a condescending way. After waiting for some color to return to her face, I reminded her that I understood English and could hear well enough that she did not have to shout. I also informed her that she was in no danger of attack, so she could remove her left hand from her hip and her right hand from my face. One of the office workers, an African-American woman in her late fifties, thanked me for not "slapping [the vice-principal] silly," and later informed the school grapevine, which made me popular with certain staff.

I began to internalize what I also sensed in the classroom: although the school was named after a socialist leader and writer, the school did not belong to the students, nor were they entitled to fully enjoy what the school might have. Rather they were allowed to mostly look and not touch, to visit Thirty-third Street and Park Avenue as early as 8:30 a.m., and to retire to whatever part of New York City they lived in after the 2:50 p.m. bell. It was logical that students like Yarius question anyone who suggested they should receive "the best," a sad lesson to learn so young, as well as for me to witness, so early in my own teaching career.

Though I wanted to fit in at Norman Thomas, I had made a conscious decision not to "pass" for heterosexual. Even before Clinton's "don't ask, don't tell" policy, I had already fallen in line: don't ask me about my sex life, I won't tell you a thing. If you do ask me about my sex life, I *might* tell. In the fourteen months I spent at Norman Thomas, I had come out to only one other teacher, a gay man himself. He, a white Latino, and I were two of a handful of men of color on a staff on more than two hundred teachers. We were also among the youngest teachers on the staff (he was 28, I was 33, with the faculty's mean age being 47). I had a lot of anxiety just talking to him, but was so hungry for an ally that I took the risk and struck up a conversation with him. After a few lunches, we somehow got onto the subject of what we did after work, and I talked about my involvement with Other Countries, a black gay men's writing group. With his help, I got over some of my fear of talking about being gay at work. While at Norman Thomas, I developed close relationships with three African-American teachers, all female, all married, and all, to my knowledge, heterosexual. I could not find the strength to tell them I was gay.

Today, almost three years later, I am teaching at City-as-School, a New York City alternative high school. I am constantly reminded of my own student days in the sixties and seventies. Everything felt possible, and nothing was beyond question. I do not think many of my present students share the same feelings about their future: their opportunities, resources, and expectations have been limited.

I wonder at times if, as a Black gay male teacher, I am really making a difference. Many of the values I hold are alien to my students. I am startled and often surprised at their frequently conservative and rigid remarks regarding sex, recreational drug use, sexuality, and other "moral" issues. Most of the time I find I am left of center, still the precocious child, the sensitive teenager, the left-wing student with the right-wing college majors; still, in the words of fellow African-American co-workers, the "too-Black" IBM sales representative. My nephew takes an HIV/AIDS awareness class that I team-teach with

Rhea Modeste, a straight African-American woman. I remember our many conversations about life, history, and politics when he was a young boy. I remember our weekend excursions to the Hayden Planetarium, museums, theater shows, movies, and ethnic restaurants. I remember encouraging him to draw and keep a picture he drew, at age four, of a dog in the park. His growth spurts are documented in several picture frames throughout my house. I have taken him on several out-of-state trips and introduced him to many gay friends, including my lover of three years, whom I make a point of inviting to all family functions. But attitudes change slowly, a fact made clear when he remarked that he "respect[s] homosexuals but wish[es] they were not so public." I was surprised and hurt by his comment. I was sad that I had not talked with him at length about my friends and lovers. I was angry with myself that I had not been more forthright about my being gay, about him having a gay uncle. I made sure I invited him to my upcoming domestic partnership celebration, in hopes that the publicness of the event will stimulate dialogue between us.

I have had more honest conversations with other students about sex and sexual orientation. Many of the gay students in the school come and talk to me about their lives and their goals. Many of the heterosexual students also talk to me about their lives and their goals. I find it especially rewarding when I can support a student or two struggling with the same issues, offering resources they were unaware of or encouraging their process of self-exploration.

I feel good about being a teacher. I feel good knowing that many of my colleagues know I am gay. While marching down Fifth Avenue, in the 1993 Lesbian and Gay Pride March, I was greeted and joined by at least seven fellow City-as-School staffers. The principal and several of my students also spotted me on an African-American cable TV talk show where I shared about being Black and gay. But, although I have never felt better about myself or my work, I still constantly struggle with feeling totally comfortable in this profession. As a gay teacher, I struggle personally as well, knowing that the successive deaths from AIDS of so many of my friends have weighed me down. I am often unable to find language to express my own feelings of loss. In April of 1991, HIV and death were unintentional motivators for me to teach. Not until an ex-lover died of AIDS did I decide it was time to get tested for HIV, the virus believed to cause AIDS. I had waited for years for some physical sign, some indicator that I might be infected. When I tested positive for HIV on November 18, 1992, I was not surprised. On that day I breathed a sigh of relief and cried three times on the way home from the anonymous testing site — once for my mother, who I did not want to see me die; a second time for my cousin Sheilah, with whom I had grown so much; and the third for my lover John, who I feared would witness me deteriorate. I was too numb to cry for myself.

When Rhea asked me to team-teach the HIV/AIDS awareness class, I was reluctant. Pressing fears about being so "out" were paralyzing. Even though many of my students know that I am gay, their remarks are often homophobic and reflect an erroneous association between HIV and being gay. But once I agreed to teach the class, I had every intention of disclosing my seropositive status. I never did. I was afraid of being perceived as the "infected gay carrier" who warns students to protect themselves from "high-risk groups," which ironically includes gay men and sexually active teenagers. I also found it difficult to echo the prevention messages routinely targeting the public which separate people into "the negatives" — those who must be spared — and "the positives" — those who will end up with AIDS and die.

Eventually, I know I will talk about being gay, how being gay, and being HIV-positive, for that matter, does not mean having AIDS. I know too that sharing this information will add to my own healing and will help define who I am. I know now that I began teaching because I was unconsciously preparing to die. I continue teaching because I am looking forward, more consciously than ever, to tomorrow.

You Can't Tell by Looking at Me

Christine Robinson

English Teacher
Phillips Exeter Academy
Exeter, New Hampshire

I am OUT ... what does that mean?

That I told my brother nearly 20 years ago in a red Volkswagen on the way to the airport. That I wrote my parents a letter some half-dozen years later. That at some point in a friendship I 'fess up. But I wasn't out, here, in my professional life, until two years ago. I had wanted to be, for a long time. But I had to figure out why and for whom I could take such a risk. I knew I was ready when the rage cooled ... when coming out could be a gesture of sharing and not (some) explosive statement ...

Okay, but *how???*

At Phillips Exeter Academy we have required, all-school assembly three times a week. Assigned seats in an austere hall. Guest speakers from university/business/law, etc. Not the right time or place. Once a week we have Meditations in the church. Free/personal/open. Safe? I'd given four in my time here and I asked for the day before Valentine's Day. I would connect my sexuality with relationship/love. Nervous and solid in my cowboy boots, jeans, and black rayon shirt.

In 20 minutes it was done.

Handshakes, hugs, some tears, some notes in my mailbox from kids I didn't know. And back-to-class-as-usual felt like an embrace. If I am known as "the lesbian teacher," I do not feel it ... do not feel any tension/knives in my back.

Feel accepted/respected/whole.

You Can't Tell by Looking at Me

You can't tell by looking at me.
My hair   skin
bone structure   dress   movement
locate me well within the BOUNDARIES of MAINSTREAM
CULTURE.
But I live on the MARGINS...
I AM a   member of a UNIQUE   MINORITY
that has no RACIAL   ETHNIC   or NATIONAL IDENTITY
that speaks EVERY language   lives in EVERY country.
A minority that has   HISTORICALLY   been both
IGNORED   and   BRUTALIZED
PUNISHED on EARTH   EXCLUDED from HEAVEN.
But you CAN'T TELL by looking at me.
I KNOW HOW TO PASS.
I couldn't pass as French on School Year Abroad
and I sure couldn't pass as Southern in Alabama.
But   acting STRAIGHT in a STRAIGHT WORLD
is EVERYTHING I've been trained for
from the   INTIMACY of family
through communities of SCHOOLING
to visual realms of ADVERTISING, CINEMA, ART,
even shopping malls...
With devastating simplicity   I learned
complex RULES of BEHAVIOR, developing elaborate forms
of   EVASION   SECRECY   DENIAL   and HALF-TRUTHS
in which the FAILURE to SPEAK becomes in itself
a FORM OF OPPRESSION.
You might carry a photo
in your wallet   of a cute guy, not too handsome,
or no one   will believe you.
You might have a friend's BROTHER take you to the movies.
After college I   went cross-country on motorcycle
with a MR. Dan Kempton.
I got enough mileage from that story to have crossed the U.S.
a dozen times.
In other words   I learned to be a pretty GOOD   LIAR.

Even NOW after all the poetry   novels   research
a GAY PRIDE   parade or two   GROUNDED in the HISTORY
and TRADITIONS of my COLLECTIVE identity,
I am reminded daily that my lifestyle is at ODDS with prevailing
ETHOS   ASSUMPTIONS   PRIVILEGES of
HETERO-SEX   U   ALITY.
So I straddle TWO WAYS of being, perceiving, and creating
MEANING.
I walk a TIGHTROPE between
ASSIMILATION and RESISTANCE   COMPLICITY and
REVOLT
SILENCE   and   VOICE.
I am   on the one hand   a member of a DOMINANT class
sharing many of its LUXURIES.
And on the other at the ROCK BOTTOM of LEGITIMACY
withOUT CONSTITUTIONAL rights   denied LEGAL
protection
and in some cases gestures of   common decency.
I have spent much of my life FEARFUL   RETICENT   too
EASILY
persuaded that   PROTECTIVE COLORATION is better than
TRUTH.
The ability to DISGUISE sex-u-ality   is both
a GIFT and a CURSE
a FREEDOM   and   a BURDEN.
For when you PASS you lose the opportunity to DEFINE
YOURSELF
because you are NOT BEING yourself...
For years I began every encounter on UNCERTAIN ground
listening for SIGNALS to guide BEHAVIOR conversation.
The advantages are as simple as SURVIVAL
sometimes PHYSICAL ... sometimes PSYCHOLOGICAL.
But to quote Adrienne Rich:
"Invisibility is a dangerous and painful condition, and lesbians are
not the only people to know it.
When someone with the authority of a teacher describes the world
and you are not in it, there is a
moment of psychic dis-equilibrium, as if you looked in the mirror
and saw nothing."

I have felt that SHADOW-Y EXISTENCE: a STRANGER to
MYSELF
and SELF-HATRED that comes from internalizing NEGATIVE
MESSAGES of our culture...
LIBERATION   of any sort can be PAINFUL   COSTLY
but also   EXHILARATING   FULFILLING.
My journey is CONNECTED to my sense of myself
as   TEACHER.

No DARK secrets to avoid telling you.
No TRAUMATIC event to provide an EXPLANATION.
There WAS a time when I needed to root out the "CAUSE,"
as though I had had NO SAY in the matter.
But   from SOUL-searching   MEMORY re-play and   TEXT
BOOKS
I have   come to BELIEVE that MY   SEX-U-ALITY
is an EXPRESSION of my FREEDOM...
It makes me WHOLE.   It is as MYSTERIOUS and
WONDERFUL to me
as rooting geraniums in glasses of water.

My childhood had a   fifties sit-com   kind of WHOLESOMENESS
with quite ORDINARY crushes.
In high school   my eye was on Scott Raine, handsome varsity
athlete.
But I had bloodied his nose on the way home from school
in the 4th grade
and when you go to school with the SAME kids forever,
such MEMORIES linger.
So I was DOOMED to unrequited gazes across the lunch room.
Until SHE arrived.
Newcomer   unaware of my social faux pas and grade school
reputation.
EXOTIC and wise,   BOOKISH and funny,
her name was ROBIN...
I shortened it to ROB and I wonder, now, if I was already learning
the DISGUISES of love.
"ROB and I are going to the movies"
sounded   NORMAL   safe   STRAIGHT...
She had wonderful gray-blue eyes   behind ugly glasses.

I would   tell her she had a smudge on her lens
rainstreaks   dust   anything
to get her to take them off,   if only   FOR A MINUTE.
We sat OPPOSITE one another in Art 102   I
would stare at her GRACEFUL fingers
making GRACEFUL lines with charcoal.
My drawings were clumsy,
I THINK because my hands were shaking.
We   had NO LANGUAGE for our friendship,
expressed by RECKLESS drives in her mother's car,
LONG quiet walks,
exchange of POETRY books
and one cheap-wine drunk.
We often passed notes in history class,
witty commentary on Mrs. McCarthy's lectures.
One afternoon she wrote "I LOVE YOU"
and quoted from a popular romantic song.
As though a HUNTER
had pulled the trigger of a shotgun,
sending birds in a swirling CHAOS of fear,
MY HEART EXPLODED ...
if she LOVED me   we were QUEER...
I felt ARC   TIC
and   without explanation
finished my senior year in NUMB solitude.
MUTE and frightened.
The ONLY thing I could do was dig initials into my desk
during English class,
C. ROB.
For this WOMAN   this GIRL   this GIFT
I was   NOT READY   for.
ROBIN CAMPBELL   who signed her notes ROB. C.
(She still does, to me anyway, although
she's been MARRIED for twenty years to a Mr. Noll)

———

Jan. 29th, 1986
"CAME OUT" to a group of students for the FIRST time.
I was in Rennes, France, teaching English on School Year Abroad.
I am SURE being 3000 miles from Exeter helped!!

I had been THINKING about this for a LONG time
and everything seemed to fall into place:
the BEAUTY of this VERY French neighborhood,
narrow, soft, cobblestone streets,
affectionate relationship with students
and the TEXT we were studying,
Alice Walker's *The Color Purple*.
THIS day   my favorite class came over to my apartment.
CROWDED around the living room   SITTING in a
CLUTTER of knapsacks, Coke cans, ashtrays,
discussing Celie.
How she EMERGES out of SILENCE
from a GIRL without a NAME to a WOMAN
who DARES to write: "AMEN, your loving sister, Celie."
THERE IT WAS...
ANON   Y   MITY   on the page   IDEN   TITY on the next
as simple and PROFOUND as a signature.
So, chain-smoking Gauloise
(which I would be doing now if not in church)
in a rather elaborate   convoluted   monologue like this one—
I   VERBALLY   SIGNED MY NAME.

After an EXCRUCIATING moment of silence,
the room erupted   locker-room kind of hooting
back-slapping CONGRATULATIONS...
Danny thought we should uncork a bottle of champagne.
(He thought that about a lot of things.)
They lingered through the afternoon,
asking SWEET   INGENUOUS   INTELLIGENT questions.
When they had   all   finally left,
I pushed OPEN the grand french windows
LEANED out to stare at the black roofs
of this city SO FAR from home   and   HER...
I took DEEP breaths of FRESH and FOREIGN air
and CRIED   for a GOOD long time.
The next few days had a GIDDY champagne feeling,
then the SOBERING headache
of writing a letter to the Academy.
I spent hours carefully wording this second "COMING OUT"
so it would sound so VERY reasonable and nonthreatening.

Perhaps trying to REASSURE   P.E.A.
that I WOULDN'T do something OUTRAGEOUS or that my
classes wouldn't disintegrate.
Perhaps I was trying to reassure myself.

Re-entry   on campus was rather AWKWARD—
I had NO idea how many people KNEW   or CARED.
I didn't know how many more times
I   WOULD   SHOULD   COULD
go through all this again.

"Coming out of the closet"   FUNNY expression.
CLOSET: a room of safety and suffocation.
All kinds of people hide in closets:
GIRLS in boys' dorms
PSYCHO-killers in B-rated movies.
CLOSETS: where you hang up your FANCY out-on-a-date BEST
clothes
and jam your   smelly   dirty laundry.
Wonderful AMBIGUITY
in the LANGUAGE and IMAGERY of my subculture,
reflecting   the HEART of all American subcultures
that must RE-SHAPE or INVENT from the stuff of a
predominantly WHITE, Western, Judeo-Christian TRADITION.

"COMING OUT"   also a mixed image,
evoking both the debutante's
Glorious   show-y   rite of passage
and a KAFKA-esque nightmare.
You roll up your sleeves   take a deep breath and
open a door to see an ENDLESS corridor
lined with a ZILLION doors—
some so tiny they belong in a doll's house,
some as TALL as this church.
A bit like stepping into Alice's Wonderland
or those old TV GAME shows:
pick the RIGHT door and win the Fridgidaire.
And you   know   early on
that some should NEVER   EVER   be opened.

I have been more often CAUTIOUS than reckless.
Today feels like one of those SEMI-SAFE times.

It has NOT been easy negotiating my lifestyle here,
maintaining a long-term relationship I define as MARRIAGE...
I have felt caught   between   POLITICAL issues of HUMAN
rights
and   the PERSONAL need for PRIVACY...
between the POWER of VISIBILITY
and the SECURITY of INVISIBILITY ...
I have often worried that in my SILENCE I have been
COMPLICIT
in allowing stereotypes
to perpetuate IGNORANCE and FEAR.

I have felt moments of RAGE
and have   FANTASIZED demonstrations
out there in the quad.   I still get WORKED up once in
a while   but I know   how   ANGER can be fueled
by SELF-IMPOSED oppression   and   paranoia.
Colleagues and students who have known   the   "SECRET LIFE"
of C. ROB   have always treated me just fine.
The more I have SHARED my life and HERS
the more PEACE   I have found in myself.
Re-discovering my sense of humor and finding
FRIENDSHIP I didn't believe was possible in this place.
I have NO desire to be a SCAPEGOAT
or some kind of preppy FOLK-HERO.
I just want to listen to my country-western songs
WRITE a poem or two   and   TEND to the GERANIUMS.

And so I wish for ALL of you,
on this day before Valentine's,
a card   box of candy   rose   or   cream in your coffee
from your sweetheart, whoever he or SHE might be...

The Life beyond the Vita

—John P. Pikala

English and Latin Teacher
Central High School
Saint Paul, Minnesota

*T*wenty-seven years is a long time to be doing anything, especially teaching. There are, of course, many reasons why I've stayed a teacher that long. But I know that one impulse in particular that motivated me to enter education. In fact, much of my life has been driven by a single aspect of my character.

Whether waiting until age thirty to begin coming out of the closet; or deciding not to buy a small hotel with my lover to become an innkeeper; or planning out every day of my nine-month travel sabbatical, leaving nothing to chance — all have been the result of this reality: I am not usually a risk taker. Many of my friends, co-workers, and students regularly say they know no one more organized than I. Structure, order, systems, schedules — they are my specialty. Confident and stable as a concrete sequential learner, I can easily be thrown off by unpredictability. A few of my friends say I'm just too anal.

A corollary to my caution is a fear of abandonment. And the result of this combination? — a professional persona of strength and steadiness that masks a lot of personal uncertainty and doubt. So let me show you why I am cautious and fearful, and let me show how my private life has intersected my public vita.

VITA

John P. Pikala is in his twenty-seventh year of teaching in the Saint Paul (Minnesota) Public Schools. On the staff of Central High School for six years, Pikala's current assignment is teacher of Latin 1-2-3-4 and ninth-grade Quest Humanities English. Pikala also is an instructor of adults in the ESL program of the Saint Paul Schools Evening Area Learning Center.

...Pikala received his bachelor's degree from the Saint Paul Seminary, his master's from the University of Saint Thomas.

———

My father relentlessly abused me — emotionally, physically, sexually. The refrain of my youth was Dad saying, "I love you, Johnny. Do you love me?" To which the required response was "I love you, too, Daddy." Dad abused everyone in the family, not me only; however, there is today still denial in my family of Dad's tyranny. One particular night of terror typifies the abuse. My parents had returned home after a night out, and from our shared back bedroom my younger sister and I heard them arguing. The raised voices were nothing new to us. But suddenly I heard my father threaten Mom and begin to throw things. When I ran to the sitting room and found Dad about to pummel Mom, I put my eight-year-old body between theirs. Amazingly, Dad backed down and began to sob. That night we all were lucky, but at other times before and after there was name-calling, taunting, hitting — and more.

My father died in 1963, at age forty-three — of alcoholism and heart failure. His was a death I had fondly fantasized, a death for which I had long prayed. And I felt guilty about my joy for years. The father who was never there even when he was at home was at last forever gone! I now believe that Dad was a closeted homosexual who was sexually active on his many business trips: he used to complain about all the faggots he saw in Greenwich Village; he never explained why he visited the Village again and again. I now know that he hated me because he saw himself in my "sensitivity" and "sissiness." I have pardoned him for his cruelty and his self-hatred. I have forgiven myself for my guilty joy.

Dad's mother truly loved me above all the other of her several grandchildren. I believe she loved me for myself; I know she loved me because I had a vocation to the Roman Catholic priesthood. Having experimented sexually with fellow grade-school boys and Boy Scouts, I really explored homosexuality with an older classmate at the seminary. John was what was called a "delayed vocation," in contrast to the "lifer"' who entered seminary life right after eighth grade. Well, I became conflicted because of my entanglement with John, who, I have come to realize, seduced me. I was conflicted because I could not reconcile "priesthood" with "practicing homosexuality." I have no conflict with this now, and, as they say, "some of my best friends are (ssshhh!!) *priests who are gay.*"

My therapist Bruce says I have abandonment issues. Yes, I certainly do! Abandoned by my father's neglect and abuse, I was later abandoned by his death. And then I was abandoned by my first therapist, a priest counselor to whom I had risked going for help over my "conflict." Father S—— had a conflict of interest in working with me: should he nurture my personhood including my sexuality, or should he support the "party line" of the Roman Catholic Church? He chose the Church and advised that, because of my continuing involvement with John, I abandon my call to the priesthood.

Filled with my own internalized homophobia, I quit the Saint Paul Seminary in 1966 and walked over to Saint Thomas College [now University] to see an advisor. "Let's see," he said. "The priesthood. Um, that's a helping profession, a social service kind of job. Teaching is a helping, social service job, too. My young man, you've come to the right place. Saint Thomas College has a fast-track graduate degree program in teaching."

And that's how I became a teacher. Someone else had, in effect, made the decision for me.

For the first time since kindergarten, I set foot in a public school. (There was no Catholic kindergarten in my neighborhood in 1950.) I was a good teacher, an effective teacher, as I still am. But from 1967, when I began my "career as a teacher," to 1974, I was asexual.

———

...Pikala was a Fulbright Scholar at the American Academy in Rome, a student at the American School of Classical Studies at Athens, a participant in International Baccalaureate Teachers' Workshops in Montezuma, New Mexico, and Edmonton, Alberta.

———

Loretta was a fellow Fulbright Scholar in the summer of 1970; she was a high school Latin teacher from New York. Even though we were both "good Catholics," our relationship did get steamy. However, we never put ourselves in situations of having or wanting to "go all the way." With another couple, Loretta and I took a side trip to Sicily during a break from the academy sessions. When our Fulbright experience came to an end, we kept in contact through letter writing.

The following spring, escorting a group of students on their senior class trip, I arranged to meet Loretta for dinner at a restaurant in Manhattan. I am amazed at those people who say they would not do anything differently if they had their lives to live over. One of the regrets of my life was not being able to risk telling this deserving person why I was just not the man for her. Here, across the table from me, was Loretta, the only woman with whom I'd ever been passionate. But there too sitting beside me was my adopted way of life, "Asexuality," who reminded me that heterosexuality was contrary to my nature and homosexuality was evil — it had driven me away from the priesthood, hadn't it? I could tell Loretta nothing. My closet door was locked tight to everyone — including myself. So now I wonder, does Loretta, abandoned by me, still believe that she was the "defective" part of our relationship?

———

...On sabbatical leave, Pikala traveled and studied in Europe, North Africa, and the Middle East.

———

My sabbatical in 1974–75 was a self-designed nine-month travel-study experience. It was a signal event in my life; it transformed who and what I am. I had gone looking for the footprints of the ancients in distant lands but also found and celebrated — at age thirty — myself as a gay person. Sabbaticals are intended to be professional growth experiences; even more, this leave provided me with a personal epiphany. Set free from the familiarity of family and friends, I gave myself permission to be the person I knew I wanted to become.

Upon my return to America, I repeatedly heard how "different" I had become, though no one could explain exactly what they meant. Now I realize that the change was in my knowing and accepting who I was. I was beginning to come out — but not yet to anyone at work.

Years and several teaching assignments later, I took a risk and participated in a weekend retreat in Minneapolis for gay and lesbian educators. My ex-lover Ken remarked often how strong and lasting an influence the retreat was on me. Not only did I discover that there were other gay and lesbian teachers in Minnesota, I also built coalitions, developed practical strategies, learned about my legal rights, examined ways to lessen homophobia at work.

The day after the retreat, I walked into my principal's office and told him about the weekend I had spent with "other gay and lesbian educators." I've been coming out to the adults in my district ever since. I've signaled my openness and celebration of diversity by displaying in my classroom a poster that reads, "Unfortunately history has set the record a little too straight," and pictures famous people whose gay and lesbian sexual orientation is not generally known: James Baldwin, Errol Flynn, Eleanor Roosevelt, Michelangelo, Willa Cather, and others.

The following year, at the 1990 Minneapolis pride celebration, representing the "Teacher Empowerment" group, I spoke to my gay brothers and sisters before the parade. As we marched, the group of teachers received the loudest cheers from onlookers.

During the process of my coming out at work — beginning with a few selected adults and now including groups of students — I've met all sorts of reactions. The most positive have been from my Latin students and their families.

With Latin students gathered in my classroom before heading out to their field trip buses, one parent chaperone thanked me for displaying the "set the record a little too straight" poster. Neither of us said anything about our own sexual orientations. I later realized that she was the lesbian psychotherapist specializing in coming-out issues whose advertisement I had regularly seen in a local community newspaper. Her son much later — after two years in my Latin classes — discovered my sexuality. I had given him as a graduation present a pocket Latin dictionary which I had put in a personal check box before wrapping. The box had my and Ken's names on it — it was from our joint account. When I saw his mom again at a fall school concert, she told me that Matt had put the pieces together and was amazed that he hadn't figured out my story sooner.

Katie, another Latin student, told me about marching for gay and lesbian rights on her vacation in Denver. A couple weeks later at a gay club in Saint Paul, a woman asked me if I was the Latin teacher at Central: the woman was Katie's older sister, happily dancing with another attractive woman.

There have been other reactions, not as positive.

There are intercom telephones in each classroom. One day, while teaching a class, I answered my phone and heard, "Is this Mr. Pikala?" ["Yes," I answered.] "You dirty homosexual! You're going to hell! DIE!!"

From time to time, students have directly asked me in the middle of a lesson, "Mr. Pikala, are you gay?" The questioners have wanted to startle or embarrass me — or have simply wanted to cause a disruption. My usual response has been something like "Would it

make a difference to you if I were? I don't talk about my personal life."
Following one such exchange a couple of years ago, I knocked on the
door of the new principal's office, found the entire administrative team
just ending a meeting, and asked them for five minutes. I said, "It's an
open secret among the adults in the district who know me that I am a
gay man. I want to be more open not only with the staff but with the
students at Central." To a person, they discouraged me from coming
out any further. Days later, another staffer told me that she heard I had
told the administrators I wanted to announce my domestic partnership
with Ken at a faculty meeting!!

This year we have another new principal who welcomed the ninth-
graders and their families during an orientation program. At Central,
she said, we celebrate diversity, and she spoke eloquently about eth-
nicity, race, religion, sex, income, ablebodiedness. When I later reminded her that she had omitted sexual orientation, she said she
regretted the oversight especially since all the printed school materials
specifically include sexual orientation.

———

*...Pikala volunteers at Grace House and the Minnesota AIDS Project, both
in Minneapolis.*

———

Mortality and abandonment — AIDS has heightened these realities
of my life. Yes, reaching my forty-third birthday was a milestone for
me; six years later, I still today feel my father's death age as a barrier
I've overcome. My back surgery in 1991 again brought me face-to-
face with death and kept me out of work for three months. But the
epidemic, especially in the past three years, has made me reassess the
meaning of my life. So many acquaintances, so many friends are gone
— including two teachers, excellent and caring educators. Neither
Bob nor David was out at work; neither, in fact, was out to many
people at all. When they acquired AIDS, both simply and quietly
disappeared from their schools and from the lives of their friends. I
later read David's obituary in the paper and called our mutual friends,
Joe and Charlie, to find out what they knew. David's death was a
complete surprise to them also; none of us had known of David's
final hospitalization five days earlier. Bob had not let anyone say
good-bye, and David had left before any of us knew enough to say
farewell.

And Bill's death from AIDS? This is the man who had nearly single-handedly created Grace House, a residential care facility for PLWAs. At the end, he was a resident at Grace, and there he died. His was the third death at Grace House within five horrific days. Most of Bill's friends had been able to come to tell him how much his energy had given life to them and how much they treasured his love of them.

Abandonment. Yes, it is an issue for me: Ken, my partner of fourteen years, and I split in 1992; a year later I made the mistake of falling in love with a man whose feelings were far from mine. My therapist also says I'm experiencing "existential grief," the sadness that comes from the realization that, even when surrounded by great friends, family, maybe a lover, each of us is in fact ALONE.

So, with all my own abandonment issues, how could I recently have so completely let down one of my ninth-graders, Edward? Fulfilling an assignment called "Elocution Contest" (prompted by our study of the novel *Betsey Brown*), he gave a presentation that included reading a poem, commenting on the poem, and saying something about its author. For absolutely no reason I could articulate, I negatively reacted to his choice, "The Star-Spangled Banner." I asked Edward to make another selection and give a second presentation. That was on a Friday.

I mulled over my stupidity and insensitivity that weekend and settled on a course of corrective action for Monday. Early Monday I had a phone call from Edward's dad — Edward was crushed; I was Edward's favorite teacher, and I had really let Edward down; Edward had thoroughly researched the making of the song, its author, its history; Edward's dad and Edward's therapist were working with Edward on issues of trust and fair play. Dad and I talked about the decision I had come to over the weekend.

That day in class, I publicly apologized to Edward and asked that he present his second poem for extra credit. (His father had told me Edward had, though unhappily, researched and prepared for another elocution.) In private, I apologized again to Edward and told him that I had at times myself been disappointed by adults and that I hoped I could somehow regain his confidence in me. Time will tell if Edward will later reflect on his contact with me as abandonment. I hope — and will do my best to ensure — that our relationship for the rest of the school year will be nurturing and fulfilling and that Edward will again risk trusting adults.

―――――

...Pikala calls himself a quester, a seeker, a searcher; he values honesty,
curiosity, compassion; he sets high expectations for himself and others.

―――――

My theme has been of a person, wounded by abandonment, who is a reluctant risk taker. I guess it is no surprise that some of us gay people, since we often face threatening situations, are hesitant about taking the risk of coming out. Gay teachers in particular feel that they are vulnerable; teachers as a group are probably the most deeply closeted segment of the gay community. We fear that, should we come out, we will lose, if not our jobs, at least the support and respect of our colleagues, superiors, students, and community.

However, I have discovered that there is less and less reason for me to keep separate my professional vita and private life: I have not been abandoned when I have risked coming out. The very few negative or indifferent reactions do not count for much compared with the overwhelming acceptance and support I have experienced.

So this year I decided to open my closet door even wider. For a couple years at Central, we've had a confidential gay and lesbian student support group facilitated by a very effective heterosexual ally, Kay. I've attended their meetings and parties on occasion. Early this year, I told the group of the decision I had come to — I would not suddenly start to shout about my gayness, but henceforth I would certainly be direct in answering student queries about my sexuality. A couple weeks later, when a student in English told a derogatory joke about gay people, I risked telling him in front of the class that his story was offensive to me as a gay man. Not only did my world not come to an end, but many other students agreed that the joke was out of line.

In fact, my closet door may be wide open. Some students have asked, and I am now advisor to the GiBLeTS, Gays, Bisexuals, Lesbians, Transgenders, and Supporters, a three-month-old group that is activist and out. I have the same expectations for the GiBLeTS as I have for my English and Latin students, the expectations my life experiences have taught me: be honest with yourselves and compassionate toward others; be questers and searchers; develop the confidence to face abandonment and to take risks.

Yes, I entered teaching almost as an afterthought — and as a protection against risk taking and as the result of being abandoned. But when I started in education I didn't know that I would be annually recommitting myself to youth. That I continue to teach young people is evidence of my belief in the motto I have on my business cards: "Qui docet, discit" — "The person who teaches, learns." A commitment to lifelong learning and the drive to be the best teacher I can be — these are among the impulses that have kept me in education for twenty-seven years.

Shelly, Hallie, Jack, and Me

Blake Respini

History Teacher
Lick-Wilmerding High School
San Francisco, California _____

As a gay high school teacher, I often think back to my own high school experience in Palo Alto, California, in the midseventies. I wasn't gay back then, or so I thought. It was just that I had enormous crushes on boys instead of girls. But I was obviously not gay — or homosexual, as we were then called: I didn't wear green plaid pants, didn't want to become a hairdresser, and hated floppy wrists. I was into kayaking and skiing, and preferred rock to show tunes. So, despite my sexual longings for the likes of Mike, Larry, and Andy, I couldn't have been gay. My crushes and feelings of true love for members of my own sex remained confusing, unnameable, and shameful in the absence of any role models or accurate information on homosexuality. I felt like a freak of nature, and found it impossible to come to terms with who I really was for many years. I felt completely, utterly, and totally alone.

When I became a high school teacher in 1982, my own experience made me painfully aware of the need for positive gay role models for both gay and straight students. As a young teacher, however, I feared for my job and my image, and chose to stay in the closet. Working in an independent school, I knew how easily I might be "eased out" of a job in a school without tenure or other traditional job protections. But the biggest obstacle was my own feelings. The thought of coming out to a hoard of teenagers brought back the old fears of taunts, ridicule, and rejection that had paralyzed me as a high school student. I wanted to be liked and respected. I wanted to be seen as cool, not queer, by my students. So I played the game of the cool young (straight) teacher, who just happened to have a roommate named Dave, who just might accompany me on a school field trip or to a school play or to a school sporting event. There may have been unasked questions, but as long as "it" wasn't discussed, "it" didn't exist, or so I thought. Perhaps the homophobia embedded in teenage culture made me feel that I should be ashamed of being gay. All I knew was that I feared being labeled the "gay teacher." So for years, I played the "don't ask, don't tell" game with my students.

For a while, this seemed to work just fine — until Shelly had a talk with me. In 1986, Shelly was one of my cross-country runners, a sensitive boy who played classical piano. I figured he was bound to be gay. One day he casually mentioned to me that many great classical composers were gay. I nonchalantly responded with something deep like, "Oh, is that so?" His comment hadn't seemed particularly extraordinary to me, so I didn't give it much of a second thought.

The next day, Shelly approached me and, in a shaky voice, told me that he had to apologize to me. It seems that he had heard and believed a rumor that I was gay. He told me he had made the comment about the classical composers in order to make me feel better. (I'm not sure why he thought I needed cheering up in the first place.) He went on to say that he now realized it was wrong to believe in rumors, and that he shouldn't have believed this one to be true. He said that there were even rumors that there were students that were gay, but that — in reality — everyone his age was just confused about their sexual identity.

I sensed that Shelly was confused and that he was dying to come out to me. I longed to tell him that whatever he felt was okay. I wanted to tell him that I was indeed gay, that you could be gay and still be whomever you wanted to be. But instead, my fears overcame me, and I simply told him that it was wrong to believe in rumors, as they could destroy careers, and that it was not really necessary for people to label themselves — especially teenagers, since their sexuality would become clearer as they grew older. I avoided the issue of my own sexuality; Shelly, rather than press for more, simply agreed with what I had said. We were both a bit nervous and awkward, and ended the conversation with some vague, general talk about the pressures to conform and the struggle of self-discovery — without ever really talking about ourselves.

I left feeling I had betrayed him. He had come to me looking for support and a role model, and I had denied him both. My own anxieties about being outed led me to refuse to even talk about homosexuality with him. My fears stopped us from having a conversation I believed we both desperately needed to have. The event stayed with me for several years, and I became determined to make sure that I never again let down a future "Shelly."

When a new headmaster was hired in 1988 and our school became a safer place, my problem became not if, but when and how, I would come out to my students. It was petrifying to imagine walking into class one day and dropping a bombshell by saying something like, "By the way, I sleep with other men." I don't think any teacher wants to initiate a conversation that leads to his or her students picturing them having sex, especially a type of sex which many still find revolting. What I needed was the right context for coming out, and something that would give me the courage to actually do so.

Teachers always talk about how much they learn from their students. Well, I learned a lot about bravery and self-acceptance from a student named Hallie, who provided me with both the context and the courage to come out. When Hallie was a junior in 1991, she became the first student at our school to come out publicly as a gay person, when she told some of her friends she was a lesbian and then put a number of "Queer Nation" stickers on her locker. This caused some controversy among students at the school, leading to the infamous "locker war," when a small group of homophobic senior boys began to decorate their lockers with signs such as "The Bible said Adam and Eve, not Adam and Steve." This led to a school ban on all locker decorations, and in an effort to raise the level of discussion, an all-school assembly on the topic of homophobia was announced. The assembly, which featured a panel of gay and lesbian people talking about their lives, was followed by small discussion groups in which all teachers and students were expected to participate.

Before the assembly, I had already made the decision that my discussion group was going to be my coming-out moment. Quite nervous about the potential consequences of this, I informed a number of colleagues and my headmaster, who all gave me their full support. My heart was racing somewhat as our discussion group began, but then students began to speak of their admiration for the courage of the panel members, who had shared so much of themselves with the school. Many also stated how surprised they were at how "regular" gay people could be, and that they now realized that there must be gay people around them who they had never figured to be gay. By the time it was my turn to speak, a serene calm had overcome me. Ready to cross the Rubicon and cast my fate to the winds, I took a deep breath and said,

"Well, guess what? I'm one of the people whom you may never have suspected was gay."

I can't remember what else I told them at that point, but I do remember that student reactions ran the gauntlet from an astonished "Oh, my God, I can't believe it. I never would have guessed" to a more sophisticated "Of course! I always knew about you and Dave, I assumed everyone did!" The main thing was that the cat was finally out of the bag.

The positive results for me were numerous. First of all, for a number of weeks I seemed to be floating on air. I had never realized what a burden it was to hide my "secret." I relaxed from a tension I had never realized even existed. Second, my relationships with my students were better than ever before. They seemed to appreciate my sharing something personal and vulnerable about myself with them, and became more open and relaxed with me in return. Finally, coming out gave me the opportunity to talk about issues that I had avoided in the past. Topics such as homophobia and gay rights now often come up spontaneously in ways that are important, relevant, and personal. As for my fears of being labeled, I don't feel I am seen as the "gay teacher." Instead, students seem to better understand me for the whole, complex person that I am.

I am often asked if I have had negative reactions. My answer is no, but one episode illustrates how my being out did turn a potentially negative situation into a positive one. At the beginning of the second semester in 1993, some new students entered my U.S. History class. During the term's second week, we discussed Lincoln's Emancipation Proclamation. We talked about how Lincoln, in his effort to advance the cause of freedom for blacks, was stuck between those who wanted him to do more and those who wanted him to do nothing at all. I pointed out the similarity between Lincoln's dilemma and that faced by the new president, Bill Clinton, who at the time was caught up in a controversy over his efforts to lift the ban on service by gays in the military. I asked students what they thought of how Clinton was handling the pressures he faced from both sides over lifting the ban, which I thought were analogous to those Lincoln had faced at the time of the Emancipation Proclamation. A new student named Jack began to spew out homophobic commentary about how disgusting gays were and so forth. For a while, I said nothing, and let other students give their opinions, which universally ran counter to Jack's. Eventually, I said that, as a gay person myself, I felt lifting the ban was very important, not because I wanted to enter the military but because the ban suggested I was unworthy and established gays as the only group officially discriminated against by the government. Jack practically melted into his seat, as he apparently had not yet heard that I was gay. Shortly thereafter he recovered and rejoined the conversation. He claimed that gays being teachers was different than gays being soldiers, and defended the ban by talking about soldiers' rights of privacy and the issue of morale. I told him I respected his opinion, and then we moved on to other topics.

After Jack was absent for the next three days, I called his home and spoke to his mother. She was quite apologetic, and told me that Jack was afraid to return to my class and thought I was going to fail him. I then spoke with Jack, who told me he had greatly exaggerated his feelings about gays in order to "look cool" to his new classmates. I told him that I did not hold his comments against him, but that he should instead use them as a learning experience to only say what you truly believe. This talk began a new relationship which deepened over the semester. Near the end of the year, a close friend of Jack's from another school committed suicide. I was the only teacher Jack sought out to deal with his anger and guilt over his friend's death. Had I never come out, I doubt our relationship would have been such that he could have confided in me. In at least this one instance, my being out enabled me to be a more effective teacher for a student who truly needed me.

All these years later, I find myself thinking back to that conversation I had with Shelly, which seemed so long ago. I suppose I truly owe thanks to him, for it was his desire to talk that made me realize the need for me to come out. I thought he had wanted to come out to me, and that gave me the impetus to eventually come out myself. Ironically, years later, I found out he wasn't gay all along.

You Can't Tell Him I'm Not

——————— "Ruth Irwin"

English Teacher
"Norman High School"
"Norman, Oklahoma" _____

I've been teaching English in high schools and junior high schools for eighteen years. I began the process of coming out of the closet with my colleagues ten years ago, but being *completely* myself in my classroom has always been a little tricky. Every so often a student will allude to my sexuality and it has always been scary; my initial reaction includes a red-hot flush and a split second of paralysis. I can't help but wonder what will happen next: a complaint from a parent, being questioned by a principal, or worse...? But most days I'm not even thinking about it; I'm too busy planning lessons, grading papers, and facilitating student work.

Last year, though, I was forced to think about what it meant to be out in my classroom when I was harassed by a student who had figured out that I am a lesbian.

Trevor was a tall, gangly fifteen-year-old who masked his lack of self-esteem by acting overly confident. He often distracted his classmates with his efforts to draw attention to himself. He was a master of the smart remark and fancied himself skilled at asking the kinds of questions designed to get a teacher off the track. I found him to be annoying at worst until his discovery about me gave him the ammunition he had been looking for to gain control of the class.

I guess Trevor drew his conclusions about me because I have reached the stage at which I refuse to lie or cover up my life. I don't make any general announcements about being a lesbian to my students, especially to sophomores, which Trevor was. But when students ask if I'm married, or if I have a boyfriend, or if I live with anyone, I answer truthfully. I tell them that I live with a woman named

Donna, two dogs, and two cats. I tell them that I am happy with my life the way it is, that I'm not interested in being married, and that my friends are my family.

I think the other clue Trevor got, as did his classmates, came from my refusal to let them use the word "fag" to put each other down. At some point I got too angry about their use of the word, and I remember explaining to them the origin of the term, thinking it would foster some empathy. But instead I suppose it led them to believe that *I* was the queer, because, after all, why would anyone but another queer defend fags?

Anyway, Trevor began to harass me each day with a different tactic. One day I was concentrating on facilitating a discussion of literature in a round-table setting when I looked up and saw Trevor's mischievous grin. He and a male cohort were holding each other's hand on top of the table so that everyone would be sure to see it, and so no one would miss my reaction to it. A blush started at the top of my head and rushed all the way through me. My chest tightened and I wanted in the worst way to explode my anger at him. But I've been at this job long enough to know that the only way to win is to act as if I'm not affected. I did my best to quickly recover, and I said only, "Very funny," and went on with my next discussion question.

Other days he would bait me with some question, including several about my stand on gays in the military. He wanted to know if I thought gays should be allowed to serve in the armed forces, and didn't I think that it would cause problems in the barracks or on the battlefield. One day he asked, "Ms. Irwin, would *you* want to be in the military if you knew that you would have to take showers with *lesbians?*" I just shook my head. By that time I was well practiced with my responses on that topic so I sighed and said, "Trevor, I think I'm a little past the age at which I'd be accepted in the army anyway. Any chance I could get you to finish reading that chapter before the bell rings?"

Of course, no one in the room knew that my partner had been discharged from the Marine Corps for being a lesbian, and no one knew the anguish it caused her or me. Every day I acted as a professional, working to keep my anger or frustration from showing, always answering questions calmly and often by asking him a question back, forcing him to disclose his motives or reveal his true intent to his classmates so they could see what kind of person he was being.

But Trevor would always leave the room acting like the victor, laughing and high on his perceived power. Neither he nor his classmates felt the full extent of my rage, or my loathing of his actions or their attitudes, and I let no one know of my fear.

But his classmates did quickly understand what Trevor was doing, and I believe that for many of them the specter of my lesbianism began to overshadow my role as teacher. This was what became the most painful part of the experience for me. Each day as I waited at my door for the students to arrive I endured the downcast eyes, the curt greetings, the snickers that hurt so much. In class the discussion was too often stiff and controlled, and the barriers some students erected were so powerful they were nearly visible. I got to the point where I dreaded coming to the job I had always loved.

The day that my rage overpowered my fear was the day that Trevor entered my classroom gesturing with his hand and his mouth to simulate a sexual act. In a split second my revulsion told me that I could not tolerate his behavior a minute longer. I saw this young man demonstrating both the degree to which he was comfortable with his bigotry and the limits to which he believed his power extended. In that moment I knew I could not allow him to continue to model behavior that was hurting everyone in the room.

I marched Trevor to the office so fast it made his head spin. My head spun too as I stood in the vice-principal's outer office writing up the incident on a referral form. As my anger finally began to flow outward, momentum took over. I took a deep breath and marched into the vice-principal's office. He was only in his second year at this job, and I had not yet built the rapport with him that would have facilitated my letting him know about my sexual orientation, but it didn't make any difference at that moment. "You need to know that I wrote Trevor up because he has been harassing me and today he went too far," I blurted. "But you also need to know that he's harassing me because he thinks I'm a lesbian, *and you can't tell him I'm not.*"

Looking back now, I believe that telling the vice-principal before really thinking through the consequences of such a statement was actually the best action in this situation. I was acting to regain my dignity, my self-esteem, and my safety, and this was simply the only way to do it.

Clearly, my vice-principal was new to this kind of situation. He didn't quite know how to react to my announcement, and it seemed to take a while for the impact of my statement to sink in. But he keyed in on the inappropriateness of Trevor's behavior and immediately called him in to his office. He confronted Trevor with his misdeed and listened while I told of the other times Trevor had tried to fluster me with his ploys. He told Trevor, "What you are doing is sexual harassment and it's against the law. Ms. Irwin is well within her rights to ask for your suspension from school because of the things you have said and done to her." When I heard him say those words, relief began to wash over me.

Immediately Trevor realized he was caught and that he would not find any support for his harassment, regardless of its basis. He began to cry, saying, "I can't get suspended! I'll get in trouble with my parents!" I must admit that the tears he shed in the office that day were gratifying to me, even though I believe they were not shed out of remorse for the pain he had caused me, but for having been caught, confronted, and given consequences. It didn't matter at that point — Trevor had admitted what he had done, the vice-principal had told him that his actions were wrong and would not be tolerated, and he was suspended from school for the rest of that day and all of the next.

When Trevor returned to my classroom he never harassed me again. Surprisingly, he became something of a brown-noser, choosing to read a feminist novel for his independent project and distancing himself from the friends he had previously drawn into his plans or tried to impress with his behaviors. Although I believe that this was mostly due to his fear of repeated and worsened consequences, it didn't matter. The harassment had stopped, and more importantly, I had stood up to it in a way that preserved my integrity. The class also understood that not only was I going to enforce my expectations regarding bigoted behavior but that I had the vice-principal on my side as well.

After the incidents with Trevor, I did meet again with my vice-principal; my assistant principal and another gay teacher were present as well. I believe my gay colleague and I made something of a difference in the administrators' understanding of the experience of the lesbian or gay teacher, of which they had little prior grasp. They had what they thought were liberal attitudes and made statements like "We're not worried about you because we know that what you do outside of school has no effect at all on who you are as a teacher." But they soon came to see that they didn't even know what questions they should ask us. We told them as much as we could about our experiences: about colleagues whose demeanor toward us would suddenly turn cold for no apparent reason; about anti-gay jokes we'd heard other teachers tell in the lounge and how that made us feel; about the colleague who insisted there were no gay or lesbian teachers in our district, and if he found out about any, he'd call the superintendent; about kids who yell names at us from a crowd in which they're hiding; about constantly pushing back the fear of losing the work we love. The principals listened wordlessly after a while; I believe that these were experiences about which they had never thought before.

That I was out to those two administrators after that was an accomplishment about which I felt very good, but as is often the case the encounter also left me with the reminder that there is a great deal that school systems don't know about lesbian and gay teachers, and that what they don't know really hurts all of us. I would like to be able to say that subsequent talks with the vice-principal and other members of the administration after this incident resulted in the writing of official policy regarding lesbian and gay teachers, but that's still a long way off. There is still no written language concerning job protection for lesbian and gay teachers in our district, and no school officials have ever even acknowledged that lesbian and gay teachers are employed in our schools. And this year all but one of our building's principals have moved on, and I have ahead of me once again the task of trust-building with the new ones.

This year I see some of last year's students in the hallway, and some still won't make eye contact or will turn away as they mumble their greetings, and that still is difficult for me. But others are friendly, and some have even told me of their plans to take other courses I teach. I know that teenagers need to know that lesbians are real people with real jobs and real lives, like me, and who win teaching awards, like the one I was given for my work in building a women's literature course for my high school. (I was one of twenty-five teachers in my state to win the award for excellence in classroom teaching, which was accompanied by a grant of several thousand dollars for curriculum building and professional growth.)

So I have come out to students who have revealed to me their own lesbianism or gayness. Once an older student stayed after class to tell me that when her peers made homophobic statements it really angered her. We talked for several minutes, as I worked to validate her feelings and to let her know that I shared them. Then she revealed to me that her mother was a lesbian and she had dealt with homophobic responses to her mother for most of her life. The more she told me the more I knew I'd be a hypocrite if I let her believe that I was straight. So I told her that I understood because I was a lesbian myself. She seemed happy that I had been open with her, and I went home that night feeling proud that I hadn't taken the easy way out. This year I am helping a gay colleague sponsor a support group that he founded for lesbian and gay students who attend our high school and other high schools in our district, and I am out to all the students in our meetings.

The result of all of this is that I have grown in my identity as both a teacher and a lesbian. The flashes of panic I sometimes had when homosexuality comes up in my classroom are fading, and I no longer worry about which of my colleagues know about me because I am finding so much strength in being out. After her experiences with being discharged from the Marine Corps, my partner is adept at teaching me how to find my bravery. With her support and the support of a strong lesbian community in my city, I feel as if I have access to the resources I need to continue my work despite any bigotry I may have to confront. I know that I'll never tolerate a student's harassment again, and that knowledge brings with it a sense of empowerment.

No one can tell my students I'm not a lesbian, and I'm glad. I wouldn't want it any other way.

Straightforward, But Not Straight

Steve Warren

Spanish Teacher
Horace Greeley High School
Chappaqua, New York

"*F*ag!*" "Hey, you're a faggot!" "Faggot!"* These insults were hurled at me as I walked across campus one afternoon at Mohonasen High School, near Albany, New York. I panicked. How could they know? Keeping my head low, I walked as fast as I could to my classroom. There I quickly set my students to work on a writing assignment so they wouldn't notice how shaken I was.

This verbal attack by students I didn't teach or even know was not provoked by any particular incident. Perhaps they were just being cruel, or maybe they sensed the one thing I had worked so hard to hide from everyone I knew, taught, or associated with. Maybe the blind dates I had gone on, the jokes I had tolerated in the faculty room, and the elaborate lies I had constructed to project a "normal" life weren't enough. It hit me how the fragile make-believe world I had created could be easily destroyed by strangers. I decided to find a new school and a new life as a straightforward, but not "straight," teacher.

On the way home the last day of school I finally got up the courage to come out to a friend I had commuted with for two years. He was wonderful, thanking me for sharing that part of myself with him. Why hadn't I done it earlier?

That was 1989. By 1990 I was teaching in Westchester County. Not knowing much about this area, I counted on its proximity to New York City to ensure a more progressive approach to teaching as well as a more inclusive attitude toward teachers.

"Why won't you dance with me? Are you gay?" An inquisitive female student asked me this at a Homecoming Dance. I was a bit unnerved, but managed to reply that regardless of my sexual orientation, I wasn't

going to dance with her. We both laughed and went on to have a pleasant conversation. By now I was halfway through my first year at Horace Greeley High School. Everything was going well, and I felt comfortable with my status as teacher. I was proud of the connections I was developing with my students, and I had not resorted to making up stories about myself. Since I wasn't completely sure that my tenure would be safe if my orientation became public, I was still evasive when my colleagues asked whether I was married or where I went on weekends. But I had left many old habits behind. I was determined not to repeat the mistakes I had made throughout college and during my first teaching position.

With some trepidation, I came out to two non-gay colleagues who have remained constant in their support. During the three years that followed they have encouraged me, cautioned me, and championed the "cause" in my absence. Unlike my last school, I wasn't waiting for my last day to be frank with the people I respected.

"Have you told your mother about your boyfriend yet?" I was asked this during a "family-themed" role-play activity in class. I don't think the student who challenged me with this had any clue as to how accurate he was. I'm sure he simply wanted to test the limits of our good-natured verbal sparring. His intent was to provoke me, expecting a firm denial. But now in my second year at HGHS I had come a long way. Even though I was nervous, I decided not to react as I had in the past. I replied as casually as I could, "No, there are a number of things I haven't yet shared with my mom." The student chuckled at what he figured was a comic response and he went back to work with his group. Later that week when a similar question surfaced I put my arm around his shoulder, steered him down the hallway away from his audience, and suggested that his fascination with my sexual orientation indicated that he had a lot of questions he should discuss with his counselor. That ended the discussion, though we continue to enjoy a very positive and lively relationship.

That same year I was encouraged when the staff development committee proposed a day focusing on diversity. That is, until I learned that sexual orientation wasn't included. I asked a few teachers to send a letter asking the committee to be more inclusive. The committee's response was disheartening. They insisted that it was a topic already covered in other workshops. Angry and frustrated, I did not pursue it. Still one year away from tenure, I walked an uncomfortable line between honest disclosure, and fear of losing a teaching position I thoroughly enjoyed.

"Just because you're straight, doesn't mean you have to be narrow." Unbeknownst to me, the Students for Social Justice chose the week before Valentine's Day to address the issue of homophobia in our school. Without the knowledge and support of the administration, the students decided to confront the homophobic intolerance that exists at our school. Over five hundred fluorescent pink triangles appeared on backpacks, sweatshirts, and ski jackets. Each day I proudly pinned one to my shirt. In the sea of pink triangles, motivated by a student-led effort to educate, my single one didn't seem out of place.

"So what are you doing to make this school a better place for gay and lesbian students?" I asked my principal following Gay Awareness Week. He had just shared his reasoning for not donning one of the pink triangles. It was more important, he felt, that one be judged by actions rather than buttons or bumper stickers. Nearly three hours later we had discussed calmly yet earnestly the challenges facing gay youth in our community as well as my personal "closeness" to the subject. I left school that day with my mind reeling at all that had transpired during those three hours and the previous three years. Though I had not yet been granted tenure, I had just come out to my principal!

By now I was much more comfortable around school. I had even invited a few colleagues over for dinner with my partner, Ed Hutchins. Some had met him during our after-school "unwinding" hour on paydays. Ed had also accompanied me to various school plays and we had worked the Softball Throw event when Horace Greeley hosted the Special Olympics.

Slowly the number of associates aware of my openness began to increase. To some I approached the subject directly, to others I some-what casually mentioned plans that "Ed and I" had made and still others noticed the matching silver bands we wore. The publication of a letter I wrote to the national AFT publication also generated discussion. In it I challenged opponents of New York City's Rainbow Curriculum to recognize the diversity of families in our society. None of my colleagues reacted negatively. I'm sure a few treated the news as hot gossip and planned to repeat it later. But instead of being frightened by this, I was actually glad to have a quicker way of spreading the good news.

"I'll be in D.C., along with about a million of my friends." It took a second before the students realized I was talking about the 1993 March on Washington. This was the first time I had approached the subject

of my orientation with students. After the march, several asked how it had gone. They were curious, but since I wasn't out to the entire student body they weren't sure whether to ask or to pretend not to know. I replied that it was an incredible feeling to be in the majority for a day, and left no doubt that it was something I was neither ashamed of nor secretive about.

"We have a responsibility to make this a safe and caring community for all our students." In 1993 I got tenure. I celebrated by presenting a gay issues packet to key administrators. It included articles describing the difficulties facing gay and lesbian youth, programs already begun in high schools around the United States, and some specific goals for the school to work towards. One result has been the scheduling of a workshop for student support personnel through the Hetrick-Martin Institute.

"Can we help increase awareness of the problems facing gay and lesbian adolescents, and find solutions? Contact Steve Warren..." Stories from former gay and lesbian students about the challenges they faced at Greeley, as well as my memories of high school homophobia, prompted me to submit an article to our local union newsletter. In it I discussed the unique circumstances encountered by gay youth in our school and asked people interested in helping to contact me. The newsletter editor included a "disclaimer" and encouraged anyone "who disagreed" to respond. Instead, the responses were unanimously positive and called on the union and the district to take an active role in addressing the needs of our gay and lesbian students. Some gay and lesbian teachers have even come out to me as a result, and our social and professional circle continues to expand. Due to some of the issues raised by this and a follow-up article, our union's executive council has since adopted a nondiscrimination policy which will be used to encourage the school district to do the same.

This year two teachers have put me in touch with two students who have come out to them. We occasionally meet informally to chat about books, movies, problems, and positive movements in the school community. What an experience to see our future in these students who have already developed such a strong sense of themselves! I think it is the most encouraging development yet.

Recently, when Ed and I bought a house together, I showed pictures of it to some students. They shared the happiness of the occasion, and one student even presented us with a set of wind chimes she had made.

"You should know that Ed will be accompanying me to the prom. And we may be dancing together." A colleague and I have been chosen to be class advisors for the Class of 1998. This four-year commitment involves numerous social and fund-raising activities. I have explained that Ed will be helping when possible, as well as accompanying me to many of these functions. Not every administrator is excited about this, but we have a long time to work out the details.

Looking back, there have been successes and there have been setbacks. But there is no turning back nor giving up. The Students for Social Justice are again planning their now-annual Gay Awareness Week. And this year I've got a drawer full of pink triangle buttons to wear proudly on my lapel.

Out in the Country

—————Kirk Bell

Humanities Teacher
The Northwest School
*Seattle, Washington*_____

I grew up in suburban Minneapolis, but my family was rooted in Iowa and my spirit rested in the lake country of northern Minnesota. As a child and young adult I had relished vacations in the mountains of Colorado and Alberta, the Dakota and Canadian prairies, and the Pacific Northwest coast. Like many gay men, I once thought that being out of the closet in large urban centers was enough of a challenge, and that being gay in rural America would be even more lonely and dangerous. I was resigned, then, to the notion that being gay required urban living, despite my stronger attraction to "the land."

In the early 1970s, many of my straight friends were moving to rural towns and farms in Oregon, Washington, Colorado, British Columbia, and Minnesota. I envied their ability to act out their dreams of rural life. I resented having to choose between the comfort of gay life in a crowded urban setting or a closeted and lonely existence in the beautiful, pastoral settings I dreamed about.

On a bicycle vacation trip to Shaw Island, a small bit of paradise in the San Juan Archipelago two hours north of Seattle, Washington, I decided to leave behind a poor relationship and to make my way in rural America. Looking back, it was a dramatic change, but was in keeping with my deeper interests and desires. Within a few months, I found work on the island and within a year I started to build a cabin on six acres of woods and meadows. Because most islanders were retired and kept to themselves, I remained quiet about my sexuality and never experienced any blatant repercussions for being gay. When I wanted contact with other gay men, I usually went to Seattle.

After three years, loneliness set in. To obtain a teaching certificate I moved to the mainland to attend university and shortly thereafter, in 1981, met my partner (and his two children).

In the fall of 1982, I was hired to teach twelve children in a K–8 one-room school on Stuart Island, also in the San Juans, and even more remote than Shaw. This is an island without ferry service, without electrical power or phones, without a town, with very few cars, and with only fifty year-round residents.

Though the prospect of work in such a remote setting sounded like a wonderful adventure, I worried that if I took the job, my partner and his kids would have no choice but to stay on the mainland and to await my weekend visits. I could not imagine people in so remote a setting accepting an openly gay man, much less his boyfriend and two kids; nor could I picture attempting to remain closeted and anonymous.

My hopeful and optimistic self wanted my family to join me ... for the kids to experience an old-fashioned one-room school ... for my partner to take a well-deserved break from the frustrations of his mainland business ... for all of us to revel in the beauty and charm of island life. Another opportunity to live in the Islands, this time with a lover!

We discussed the situation. My partner wanted the adventure of island living for his kids and for himself. I certainly wanted to return to rural life; so I accepted the position but waited to talk openly about my family until securing a place to live. Because there were no homes available to rent on the island, I resigned myself to camp at the school for three long months until the school district arranged for me to live at the Lighthouse on a dramatic, wind-swept, and stunning point of land on the northwest tip of the island, two miles from the nearest neighbor. I was pleased that my family could join me; but I then had the onerous task of divulging to islanders that my partner was a *man*.

My approach to telling the truth was to work the subject slowly into conversations over a period of several days, first with those I assumed might be open-minded. To my surprise, the response was not at all negative. Several people indicated their satisfaction with my performance as a teacher. They particularly liked my emphasis in teaching through art, music, and theater and my strong efforts to individualize instruction to each student's needs. A couple of folks mentioned having gay or lesbian friends and acquaintances in Seattle. Others professed "liberal" attitudes about the subject even though there appeared to be some hesitancy in their voices. Everyone, however, was *elated* at the prospect of two more children for the school. With only twelve children at the school and usually one per grade level, any additional students were valued by other students as new friends. This gave us an easy entree into island life.

From the moment my family arrived on the island until we left two years later, we were not only tolerated but were openly embraced as friends by parents and other island residents. It was a fact of remote island life that few could make it on their own without support. We relied on others' help with traveling by boat to the larger islands for supplies. One Christmas, when the winds had been blowing hard for days and many folks could not get off the island to travel, we hosted a spontaneous potluck dinner of salmon, king cod, and beer for those thirty-five of us left on the island. It was frigid outside but full of warmth and camaraderie within. Others relied on us to help with building projects and with farm-sitting. One family trusted us to care for their pigs, chickens, geese, sheep, and a donkey while they were gone for a week. Ever chased a loose, stubborn pig through a large garden on a cold Thanksgiving Day?

The school was the only space large enough for community dances. Old folks, young folks, dogs, and even a donkey attended these frequent events. People were there to have a good time and tended to dance regardless of gender. The sense of community was strong and our presence as a gay couple never seemed to dampen conversation.

Adults of the island looked out for each others' kids, when necessary. We were instantly included in that network. We accompanied kids on their walks home from visiting our kids at the Lighthouse when it was too dark and late for them to go alone. We never felt shunned nor distrusted with regard to others' children. We also could count on others to watch out for our kids when they were elsewhere on the island. The kids of Stuart Island treated my partner's kids with respect and even with some adulation because of their skills in sports and academics. All of the kids voraciously devoured soccer practices, undeterred by the tiny, sloping field scattered with trees. Never did I hear from the playground any use of anti-gay derogatory language.

In 1984, my partner and I decided amicably to separate. We each moved back to the mainland for professional and personal growth. My partner and his kids moved to Seattle. I got a job teaching in Orting, Washington, a small town of about twenty-five hundred people, located in a gorgeous valley at the base of Mt. Rainier, about forty miles from the city. I found a quaint little house in Orting with a great view of the mountain and of daffodil and pumpkin fields. Imagine my surprise, my first weekend there, when the main street of town had been taken over by a fundamental Christian revival meeting! "Oh my God!" I thought. "This may be a lot different than living on the island." And, indeed, it was.

I discovered an insular community of people, many of whom expressed distrust of anyone who seemed different. Even a "bicyclist" was hung in effigy when a bike route was to be run through town along the old railroad tracks. Going for meals at the local fast-food joint, I was gawked at by other customers as if I was some alien from a distant planet. At the local laundromat, the proprietors never bothered to greet me in a neighborly, welcoming way. Instead, they stared at me for the duration of my chores.

At school, there was an indication early on that diversity was not tolerated by students or adults. Playground insults of "faggot," "queer," and "cocksucker" were common among even six- and seven-year-olds. Such words, it seemed, should not have come from truly devout Christian homes. Any child who appeared different in dress, action, or identity ended up bearing the brunt of constant verbal attacks. One bright, artistic, but soft-spoken boy continually suffered taunts and jeers for a couple of years. His parents eventually removed him and sent him away to a conservative Christian school. News from former colleagues is that at fifteen, he is now in juvenile detention for selling drugs.

Where island kids seemed to foster among themselves a recognition and acceptance of eccentricities and individuality, Orting kids demanded of each other and themselves a uniformity of behavior and appearance. Many kids who were frustrated swore at and insulted teachers as well. When one boy screamed at me to "Fuck off," his father, after being contacted, justified the action by saying that he, as a boy, had been the same way. "Boys will be boys."

Gay friends from Seattle who had visited me in Orting expressed disappointment. They appreciated the scenic beauty of the valley but instantly sensed a cultural ugliness in the townsfolk they had encountered. Two friends likened the experience to entering the "twilight zone." While I understood my friends' lack of interest in continued visits, I was frustrated that my life was again split in two — a closeted life in Orting, and visits to gay life in Seattle. My intuition consistently indicated that it was appropriate to keep the closet door closed most of the time.

My colleagues at the school were nice people but there were only three with whom I could be at all open and honest about myself. None of them lived in the town. The teaching staff relished social events — wedding and baby showers and staff and family picnics. I was expected to participate in the rituals and in the purchase of gifts for such occasions. I never felt comfortable bringing any of my gay friends from the city to such events, even though many others brought spouses and other friends.

I continued to work in that town for five years for professional reasons. The difficult situation somehow helped me grow as a teacher. I was determined to make the most of my experiences there. My sense of strong, personal self-esteem, however, was held in limbo. During my last year in Orting, after having participated for four years in others' gift-giving events, I made my first and only request for support from the staff at the school. I wanted to participate in an "AIDS Walk" in Seattle and needed sponsors. Not one of my sixty colleagues were willing to help out. I was devastated and angry. That single event encouraged me to look elsewhere for employment. The following year I took a job back in the city.

I now work at a small independent middle and high school in central Seattle. It is a place where homophobia is "not cool," even among thirteen-year-old boys. The atmosphere is one of tremendous support for individual eccentricities among students and faculty. My personal and professional lives are happily integrated. In the classroom and in contacts with students I am encouraged to be a positive role model as a gay man. The school has an extensive outdoor program through which I am able to get out into the country with other faculty and with students.

———

Looking at my experiences on Stuart Island, in Orting, and now in Seattle, I wonder why openness and acceptance come so readily to the island and to the small school in Seattle but not to the valley town. While pleased with the situation at the Stuart School and the North-west School, I'm saddened by continually hearing stories of Orting kids with great potential who have not had the chance to embrace their individuality. What is important about Stuart Island and Northwest School folks is not so much that they have accepted homosexuality. Many of them, indeed, may not advocate homosexuality for themselves or for their kids. But it is consistently clear that they expect acceptance of diversity and individual differences among people. In Orting, repressive religious beliefs and a strict social code of uniformity have bred mistrust and cynicism for anyone not fitting in.

Living in two different rural worlds and now in the city, I've learned that openness about gays and lesbians is certainly not limited to nor a product of urban living. It is a quality that comes from within people who are comfortable in themselves, wherever they may live.

I'd Rather the Honesty

Sara Ford

English Teacher
"The Mountain School"
"Puyallup, Washington"

This fall, the counselor at my school suggested that my partner and I tell the administration about our relationship. It would be far better for them to hear it from us than from someone who happened to see us hand in hand in Olympia (because we like to hold hands sometimes when we walk; we like to stop now and then and hug, lean into a kiss). What if a student — or god forbid, a parent — saw? And went complaining to the school about those nasty women teaching their children immoral things? Forewarned is forearmed, she said.

Like so many schools, ours talks about the importance of community, of creating a supportive environment for students and teachers, of learning to understand and respect difference. Words like these are written into the mission statement, which sound so much like the mission statements of countless independent schools these days.

At the opening faculty meetings, the headmaster made a big deal of including sexual orientation as a critical diversity issue and homophobia as one of the "isms" we had to work to eradicate in our school. He talked about how intensely moved he'd been at a national conference on diversity held in Pennsylvania last summer. He wrote an equally forthright letter to parents.

Hearing such a clear message from the headmaster, Ruth and I felt hopeful. The counselor told us that the administration would be supportive.

Yes and no. The headmaster was carefully supportive. For various reasons, he already felt a strong connection to Ruth and said how much he respected her and cared about her. He said he needed to mention our relationship to the board, but that he would do so in a positive way.

"Of course, we know you'll be careful, professional. You won't kiss — you know, that 'have a good day' kiss — around the kids." He was only a little uncomfortable saying this, the discomfort showing in his smile. My throat hurt, the ache of tears quite sudden. The closet door had hardly opened at all, and I wondered whom he was asking us to protect with our circumspection.

"Alan," the assistant headmaster, was genuinely pleased. Alan is in charge of hiring and firing staff, and of curriculum development. An elfish man with masses of light brown and gray curls, Alan is thoughtful, nutty, and warm. His personalty exemplifies the attitude of openness the school claims to have. Like me, he's a writer. I talked with him once about the frustrations of trying to write while teaching. We promised to nudge each other. He is the administrator to whom I've felt the closest.

When Ruth and I told him, he beamed. He knew we'd both had personally difficult times last year and said he could see the happiness in our faces. With him we felt safe to let the power of our feelings show on our faces. He also told us, gently, to be careful. "Affection between gay people is different than affection between heterosexuals. Whether that's right or wrong, it is."

Yes, it is. So sometimes we sneak. I'm forty-three and I'm sneaking. I'm suddenly one of "those kinds of people." I am also something of a problem to the school, because, unlike my partner, I changed.

Ruth was hired as the drama teacher and entered the school as a lesbian. That had its consequences, put her into a different category. But she was in theater, and people tend to make allowances for theater types. She also wasn't out, and though some people knew, they didn't talk about it. The gay kids, mostly in her drama class, eventually found her, with tremendous relief. They were silent, too, for different reasons. Protective — of her, of themselves.

I came into the English department. Academia makes fewer allowances for "aberrant" behavior. I also came into the school straight, married, a teaching wife, a teacher's wife. Last spring I fell in love with Ruth. At the age of forty-two, after having been married three times, I finally acknowledged that I am a lesbian.

For me it was a relief. I felt like I'd come home, in the arms of my lover. (Is this too personal? Who writes about the wonder of gay sexuality? Who reads it? Who flinches?) I can trace my journey, remember women falling in love with me, scaring me, giving me dreams; remember falling in love with a woman one summer in the country, scaring her away; remember the novel I started about the journey of two women toward each other. The last time I married I bought a goddess ring and didn't change my name. These were signposts.

People at school couldn't see these signposts, of course. Nor were they privy to the many conversations with my ex-husband as we worked through our relationship, the core of which was our friendship. He was not surprised that I was a lesbian; nor was he hurt, angry, or disgusted. We grieved together because of the letting-go of the familiar, the day-to-dayness of living with one another. We have also stayed the best of friends. Colleagues were probably confused by our comfort with each other, especially here at school, but even if they understood it or knew something about my journey, I don't know if they would be any less threatened by my changing from a heterosexual woman to a lesbian. I think people were able to tuck Ruth's sexuality away where it wouldn't bother them, where they wouldn't even see it, because she didn't *do* anything, she simply was. I did something. I did something unexpected, huge.

Perhaps if I'd looked the same when school started in the fall, my changes would have seemed less dramatic, but I'd cut my hair, from the middle of my back to an inch from my head. Over and over, students and adults asked me why. I did it in June, right after school had ended for the summer, several months after I came out to myself. It was a gesture of independence, freedom. No more wisps, no more loose hairs tickling my face when the wind blew, no more weight. But it had an impact, turned heads, caught their attention, put them on guard. I'd left for summer break with long hair and come back in the fall with short. I'd left a straight woman and returned gay, and I wanted to be as open about that fact as my face had become without the curtain of hair hiding it.

If I could change, could they? Is this what makes people go silent? Is it suddenly too real, no longer an abstraction? Is this the fear? No one talks about it, and I'm not sure they even could. Some fears are subterranean and nonverbal.

The shift in attitude toward me was subtle — little things, small professional slights, a quiet isolation. The headmaster never responded to a letter I wrote him concerning my appointment to the Gender Committee and my request to move into the upper school, where there is currently only one female English teacher and she is leaving. (I explained that I no longer want to teach middle school and that of my twenty-one years of teaching experience, more than half of those have been in the upper school.) Although he didn't answer me directly, I heard from other administrators that he was angry. I finally had to go to him to clear the air.

He apologized for not getting back to me, but denied that he'd been angry. He explained that because the upper school English position had now become linked with the newly vacant department chair position, he couldn't automatically move me up. I reminded him that the year before, the school had appointed a middle school history teacher chair of the history department without ever publicizing the position. He shrugged and said that there are always some inconsistencies in schools. In the case of the English position, there would be a genuine search. He promised to be as helpful as possible if I decided to look for work elsewhere, though he didn't want me to feel that he was in any way suggesting that he wanted me to leave. The meeting was civil; the undercurrents of tension, unmistakable.

Throughout my years in education, I have been passionately committed to and outspoken about issues of diversity; I have been on the school's Diversity Committee and created, organized, and ran several in-school diversity events last year. Nevertheless, the school rejected my request to be sent to the Teachers/Students of Color conference in Minnesota in December, choosing instead the same man who had been made history department chair, though he'd never served on the committee and had done nothing active in this area of the school. The assistant headmaster, to whom I'd mentioned several times how much I wanted to go, pulled me aside in the hall one morning on my way to class to tell me the decision. He never explained why.

The shift in attitude could be explained by the fact that I am an outspoken woman in an upper school that is filled with almost all men, but I am now also an outspoken woman who has chosen to be with women instead of men. I push people's buttons, yet they could find all sorts of rational, reasonable explanations for any of these experiences. I have no grounds for accusation; I'll not be asked to leave. It will be my choice, but I am convinced that it would be easier for the school to have me gone. Ruth's lesbianism then could become comfortably forgettable again.

I'd prefer the "straight shooting" of most of my middle school kids. Perhaps because of their age and preoccupation with themselves, they haven't learned the art of subtle innuendo. They do not know that I am gay, but I know where they stand. They have a fascination with homosexuality, and some of them can be frankly cruel. "I saw two guys kissing. Yuch. It made me sick." I listen.

Last year one of the girls told me she has no problem with homosexuality because, after all, "a gay person can't help it." Bisexuality is wrong, though, because bisexuals are choosing to have sex with someone of the same sex when they don't have to. I listen to the assumption underlying her "tolerance": there is something inherently ugly in the act, but it can be forgiven as long as you have this biological excuse.

Should I be hurt? Angry? I feel a quick desire to shock them. I have a relationship with these kids. I'm a good teacher, and I care about them. They know it; they know I respect them, give them lots of room for their voices. I am not sure if they would give me room for mine.

This spring one of the reading choices will be *The Drowning of Stephan Jones* by Bette Green. The book is set in Arkansas. Two gay men have moved their antique business from Boston to Racketville, to get away from the frantic pace of city life. The story is told through the perspective of sixteen-year-old Cara, who believes deeply in justice and equal rights for everyone. However, she is also in love with a boy who leads a hate campaign against Frank and Stephan, the gay couple, which ultimately leads to Stephan's drowning. During the trial, Carla has to decide on the depth of her commitment. Some of last year's seventh-graders read it, and it had a big impact on them. Perhaps this year it will be the catalyst for a conversation, but I wonder, will they as be as honest with me if they know I am gay as they have been in their ignorance?

Just yesterday I had my first honest conversation with a parent. "Joyce," whom I know through our Diversity Committee, is a fundamentalist Christian. She is also an African-American. Last year, she expressed her anger that homosexuality was being made part of the Diversity Committee's agenda. Personally, it went against her religious values. Politically, she felt it diffused the race issue. I listened, trying to learn. I spoke about the isolation of gay and lesbian kids who are invisible even to one another and who so desperately need each other's support. At least when you're black, you can see other black people. She listened too.

I wanted to talk with her because I knew I could have an honest discussion, even though it would be difficult. She's that kind of person — straight to the center. So we got together yesterday and only just started. It was a good talk, because it was real. I know that my revelation gave her pause, but didn't turn her away.

"Joyce" believes that even if one is born gay, one still has the choice to be actively gay or not. One doesn't have the choice to be black or not. I see her distinction. I am not and cannot be black. I am a lesbian, but I could and did, for so many years of my life, choose to act as a heterosexual. But I also know the terrible cost and loss of not being myself. How can one say, choose not to be who you are? Is my identity any less real because it can be invisible, can be denied?

She still struggles with the politics, does not want sexual orientation to become a civil rights issue. And I recognize how deeply homosexuality goes against her religious values. For these reasons, I couldn't ask her, just yet, where she stands with the Washington state initiatives. These initiatives, modeled on the ones that were barely voted down in Oregon last year, are designed to prevent homosexuals from having "special rights" or minority-group status. Among other things, they would deny the right of gays to adopt children and force those who have done so to give their children up. The initiatives also state that schools cannot in any way suggest that "homosexuality is a positive or healthy lifestyle, or an acceptable or approved condition of behavior."

If they passed, it would mean that Ruth couldn't keep her two children. Her former partner couldn't have them either. It would probably mean that my thirteen-year-old son, who lives in New York with his father, couldn't come and live with me for his high school years. When I think of these possibilities, I get cold with despair and rage. I don't believe that the initiatives will pass, but it frightens me that I could even hold a photocopy of them in my hand.

At bottom, these initiatives are about hatred and violence against human beings, and in this "Joyce" and I share a common ground. We are already bound together as women. Maybe sometimes I'll be able to tell her that loving a woman is as natural as breathing. I think she will listen. I don't think she will agree, but that will be okay. These feelings are tremendously complicated, but at least we are talking about them. Up front.

I'd rather the honesty.

Yes, I Am

Jim Bridgman

Latin Teacher
Northampton High School
Northampton, Massachusetts

The first time a student asked if I were gay, I lied. "No," I scoffed, trying hard to sound convincing. It was 1983. I was twenty-five years old, deeply closeted, and stunned by the question, which echoed in my mind for days.

The next time a student asked the same question was just a few months ago, in 1993, and I didn't lie. "Yes, as a matter of fact, I am," I answered. This time what echoed in my mind afterwards was not the question but my response, more precisely the pride with which I had responded.

Both occasions are memorable. Both occasions brought forth deep emotions. But the fear and shame of 1983 has turned into exhilaration and pride ten years later.

I am a late bloomer in respect to coming to terms with my homosexuality. I have always known that I am gay, ever since I was ten or twelve years old and felt attracted to the other boys in gym class. But I always lived a life of denial, trying hard to convince even myself that it wasn't true.

For many years before and after the 1983 incident, I had every intention of living my life as a heterosexual person, and for the most part I succeeded. It wasn't until my early thirties that the facade started to crumble. The strain of living a lie was taking its toll.

Finally I sought the help of a therapist, a gay man who not only helped me through some rough times, but also taught me to view my homosexuality as something special, a unique gift that has allowed me to grow in ways I might never have experienced if I hadn't grown up an outsider, if I hadn't always been different.

I immersed myself in the local gay community, forged new friend-ships with gay men and women, read as much recent gay literature as I could get my hands on. I came out to my old friends, my straight friends, and even my parents.

The only area of my life in which I remained closeted was my job, and for a long time I was convinced that I could never come out at school. The risks were too great. Harassment by students, ostracism by fellow teachers, even the possibility of losing my job were threats that kept me in the closet at school.

But it was not easy living a double life, especially since I live and work in the same town, and in a town that has a growing reputation as a mecca for gays and lesbians. Increasingly, I was running into stu-dents or parents in downtown Northampton, when I was with my gay friends or with a date, and it was becoming more difficult for me to lie about who I was with, more of a strain to pretend to be straight.

Finally, I decided that I could hide no longer. I made up my mind that, no matter what the cost, I would live my life openly and with pride.

———
———

I thought a lot about the "why" and "how" of coming out at school. The "why" was easy. I wanted to come out because I could no longer abide the closet. I felt a growing pride about my sexuality, and if other people had a problem with that, it was their problem, not mine. To continue to deny my sexuality at school would be to continue to accept society's intolerance of gay people. I could not hold my head high in my private life if I continued to cower in fear in my professional life.

There was another reason I wanted to come out at school. I was a gay student at Northampton High School twenty years ago, and I remembered how scared I felt, how isolated and lonely, and how much I hated myself for what I was. I didn't want those who followed me to go through their teen years as I did, frightened and confused, with no one to turn to for support. I wanted the Northampton High School I taught at to be a different, better school than the one I had attended as a student.

The "how" of coming out was more difficult. I decided that I did not want to make a public announcement to my classes. I have always believed that "the truth sets one free," that confronting difficult situ-ations head-on and talking openly and honestly about them averts whispers and gossip. Nevertheless, I suspected that, in announcing my homosexuality to my classes, I would be exposing myself to the censure and reprobation of homophobic parents. Northampton may have a growing reputation as a haven for gays and lesbians, but as a lifelong resident I know that homophobia thrives in some of its darker corners. Every bigot in town would be galvanized into action by the news that a "faggot teacher" was "recruiting" in his classroom. I did not want to expose myself to such attacks. When the accusations and insinuations came, as I felt sure they would, I wanted to be able to say that never once did I spend academic time talking about my sexual life, that I had always carried out the duties of my job with professionalism and responsibility.

Finally I decided that the best way for me to come out was to live my life openly and proudly, and to answer any questions that students or faculty might ask with complete honesty. I never doubted that one day someone would ask me if I were gay, and when that day came I wanted to be able to say, "Yes, I am!"

———

I didn't leave my coming out all to chance, however. I prompted things along by placing a pink triangle on the bumper of my car. Pink triangles, the symbol of gay pride, are common in Northampton, and I was certain that sooner or later a student would see it and recognize its significance.

It took several weeks before anyone approached me with a question about the pink triangle. When it did happen it was a girl in my Latin III class, a junior, who had spotted it one day when I was driving through town. The next day, after class, she came up to my desk and said, "Mr. Bridgman, can I ask you a question?" There was a hint of something personal about her manner, and I felt a small rush of adrenaline. Was this it? Was this the big moment I'd been dreading, yet longing for, for so long?

"Did you buy your car new or used?" she asked.

Well, that certainly wasn't the question I had been anticipating.

"Used," I said, beginning to suspect what she might be driving at.

"Are there any bumper stickers on your car?"

"Yes, there are."

"Were the bumper stickers on your car when you bought it?"

"No, they weren't." I thought she might actually ask the big question, but she didn't pursue the conversation any further than that. I assumed her question was answered.

In retrospect I wonder at my confidence at this point. I was making a major life decision, and once out of the closet at school there was no returning. My sense of happiness that I would no longer have to lie, however, seemed to overpower any feelings of fear or uncertainty about the future.

———

One day I confiscated a note from a girl in my Latin II class written to the girl who had asked me about my car, and when I looked at it afterwards I was amused to see the last sentence. "Oh, and I have a sticker we could use maybe to cover up that pink triangle." It was clear that word was beginning to spread, but just how quickly and how far I couldn't judge.

———

One Saturday morning I went out to my car and the pink triangle was gone. Someone had painstakingly peeled it off. I suspected who it was, the same girl who had asked me whether I had bought my car new or used. She lives near me, and was clearly bothered by the pink triangle.

The following Monday I asked her to stay after class. I asked her outright if she had removed the pink triangle. She denied it without a moment's hesitation or surprise that I would be asking, confirming my belief that she knew all about it. I asked her again, and she continued to deny it, but the look in her eye confirmed my suspicion. Finally I said, "Well, if you did take it off, please don't do it again. I had to run out last night and buy another one."

After she left I felt almost light-headed with emotion. The thing that I had feared for so many years, being "found out" by students, no longer seemed to hold the same power over me as in the past. I was beginning to perceive the sense of freedom that I would gain with coming out.

———

Later that week it became clear to me that rumors were starting to spread. One afternoon four seniors, whom I had previously taught, came to my door asking if they could talk to me for a minute. They looked solemn and said they had something they wanted to ask me. I was teaching a class at the time and told them they would have to come back later, but it was clear to me what they wanted. I felt excited, but also a little scared, that the question was obviously about to be asked. Would I still have the courage to answer honestly and, more importantly, with pride?

————————

I didn't have to wait long to find out. The next day it finally happened.

It was after the final bell of the day and I was in my room alone closing windows and shades for the weekend. A senior boy and a junior girl came by to ask if I were going to the football game that night. When I said no, that I had dinner plans for the evening, the girl asked me where I was going to dinner. The boy, who was never shy about asking personal questions, asked with whom I was going to dinner. When I told them I was going out with my friend Beth, they were both visibly confused. For several years various students had seen me around town with Beth, one of my closest friends, and since I was closeted at the time and wanted to remain so, I did nothing to dispel the rumors that she was my girlfriend. These two students, now suspecting that I was gay, evidently were having trouble understanding how I could still be going out to dinner with a woman.

"Look," I said, deciding not to let the opportunity slip by, "I know what you're thinking, and I know what you want to ask."

"Well, then," said the boy, "what's your answer?"

"My answer is yes." My knees were shaking so hard I thought I might fall down, but I tried hard to mask my nervousness with a smile.

Their reaction was entirely different from what I had anticipated. I think I had expected smirks or comments like "That's so gross," but instead the boy said, "So what's the big deal?"

I suddenly thought that maybe we were misunderstanding each other, so I said, "Are you sure we're talking about the same thing here?"

He said, "I think so; you know the...," and he made the symbol of a triangle with his hands.

"That's what I thought we were talking about."

"Well, so, are you...?"

"Yes, I am," I said, my courage staring to grow.

At this point the girl spoke up and said something about how she always respects other people's choices. Of course, I responded by saying that it isn't a choice, that there's growing evidence that people are born with their sexual identity already determined. They looked like they didn't quite believe that.

When they were leaving the girl looked a little troubled and asked, "So, are you going to tell Beth tonight?" I think she had this image of two lovers holding hands across the table, gazing into each other's eyes, when the man suddenly says, "Honey, there's something I have to tell you."

"Oh, Beth has known for a long time," I said, "and she's totally supportive."

———

After that conversation I felt exhilarated. I spent the weekend hiking in the mountains with some gay friends, and I couldn't get the conversation out of my mind. By the end of the weekend, however, the initial exhilaration had worn off a little, and I had moments when I questioned the wisdom of coming out to my students. I was sure that they would spread the word, that everyone at school would know by Monday. I kept having an image of walking down a crowded corridor pursued by the catcalls of homophobic students. "Faggot! Faggot! Faggot!"

———

Despite my fears of Sunday evening, the walls did not come crashing down on Monday. It was only in my Latin IV class in the afternoon that I sensed anything different. When I walked into class at the beginning of the period, I noticed that one of the girls was whispering to a small group of boys. I heard one of the boys say, "Oh my God, you're kidding," and they all turned and looked my way. But no one said a word and class carried on as usual.

Word was clearly beginning to spread, but not as quickly as I had imagined. I really thought that once a few kids found out, the news would spread like wildfire. It didn't, and I kept wondering why. Was it really not an issue for them? Were the ones who knew not talking about it in an effort to protect me? Were they in denial?

I found myself wishing that more kids knew, and then found myself wondering why I wanted more kids to know. Was I on some kind of ego trip? Did I really want to be a role model for young people, both gay and straight, or was I seeking the sexual validation that I had been denied as a closeted gay teen twenty years ago? What really were my reasons for coming out at school?

I realized that I was probably coming out for a combination of the above reasons. But even if it were for purely personal reasons, to satisfy a need in myself, were there not still benefits for others in the school? Wouldn't the gay and lesbian students who are scared and alone find comfort in an openly gay teacher? Wouldn't the straight students who are growing up in a homophobic world learn tolerance? Wouldn't the faculty and administrators who prefer not to think about homosexuality be forced to address the issue?

———

I had the feeling that my students thought this was some kind of big secret, that they were afraid to bring it up because they thought I would be embarrassed or ashamed. This was not the image I wanted to project. Maybe my decision to not make an announcement to my classes was a mistake. Maybe those teachers who do make announcements about their sexuality, coming out in front of a class or in a schoolwide assembly, for instance, have the right idea. One certainly can't mistake the fact that the person feels pride. The way I was doing it, by bits and pieces, letting the rumor spread the word, slowly, sporadically, and in whispers, was creating an environment of "dark secrets" and "shame."

———

As of this writing I have not officially come out in front of a class. Many individual students have asked me if I'm gay, and I've always answered with honesty. I'm quite sure now that most of my students know, and their attitudes toward me seem not to have changed, but I regret not talking openly with my classes about my homosexuality. I think that an honest discussion about homosexuality would be a healthy thing for everyone, and I still hope one day to do it. What is holding me back, I think, is the fear of being accused of spending academic time talking about a controversial issue when I have been hired to teach Latin.

The discussions I've had individually, or with small groups of students, have always been positive. I have found that students are full of curiosity about the subject of homosexuality, and are excited to have an adult, a "real, live homosexual," who is willing to answer most of their questions. "How do you know you're gay?" "How long have you known?" "Did you know you were gay when you were our age?" "How do you meet other gay people?" "Can you tell if someone is gay when you meet them?" These are the questions I hear again and again. They are good questions that need to be discussed openly with young people, and it's been exciting for me to have the opportunity to do so at least in some small way.

I am lucky to be teaching in Northampton, a town recently made famous by the national media as a haven for lesbians. Despite the bigots that I know live in this town, tolerance is definitely higher here than in most small communities. Most of the faculty and administration at Northampton High School are tolerant, and I know several gay-friendly residents who are eager for the school to start addressing the issue of homosexuality openly. Most importantly, my greatest fear in coming out at school has not been realized. Never once have I been called a "homo" or "faggot" as I walk down the halls, never once have I found derogatory graffiti scrawled on desks or the chalkboard.

Now that I am no longer afraid of being found out, it's exciting to walk around downtown Northampton with my gay friends, not caring who sees me or what they think.

One recent evening my friend Scott and I went out to dinner and then to a local cafe for dessert. One of my students, who knows I'm gay, was working at the dessert counter and was clearly curious about who my friend was. The next day at school I walked into my classroom after lunch and found this boy and a small group of other students waiting for me.

"All right, who is he?"

"Just a friend," I assured them.

"Yeah, right!"

It seems that the boy who had seen us had exaggerated, actually downright fabricated, telling the other students that Scott and I had come in arm-in-arm, were feeding each other bits of chocolate cake, and were gazing into each other's eyes. Scott and I are just good friends, and I assured the kids of this.

"Oh, that's too bad," said one. "We were excited because we thought you had found a boyfriend."

Coming Out of the Cloakroom

Gary Campbell

Union Representative
United Teachers Los Angeles
Los Angeles, California

I envy famous people. They come out on television or in a magazine article and never have to do it again. For most of us, however, coming out is a difficult and never-ending process.

People didn't talk about homosexuality when I grew up in the 1950s. But if you were a boy who wasn't good in sports, cried when you hurt, and liked school, you were called a sissy. As I got older, names like "fag" and "queer" were used to taunt me and I became very much a loner. The more I was taunted, the more determined I became to prove I was not gay.

To get away from the pressures of dating, I took after-school jobs that prevented me from attending school activities. I satisfied my need for acceptance by being the best worker that I could be. Adults didn't call me names and genuinely appreciated my hard work and abilities. I sublimated my social and sexual life and immersed myself in my work.

When my draft notice came in February 1969, I dutifully joined the air force although I couldn't imagine myself ever killing another human being. I began to question my sexuality while I was in the air force. I had been recommended for a job at the White House and had to take a lie detector test. My reactions to questions about my sexuality triggered something during the lie detector test. I was given the option of stopping the test and forfeiting the White House job, or continuing it and undergoing questions that would delve deeply into my sexuality. I was terrified that the test would reveal my homosexuality and get me thrown out of the service in disgrace, so I forfeited the White House job. The examiner was very apologetic and explained that they had to be extra careful, as no one could allow a scandal to occur at the White House. As it turned out, Richard Nixon did not need me to cause a scandal for him.

After my honorable discharge in November 1972, I returned home, did graduate work, secured a teaching job, and devoted myself to it. I also took care of my mother, who was dying of cancer. I developed into an excellent teacher. These children were the substitutes for the children that I would probably never have, and I devoted myself to trying to help them succeed. I received excellent evaluations, was well respected by my peers, and was popular with both students and parents. My personal life was totally consumed with school and caring for my dying mother.

It was just before my mother's death that I began to deal with my sexuality. For me, the most difficult coming out was when I admitted to myself that I was gay. I was almost thirty when I finally accepted my sexuality, and had been teaching at the same school for a number of years. At first, I was paranoid that someone would find out and I would lose my job. I was so paranoid that I hoped any gay men I met would not ask me what I did for a living. If it was summer vacation, I often replied that I wasn't working at the time.

I taught in a small elementary school then, and I never did figure out how to tell my colleagues that I was gay. I felt so all alone. I wanted desperately to meet other gay and lesbian teachers. One day I saw a small listing in the classified section of a local gay newspaper about a group called Gay Teachers of Los Angeles (GTLA). My boyfriend at that time was in the entertainment industry. He always claimed that "the industry" was accepting of homosexuality and that nobody cared if he brought a male date to the Emmy awards. Not once, however, did he take me. When I told him I wanted to go to a GTLA meeting, he was horrified. "They'll have you parading up and down with picket signs outside of the schools and you'll lose your job." He lectured me on the value of being discreet. I never got rid of my desire to be with other gay and lesbian teachers, but I quickly lost my desire for that boyfriend.

———

I felt I had found my niche when I became active in the gay and lesbian education movement. While I headed GTLA from 1983 until 1986, we built it from a group that had dwindled to a dozen members into Gay and Lesbian Educators of Southern California (GALE), with a mailing list of well over three hundred men and women and chapters in several Southern California areas outside of Los Angeles. Despite the increase in numbers, most of our members were closeted, and I found myself doing everything from writing the newsletter to visiting school board members.

I was already involved in the local teachers union and saw it as the way to expand our movement. I expanded my efforts from being our building representative to serving on the union's House of Representatives. When several teachers asked me to run with them for the union board of directors, I made sure that they knew I was gay before I agreed, as I knew it could be used in the campaign against all of us. My opponents did make some comments about my sexuality behind my back, but if anything, it backfired on them: only a couple of incumbent area directors received more votes than I did in that election and I was easily elected. This stunned a number of the longtime activists and I soon found myself being courted by the inner circle of union leadership.

My lover, Ralph, assisted me in my union activities. In fact, Ralph was so constantly at my side providing support at GTLA meetings that when I eventually became its president, we often jokingly called him GTLA's "first lady." We attended union events as a couple and worked for union-endorsed political candidates together. My first real union coming out was when a union-endorsed school board candidate in her victory speech at the union hall thanked the members of her gay and lesbian committee and then named most of us. I saw several eyebrows go up and wondered how the union activists who did not know about me would react. To my surprise, people who had never said much to me before now went out of their way to be friendly. I had been warned that closeted gays would shun me like the plague. Although a few were careful not to be seen with me too frequently, far more people that I did not know about before came forward, as well as some deeply closeted people (that *everyone* knew about) who would pull me aside discreetly and tell me that although they could never come out in public, they admired what I was doing and would support my efforts with votes whenever they could.

Despite this increasing visibility with being out in the union, I was still pretty closeted at school. I never figured out how to come out to people that I had worked with for so long. I feared that I would jeopardize my hard-earned career. I was afraid I would lose the parental support that is so important to a teacher. I didn't know what was appropriate to tell elementary-age children. I'm embarrassed to say that I never did formally announce my sexual orientation, but I did hide it less and less. The first eyebrow-raiser at school came when a picture of Ralph and me campaigning for a union-endorsed candidate was printed in the union newspaper and mistakenly identified us both as teachers at my school. When co-workers asked who Ralph was, I simply stated that he was my roommate. Soon, however, the way I spoke about my home life at school subtly changed also. While I had never been one to make up stories about girlfriends or change my pronouns, I had been one who had been careful to use the pronoun "I" when discussing my out-of-school activities when "we" would have been used by a heterosexual. I began to feel comfortable using "we" and even saying "Ralph and I."

I'd like to tell you that this gay educational activist who fervently believes in the goal of being out finally took the final step and came out to his faculty. However, the closest I came at that school was in my reaction to a colleague telling a joke in the lunchroom. I was talking to another teacher when I overheard her say, "Did you hear about the miracle of AIDS? It turns fruits into vegetables." I was stunned, but before I could even think how to react, the bell rang and everyone left for their classes. All afternoon, I thought of what she had said and I became more and more angry. I was especially angry that I had not confronted her about her remarks and I resolved that I would talk to her after school. I saw her in the main office by the teacher mailboxes. As I signed out, I told her that I was shocked at the joke she had told in the lunchroom and that I didn't understand how she could joke about people dying such a horrible death. She smirked an "I told you he was" look at another colleague and proceeded to defend herself by saying she was just repeating a joke her husband had heard at work. The smirk on her face enraged me even more than this ridiculous defense. I don't remember all that was said, but it was a loud and angry exchange. As I stormed out into the main room of the office, I noticed that numerous other teachers had heard our conversation. They, along with the three office clerks, just stood there with their mouths open and their eyes bulging. They all appeared stunned and did not utter a word. As I got in my car, another teacher pulled up beside me, rolled down her window, and said, "Good for you!" Although no one mentioned the incident the next day, I had no negative reactions and I never again heard a homophobic or AIDS-phobic remark in the lunchroom. I learned from that incident that if we don't speak up, no one else will, and I vowed never to sit by silently again.

I was determined to not be so closeted at my next school. Shortly after my arrival at the new school, a young teacher approached me with the question "Have you marched in a parade lately?" When I said yes, he replied, "Last June?" He had seen me marching with Gay and Lesbian Educators in the Christopher Street West Gay Pride Parade and had told his friend, "I think that's the new teacher that's coming to our school in September." Within a week, two other teachers, who knew my name from the GALE newsletter, also came out to me. It was wonderful to be working for the first time at a school where I didn't feel alone, even though all three of the other teachers were scared to death of being "found out." Thus, I was pleased to see one of them at the 1993 March on Washington and learn that he had told the principal where he was going. Her reaction was "Don't tell me that. You're just taking sick days, but have a good time."

When I attended my first National Education Association convention in 1984, I noticed that they had many caucuses, which ranged from the Irish Caucus to the Beer Drinker's Caucus. I figured that if the NEA could have a Beer Drinker's Caucus, it certainly should have a Gay and Lesbian Caucus. However, I had a hard time figuring out how to launch one. It was not until a convention in Louisville, Kentucky, two years later, that the method arose. I had written a motion to get the NEA to endorse against California's LaRouche AIDS Quarantine Initiative and spoke for the motion on the floor. After I spoke, a man approached me and invited me to a dinner held by the Ichabod Crane Debating Society. The Society was an underground and unrecognized gay group that had formed and began meeting each year at the convention after a previous attempt with a gay and lesbian caucus had fizzled. I grabbed my friend Jeff Horton, told him about the Society, and asked if he would help me form an official caucus at the next year's convention in our hometown of Los Angeles. After the dinner, the group asked for volunteers to plan the next year's dinner. Jeff and I raised our hands and also announced our plans for the caucus. There were many negative reactions from some men who felt we would ruin their pleasant yearly dinners by going public. However, we did get a list of names, and in 1987, the next year, the NEA Gay and Lesbian Educators' Caucus was born.

Shortly after the birth of the caucus, I was offered a job in my local (despite being very openly gay) and was not able to continue working with the caucus. However, thanks to Jeff Horton, Carol Watchler, and others, the caucus has grown into a large and effective organization now known as the NEA Gay and Lesbian Caucus.

———

Today, by working with other gay and lesbian teachers, we are seeing things improve for lesbian and gay educators and students. The National Education Association, American Federation of Teachers, California Teachers Association, and United Teachers Los Angeles all have gay and lesbian groups and often take pro-gay positions. The Los Angeles Board of Education has added sexual orientation to its non-discrimination clause; Parents and Friends of Lesbians and Gays was placed on its approved classroom speakers list; domestic partner language was added to employee leaves; hate language has become a suspendable offense for students; Project 10 (a counseling group for lesbian and gay teens) and the EAGLES Center (an alternative school for lesbian and gay kids) were established; a lesbian and a gay man were elected to the school board; June has been named "Gay Pride Month" in our schools; gay and lesbian issues have been added to the recommendations in our multicultural task force; and the UTLA Stonewall Scholarship Program, for high school kids who submit entries on gay and lesbian issues, now exists. This was all accomplished by the efforts of a few brave lesbians and gay men.

I hated the days when I was in the closet. It made me feel inferior, isolated, and deceitful. I didn't attend most social activities, because I wouldn't bring a heterosexual date or attend alone without my lover. Today I feel like a whole person. I haven't totally eliminated homophobia from my workplace, but most of the blind ignorance of homosexuality is gone. I'm pleased that my colleagues respect me and try to include and understand my issues. My employers and colleagues know that when an activity includes spouses, my lover is to be included. Most of all, I have a great deal of pride in knowing that because of my openness, things are changing. More and more gays and lesbians are becoming active in the union and are coming out at school. And, just by being myself, people who know me are forced to be more accepting and question some of their prejudices. Think what could be done if we all came out!

Part Three:

Struggles

"The price of increasing power
is increasing opposition."

—LAO TZU

One Teacher in Ten Thousand: Out in Kentucky

———————Tony Prince

English and Drama Teacher
Waggener High School
*Louisville, Kentucky*_____

> *For Gay Rapley, mentor and friend*
> *and Brent McKim, ethics incarnate*

I was never really "in the closet" at school.

No, that comment reeks of self-denial. It carries the echoes of those thousands of gay teachers who say, "I'm not closeted. It just never comes up." Yeah, right. Never. Never ever.

In truth, I guess I was closeted, at least for the first month of my employment. But I was closeted with my hand on the doorknob, just waiting for the appropriate opportunity to fling that sucker open. That chance came at the end of October 1992, one month into my employment. I was discussing the upcoming presidential elections with one of my freshman classes. I was gearing the class around issues the students felt were important. One of these issues was racism. The talk soon led to interracial dating. One student, an often angry young black girl, asked if I could see myself dating a black woman.

"Here we go," I thought, but I said, "Well, that's a really complicated question to ask me."

"No, it's not *complicated* at all," she replied, somewhat scornfully.

I had always had a very good relationship with the black kids in my classes. I think it stemmed from my respect for their anger and their right to it. However, because of my hesitation in answering this question, I felt I was losing them. They were deciding I was just as racist as they perceived some of their other teachers as being.

After a moment, I spoke. "Well, the answer is no. I can't see myself dating a black woman. But I don't date women."

There was dead silence in the room (probably for the first time all year), followed by a whoosh of energy. Two boys leapt up to leave the room. Though my heart was pounding, I smiled and laughed and asked them to sit back down, which they immediately did, so that we could talk about it. They knew I was being honest with them in a way few people are, and I'm sure they were dying to know what in the world I'd say next.

The students proceeded to ask me a few questions, some of them silly, but all of them sincere. The first one was a very telling one: "Does your mother know?" "Yes," I responded, and went on to tell of my mother's initial denial and current wholehearted support. I kept answering their questions in a fog of trepidation, trying to sound calm and reasonable, while at the same time tying to hide my wet and shaking hands in my coat pockets.

The bell soon rang and that (for me) historic class was over. As I was packing up my belongings to move on to lunch duty (I was a "floating" teacher at that time, with no classroom of my own), a young white boy approached me. On the previous day, this boy had loaned a pen to another classmate, a black male, who refused to give it back to him because he felt he was entitled to keep it as a small recompense of "hundreds of years of oppression." Obviously I could not argue over the issue of racial oppression, but I did take a few moments with him to discuss the concept of focusing and directing one's legitimate anger. The pen was returned, but the young man who had lent it was still extremely upset and had begun to cry. It turned out that the pen had been a gift from him to his grandfather, who had returned it to him while dying.

It is not an easy thing to cry in front of your classmates over a pen when you are a fourteen-year-old boy. It reminded me of a time when I was that age and a gym teacher yelled in my face so angrily that I wet my pants a little bit. I don't think I'd ever felt so abused and humiliated as I did that day. It was with this incident in mind that I asked this young man if he needed to stay in the room for a few minutes before going to lunch. He said he did and continued to cry. Knowing that relieving human suffering is more important than fear, I sat next to him and held him as he wept. I had met his parents at an open house and knew that, although they were kind and loving people, they were also fundamentalist Christians who would probably not relish the image of their child sobbing in the arms of a gay man. I also knew that, at this moment, tenderness was the only moral response possible.

I had no idea what this young man's response would be when he approached me the next day after my self-outing. I was relieved and moved when he simply but strongly shook my hand and said, "I think you're a very brave man, Mr. Prince." That day, it was my turn to weep before going to lunch. The only difference was that I knew I was on my own, and that I could not count on someone more powerful to support me in my time of need.

When I at last went to my lunch duty, I had images in my mind of food flying toward me whenever I turned my back, thrown by homophobic kids proving their "normality." To my surprise, it turned out to be a day like any other, without incident.

The next day, word began to circulate a bit more and I began to get some student feedback. There was no hostility at all. Frequently, a kid I had never seen before in my life would approach me and say something like "Mr. Prince, I just heard something and I just wanted to ask you — are you gay?" I would just look back at each student with a calmness that was actually slowly becoming genuine and blandly say, "Yeah." The student would then say something equally bland like, "Oh, okay, that's cool. I just wanted to know," and then go on about his or her way. My junior and senior classes responded by politely not mentioning that they had heard anything about it. No one requested a transfer to another English class. In fact, students continued to request transfers *into* my classes. The administration did not respond to any of this at this point. I was living in a Twilight Zone of nonplused acceptance ... but not for long...

———

With the coming of winter came the frosty insurgence of homophobia. In the fall of 1992, another local high school invited volunteers from the Fairness Campaign, a Louisville organization which lobbies for local gay rights legislation, to speak as part of a social studies unit. This inspired the wrath of a few self-styled "community leaders," despite the absence of parental complaints. Our conservative superintendent then suggested an elaborate "controversial speakers" policy clearly intended to intimidate teachers, unveiling it at a February countywide principals' meeting. Before the next school day, my principal called me at home with a bit of homophobic intimidation of her own. Since this meeting, she had suddenly decided that my mentioning the lesbian relationship between Celie and Shug in *The Color Purple* (a lesson she had observed me teaching) was "not appropriate" and in some undefined way not in accordance with the Jefferson County Public Schools curriculum. She further stated that I was not to consider students "captive audiences" for my own "personal agenda." I was both insulted and offended, and began to realize how much the school system wanted to keep gay people literally invisible. Unfortunately, this was only the beginning.

————

With the arrival of spring came the realization that I really wanted to attend the March on Washington in April. In fact, I was desperate to go. I was doing so much fighting alone that I longed for the comfort of having genuine comrades surrounding me. I was surprised and moved when my best friend at Waggener, a straight physics teacher, and his wife, a math teacher at another local high school, said they wanted to go with me to show their support. We bought tickets to ride on the bus chartered by the University of Louisville gay students group and were all set to go.

Since the trip required that we each take two days off from school, we decided to tell our students where we were going and when we'd be back. The schools' administrators could say little about these requests, as they were contractually agreed-upon "personal days." The students responded to the news with little surprise, but were quite interested in the march. Some were curious as to why straight people would want to go to a gay march. My friend patiently explained his and his wife's love for me and their firm commitment to all areas of civil rights. One straight female student said she wished she could go because she knew there'd be a lot of "really cool people" there. (I'm constantly amazed at the leap I see us making, from social pariahs to "really cool people" in the eyes of many young people.)

When we returned to school, wearing our t-shirts and buttons, several students informed us that they and their parents had watched the rally on C-SPAN to see if they could spot us and found themselves getting caught up in the event itself. The two most common questions they asked were "Did you have a good time?" and "Did you meet RuPaul?" The answers were an emphatic "Yes!" to the former and an unfortunate "No" to the latter.

Superior even to the joy of the march itself was the feeling of being welcomed home by my students and fellow faculty members. We received nothing but warmth and acceptance. I felt like I was living in a wonderful dream world of love and openness. It was a wonderful preview of the world that is within our grasp if we but reach for it with our arms wide and trusting, unafraid of the chasms which may exist beneath our dancing feet.

———

About three weeks later, on May 19, 1993, I was informed by my principal that she was implementing "the significant deficiency process" with me. This is a serious and threatening evaluative procedure that can result in dismissal. She mentioned to me that one of her reasons for instigating this process was that she had observed me showing cartoons to my class. The "cartoons" she mentioned were a video of *Animal Farm*, which I was showing as a review of the book, which we had just finished reading. In the official deficiency notice, I was no longer criticized for showing "cartoons" but because "the audio was high" and, according to her, six students had their heads down. The principal, at a later meeting arranged by my union with the assistant superintendent of schools, elevated this figure to "over half of the class." I was also again criticized for not sticking to the JCPS curriculum, although no specifics were given. As part of the procedure, I was to be assigned two people from the school system to "visit" and "assist" me.

The most interesting and significant aspect of this procedure was the student response to it. Since I knew from the start that I was not "deficient" as a teacher, I felt no shame about this process and had no qualms about talking about it with faculty, students, parents, or anyone else interested in it. Some people prefer not to work in the light of day and so my principal issued me a gag order that forbade me to share information about the procedure with "students, parents, or anyone else who might use it to disrupt the school or the educational process." I was shocked that she felt she had the authority to take away my constitutional right of free speech in my home, or in the homes of my students and their parents, with a mere declaration.

The gag rule was imposed because, after hearing about my "deficiency," students began to circulate petitions and wear pink triangles as a sign of support. Needless to say, the administration was disturbed, responding not only with the gag rule but also with an unwritten policy that students could not give out pink triangles unless someone specifically asked for one. For me, the most moving moment of all was when I walked into my department chair's room to ask for some supplies, and found that he had attached a large pink triangle to his shirt. I knew then that he would support me publicly, not just whisper private encouragement while maintaining public distance, as many others had done.

The controversy climaxed at the end of May, at an academic awards banquet. Much to everyone's surprise (including mine), over a dozen of the award-winning students, including the school's valedictorian, attended the semiformal banquet wearing large pink triangles. There they sat, with their parents, wearing these ostentatious signs of support! I felt equal parts embarrassment and pride as each one rose to their feet to accept their awards from the principal. My sense of unreality was almost palpable. They had nothing to gain personally from doing this. It was done out of a sense of justice. I'd never felt a greater sense of comfort than I did on that night. I could see and feel the power of love turning the tide of fear and secrecy.

My first "significant deficiency" visit came on the last day of classes in June. I had not received notification of this impending visit in time to tell my students that an observer would be present. I decided to make no special plans but simply to help them finish up the resumes they had been working on for the past couple of days. Nevertheless, the observer reported that she "enjoyed the class" and had no criticisms of my planning or teaching.

At the beginning of the next school year, in September of 1993, a meeting with an assistant superintendent was arranged through the teachers union in order to protest my gag order. The assistant superintendent apparently agreed with me about the inappropriate, and possibly illegal, nature of this order, as he not only recommended that it be rescinded but in fact also told me that I could "burn it."

As the fall term wore on, despite the fact that I did not change my teaching style and explored a wide range of social issues in my classes (including gay issues, when appropriate), my observers continued to report that they could find nothing in my teaching which constituted a "significant deficiency." On the contrary, they were enthusiastically supportive of my high expectations for students as well as the caring environment I had created in my classroom. Consequently, the "deficiency" was withdrawn by my principal on October 13, 1993.

————

Throughout the spring of 1993, I had also been meeting with several other gay teachers (none of them out) about the possibility of forming a gay and lesbian teachers' caucus through our union. Much to our surprise and relief, union officials were extremely supportive, consistently going above and beyond the call of duty to assist us in any way that they could. The union's board of directors unanimously approved our caucus in June 1993. After years of being outsiders, we have now carved out a place for ourselves within this mainstream organization. Unfortunately, as of this writing in February 1994, I am still the only out teacher in Kentucky and, as such, continue to be subjected to much scrutiny.

I feel often as if I am working beneath a microscope. For example, a parent recently complained about my loaning of Deborah Hautzig's *Hey, Dollface,* a teenage lesbian novel approved by the National Council of Teachers of English, to a student to read for her response journal. I had informed parents through a letter sent home at the year's outset (and distributed again at the open house) that students could read any book they wished for their response journals and that parents should communicate with their children about what they were reading. I personally would in no way dictate or censor their selections. This parent, however, was not satisfied with merely taking the book away from her daughter but insisted that I not loan her "such books" again in the future. She insisted the books with gay characters not be available in my classroom at all. Although gay people are rarely mentioned in my class, any inclusion at all seemed to be inordinate emphasis in the mind of this woman. It seemed unimportant to her that no student, not even her daughter, had ever complained of this. The fact is that breaking the conspiracy of silence at all induces panic in some parents and administrators. My principal said that "simply informing parents prior to giving such a book [one which may be perceived as controversial by parents] would alleviate any problems that might arise." However, she refused to state which issues she would consider necessitating such notification and which issues she would not.

So much of the oppression we face as gay educators stems from these kinds of vague, euphemistic policies that try to intimidate us into self-censorship. Of course, I realize that, to my principal and other like-minded people, controversial equals gay. They're not talking about books where someone uses a handgun or gets the death penalty when they say "controversial": they're talking about books in which someone is gay. But if they really want to ban all books with gay characters from public schools, they need to accept the responsibility for their actions honestly and openly, not by relying on teachers to give in to vague and cowardly directives that rely on internalized homophobia for their successful implementation.

When, in the later eighties, I decided to go back to graduate school to become a teacher, gay issues were not paramount in my mind, nor do I choose them to be now. My openness has simply swept me up in the current of the times. There are many other equally important issues for progressive educators to address: de-tracking, nonpunitive discipline, multicultural acceptance (*not* tolerance), and many others. However, those issues, while far from totally accepted, have made great inroads in our schools and now have powerful, high-profile adherents. Few people are willing to speak up yet for gay students in the same manner. Day after day, in my school and others, I see kids with little official power or influence standing up for equal rights for gay people, while gay adults continue to cower in fear of their own shadows.

The future beckons. This is our battle, and we must lead it. It's certainly not been easy for me, but if you step out into the sunlight where there's love and hope, you will discover, as I have, that there are kind and loving people of all ages and orientations ready to support you when you need them. It's within our reach and the emperors we fear, in reality, have no clothes.

Ms. G. Is a Lesbian

────────Teri Gruenwald

Social Studies and Language Arts Teacher
"Altameda High School"
"Altameda, California" _____

*I*t was only the second week of school, and already I had to do my homophobia lecture. During a fire drill, I heard one of my eighth-grade girls whisper to a boy under her breath with such vicious disdain it surprised me, "Fag."

He taunted back, "Dyke."

I spoke to them individually about the inappropriateness of their words, but didn't say anything to the class. However, the next day, during an activity, I heard the word *"Jerk!"* flying about several times.

I stopped the class and lectured them on how to respect each other. I spoke with emphasis on how it wasn't okay to call each other names like *jerk* or *idiot* or say something was stupid.

"But I've been hearing worse things," I said softly, so the kids had to strain to listen. "Yesterday, I heard a girl call a boy 'fag' and that boy call the girl 'dyke.'"

Some kids started to giggle and others looked around askance.

"I'm not going to say who did it, so don't even ask. That's not what this is about, because all of you have the potential to name-call like that and I want to talk about why it's not okay."

I then told them about a gay man in Maine who was attacked by some thugs who chased him to a bridge. "They surrounded him and made him jump off the bridge. He didn't know how to swim, so he drowned."

There was absolute silence in my class. And on some of the faces, I could see horror.

"Those gay-bashers were caught and tried for murder. What do you think they got?"

The hands shot up around the class. I called on several individuals and got predictable answers. "The death penalty," said one girl, and a number of kids nodded their heads. Several hands were lowered.

"Nope."

"Life in prison without parole," said a hopeful boy.

"Nope." Around the class, kids started to make sounds in disagreement.

"Life in prison with parole?" asked a girl tentatively.

"Nope, again."

Other kids guessed forty-five years, or thirty-eight years. Finally, I said, "They got off."

The kids were outraged.

"The judge ruled that it wasn't their fault the guy died," I explained. "After all, they didn't know he couldn't swim. But one of his attackers now feels remorse. I read an article about him this summer and he says every morning he wakes up with the knowledge that he helped kill an innocent man. And he goes to sleep at night with that same thought. He wishes he was in jail now."

Then I explained how calling someone a fag or a dyke, although not murder, is present on a scale of hateful acts or hate crimes.

I think my students got it. At least they got it enough not to say these things in class. But they don't always "get" it.

Last year I was lucky to have Garret, one of the brightest boys in our school. He is African-American, from a middle-class Christian family, and like so many of my students, he has adopted hip-hop culture. He identifies deeply with gangsta rap and rap stars. One day, while we were watching a movie about the civil rights movement, he asked, "How come they don't make gays sit in the back of the bus the way they made blacks sit in the back of the bus?"

I explained the difference between being visible (because of skin color) and invisible (because one's sexuality isn't necessarily obvious). That seemed to satisfy him for the moment.

After watching a painful episode about the murder of Emmet Till, he said, "How come gay people don't get lynched for being gay the way black people do?"

I told Garret's class the story about the gay man forced off the bridge. His reaction was, "You mean it's okay to kill gay people? You can get away with it? Cool."

I was stunned into silence. The whole class watched me, awaiting my answer. Some of his response was simply bravado and deliberate devil's advocate game playing. But he also mirrored the thoughts of others, and I knew that as I looked around my class. On some faces I noted the familiar half-smile ready to explode if my answer didn't put Garret in his place.

I took a breath and said, "Well, that's the same message white supremacists in the South had toward killing black folks. Do you agree with that?"

Now it was his turn to be silent. Around the class, I saw students settle down, ready to continue with the movie. Later I spoke to him about his comments. I wanted to know why he hated gays so much. He told me his cousin was gay and he hated his cousin. In fact, his whole family hated his cousin.

"So, because you and your whole family hate your cousin, you're going to write off twenty-five million people?" I asked.

His eyes grew wide. "That's how many gays there are in the world?"

"No," I replied. "That's the estimate of how many gays there are in the United States. And you're going to hate all 24,999,999 of them because of your cousin. That doesn't seem very open-minded of you."

He agreed it wasn't. But he also explained he couldn't help his feelings. And besides, his mother and his church said that "gays were to be reviled."

I've encountered this before. I've had students tell me their ministers or priests, as well as their parents, say it's perfectly all right to hate gays and lesbians. Despite my differences with Garret, I know he respected me and enjoyed my class. And I know he figured out that I am a lesbian. He wrote about it in his journal. It wasn't a thoughtful response. He was doodling in his journal one day and wrote, "Ms. Gruenwald is a lezzie," several times. Then he thought better of it and erased it. However, he pressed too hard and when I collected their journals, I could make out the shadows of those letters even though he had written over it.

I was angry when I read those words. I wanted to write, "SO?" in big bold capitals and then erase them like he had done. But then I calmed down and thought more about the implications of his actions of both writing it and then erasing it. I figured he had written it after one of our numerous discussions when I was forcing him to rethink his preconceptions. But had he attempted to erase it out of respect for my feelings? Or because he was afraid he'd get into trouble? Or was it simply that he had worked out some feelings and now had second thoughts? I responded to his comments on *Flowers for Algernon,* which was the topic and about which he had written very simplistically. And then I added that the meaning was often hidden in not what was written but what was not. I added that I thought he understood what I was getting at and that this particular section of the book deals with a specific form of discrimination that people in the world have to deal with because they may be different. The author seemed to be suggesting that compassion and tolerance for difference were the appropriate responses, a lesson more of us need to learn. We never discussed his journal, but he did read my comments when I returned it. He never wrote anything like that in his journal again.

My students have very specific ideas about lesbians and gays that are formed, not just by their families and churches, but by the presence of a large and vocal community. Because I teach near San Francisco, my students are more aware of lesbians and gay men. Many of them have been to San Francisco and have seen gay men and lesbians. Our lesbian and gay pride parade is the largest in the country and receives ample television coverage. Many of the smaller cities around San Francisco have visible and active gay communities. They know that gay men and lesbians look like "everyone" and not just like the stereotypes of the swishy man or butch woman. My gay and lesbian students also know there is a diverse community for them when they are old enough to explore on their own. But I realize it also opens up the arena and students can think I'm gay, too.

Only once has a student ever directly asked me in the middle of class if I'm gay. Drew wanted to know if the reason I was always defending gays was because I was one. I was quick to respond that I defended all people against inappropriate and prejudiced remarks. I asked him if it was okay to be prejudiced against Filipinos.

"No!" he said vehemently. "I'm Filipino!"

"How about Mexicans?"

"No! I'm Mexican, too."

"How about blacks or Vietnamese or Indians?"

"No, I'm friends with them."

I decided to be bold. "So did you ever think that one of your friends might end up being gay? What would you do then?" My heart was pounding and my hands felt as if I had just plunged them into a sink full of ice water.

That possibility was so far away from Drew's imagination it quieted him. But I saw him pondering that thought. I watched his eyes move and his mouth frown and I knew he was doing some rethinking. Other students wanted to pick up where he left off and I explained that one in ten people is probably gay; therefore, the odds that they would know someone gay or even be related to someone gay are very high.

Every year, I have had students tell me they have gay relatives. Twice the relatives have died of AIDS. Sometimes those students are my biggest allies. But not often. Usually they are very quiet during discussions about gays. It's only afterwards that they may come up and share their personal experiences. When I spoke with Garret last year about why he hated gays, I made sure he understood that another student in class had a gay uncle who she loved. "I want everyone to feel safe in class," I said. "I don't want anyone to feel bad because someone is either putting them or their relative down."

I wonder how it is for my lesbian and gay students in class. I would like to think they appreciate my positive remarks, that their chests fill with pride or that they simply sigh in relief. But I have noticed that some students whom I have suspected are gay don't appear to be listening to my words. I know they are, but I worry that they may be afraid that I'm drawing attention to them, that other kids may figure them out. I fear that they may feel less safe instead of safer in my classroom.

Last year, Victor was a gay student in my class. He was a troubled boy and he chose to be the class clown. He fooled around and drew attention to himself whenever possible. He interrupted me constantly, made silly or inappropriate remarks, and thrived on the kids' laughter. Some of his antics were very campy, such as doing Barbara Bush in drag for a skit. Students made fun of him for being fat, for acting queer. I spoke to them about it, of course, and it stopped around me. On the surface he acted oblivious to their comments, although he did produce a picture of his "girlfriend from another school." But he was failing all his classes and had very few friends. The only time he was silent in class was when I spoke about gays and lesbians. He would sit still, head looking intently down at his desk. Yet, as soon as the discussion was over, he would bounce back to his normal, disruptive self.

I tried to get to know Victor, to help him do well in school, to help his self-esteem. But he was a hard one to reach. When I filled out his final grades of F in both my classes, I felt that I had failed him, not just as a teacher, but as an ally. He hated me and told other teachers and his counselor quite often. I don't believe he hated me because I got on his case to do his work. I think my teachings on tolerance gave him one more reason to feel uncomfortable about himself. Perhaps my words reminded him that in yet another way he was different from the other students.

As a Jew I am a distinct minority as well as a novelty to my students (who are Catholic, Christian, Sikh, Buddhist, Muslim, Hindu). I see a similarity between being a lesbian in this straight school community and a Jew among a faculty that is overwhelmingly Christian and a student body whose diversity doesn't include Jews. I am very out as a Jew. One day, in the middle of telling a Christian colleague about the first time I realized there were non-Jews in the world, a thought which truly intrigued and amazed him, I suddenly realized that I am so out as a Jew because I am so closeted as a lesbian. My Jewish identity has become stronger, almost exaggerated, to make up for the pain I feel as a closeted lesbian. I quickly ended the conversation with my colleague because I felt, in some very particular way, as if I were exploiting myself. I felt a sudden, overwhelming sadness. If I were to have told him at that moment that I was a lesbian, he would have been sickened. In the past he has made negative comments about gay people in my presence. I don't let him get away with those comments, but neither do I tell him he is talking about me. He always shrugs and smiles and says, "I know. In this age of political correctness, I shouldn't be saying those things."

I walk around with a lot of repressed irritation that periodically bubbles into anger. Then I complain to one of my colleagues who knows I am a lesbian. But that is only momentarily satisfying. Because as I am sharing my feelings, I am also educating straight people about their own homophobia. This became clear to me one day when I expressed my anger to two of my colleagues, Mark and Elaine, about gifts and celebrations for four newly married teachers.

"Karen and I registered as domestic partners and flew to Baja for a long weekend as our honeymoon. Did I get any acknowledgment? No, of course not," I steamed, "because so few people even knew because I can't come out openly to everyone. And if I did make an announcement, some people wouldn't consider it the same thing. You people are always congratulating yourselves on being heterosexual. Not only did they get engagement gifts, then they got wedding presents. I can't even get married legally. The best I get is a little piece of paper that affords me no rights. I'm tired of being a second-class citizen!"

Both Mark and Elaine apologized for their people's insensitivity and I knew that I had genuinely moved them. However, it wasn't enough for me. I carried that bitterness around for days.

I am lucky to have a lesbian carpool buddy. And from the moment we are out of the parking lot of her school or mine, one of us begins a catalogue of feelings and injuries. These are moments I cherish. Because of the insipid and relentless heterosexism, I begin to carry around the baggage of shame and self-loathing. I fight it constantly. I make myself mention lesbians and gays in my classroom. At an in-service on diversity, in front of half the staff, I raised the issue of homophobia because everyone else was silent. And I have begun to tell more and more of my colleagues that my partner Karen and I are buying a house.

In all the time I've been teaching, I have come out to one student. Lynne was my student in both seventh and eighth grades. Consequently we got to know each other well. Her family life was difficult and she confided in me regularly. Her older sister was a lesbian, and early on, she guessed I was, too.

Later on, Lynne was seeing someone but wouldn't tell me who. I guessed she was dating a girl (her care not to specify a gender was my clue, I explained). She asked me, "So have you ever thought about dating girls?"

I turned away, suddenly straightening a stack of papers. "I've thought about it," I said slowly.

"And you decided it wasn't for you?" she probed.

It was after school, and I longed for the custodian to arrive or the phone to ring. But the only interruption was Lynne's observation, "You're not answering me."

I didn't know how to answer her. I didn't have tenure yet and was desperately afraid that, if I told her, she'd tell a friend or two with the promise, of course, that they'd keep it a secret. Secrets like that echo long after the person is gone. Still, I understood the importance of this moment. She respected me, trusted me, and she needed to know that both she and her sister were normal.

I explained to her that I wasn't going to answer the question right then because anything I said could easily be misinterpreted and although I trusted her, she might blurt out information that could be harmful to my career.

"Well, you've just told me," she shot back. She was hurt.

"I haven't admitted or denied anything, Lynne."

"Will you ever tell me?" She looked at me hopefully.

"On the last day of school," I answered.

At her graduation, she came running up to me with her sister not far behind. "So, are you or aren't you?" She laughed. "I bet you'd thought I'd forget to ask you."

"Not for a minute." I laughed, too. "Yes, I am."

"I knew it," she said with immense satisfaction and introduced her sister to me.

After that, Lynne told me many of my other students had figured out that I'm a lesbian because I talk about lesbian and gay issues in my classroom. "The only people who talk positively about lesbians and gays are lesbian and gays. None of the other teachers talk about it," she explained.

Every year my students ask me if I'm married. This causes a quandary for me because I consider myself married to my partner Karen. In the last few years I've begun saying yes, I am married. I decided it was more of a lie for me to say no, meaning I'm single, than for me to say yes, even though I know they'll imagine I have a husband. Until recently, my students never have asked me about my marriage, perhaps because I cut them off. Lately, however, a new student is obsessed with my "husband." So far I have managed to avoid answering questions about my "husband's" name.

The way this latest incident of curiosity happened is that some of my students, during a break, overheard me telling a colleague to whom I am out, something about the house my partner and I are in the process of buying. I used the term "we" and several students wanted to know who the "we" meant. I smiled, and one of my students, Kathy, said, "Her husband, stupid."

"You have a husband?" asked Ricardo rather incredulously.

My heart fluttered as I answered, "I have a spouse." For Ricardo's sake, I wanted to keep it deliberately vague and full of possibilities because I believe he is gay. He has a certain innate quality and gentleness that I don't see in most straight boys and men. I don't know if I imagined or indeed saw a flicker of disappointment or surprise shade his eyes for a moment. But I felt I had just betrayed him.

Since that conversation, I can't shake the feeling of repulsion at the thought of "my husband." I want to scream, "I don't have a husband! I am married to a wonderful woman!" I cringe when I hear speculative whispers about "my husband." Several students have asked me if he is also Jewish and can I bring in a picture of him. I answer vaguely, with concealed disgust. I am consciously collaborating in my own misnaming. It leaves me feeling bereft, alone, and weak. My identity as a strong prideful lesbian cowers behind my fear of being found out.

More and more of my colleagues know that I'm a lesbian and that I am in a committed relationship. They ask after Karen and have extended invitations to her. Still, I don't ask these colleagues to show their support for us in their classes. And they don't ask me how they can be more supportive in their curriculum. This silence is what makes me saddest. I worry about the Victors, Lynnes, Ricardos, and other nameless students who will grow up in a world of silence, denial, and hatred unless more of us come out of the closet. And yet, I am paralyzed to tell my students my "husband" is a woman. I hesitate and have to decide whether this year I will announce that Walt Whitman was a gay man.

I feel lucky to have found my right livelihood. I love teaching with a passion. I know I'm a good teacher because my students tell me so and because I see them excited to learn. But sometimes I wonder how long I'll be able to continue teaching. I live two lives: one in the classroom, and one at home. And at times, the distance between those two lives seems insurmountable. It is a chasm so deep that I fear it will swallow me up. I worry that I may be forced to choose between being a teacher and living my life.

Jewish people were exiled from Jerusalem for millennia. The phrase "Next year in Jerusalem" came to symbolize for many Jews the longing to feel whole. Each year of teaching I come closer to ending the fragmenting exile of the closet and finding my own Jerusalem.

So What Does Happen When You Answer "Yes" to the "L" Question?

Jacqui Griffin

Science Teacher
Sydney Public School System
Sydney, New South Wales, Australia

The issue that is constantly on my mind as a lesbian teacher is one of visibility. "Will I?," "Won't I?," and "How much?" are the questions I have struggled with throughout my career. Looking back over eleven years of teaching, there have been clear highs and lows, depending largely on the school at which I was teaching at the time.

I began my first year of teaching in my hometown of Darwin in the Northern Territory — Crocodile Dundee land, to film buffs. That same year I came out as a lesbian. I was twenty-one years old. I was fearful of being "found out" at school, and consequently never mentioned the "L" word in the two years I taught there.

Looking for a different environment, I moved to Sydney at age twenty-three and began teaching in a suburban high school. That school was a shock to the system. The students, particularly the boys from army families, were aggressive, and I just managed to survive during the two years I taught there. I never came out as a lesbian to my students, but the seeds of visibility were starting to be sown. I showed films on gay and lesbian youth as part of the science sexuality curriculum, the news of which quickly spread around the school. A group of year-7 girls as well as one year-10 girl began harassing me. While I was never called "leso" or "lemon" (Australian slang for "dyke"), the harassment was unmistakable. Subtle comments like "What does your husband wear? A dress?" were more of the norm. I didn't handle this well, trying initially to ignore it, which seemed only to signal them to "go for it." After a year, I finally called one of the girls' fathers and told him that his daughter was being extremely rude, without sharing any details.

Although this call ended that particular harassment, I still had to deal with a sexist and homophobic fellow teacher. I finally contacted a grievance officer at the Department of Education when this "colleague" called me a dyke. The office organized a meeting where I requested an apology, which was forthcoming three hours later. While I doubted this "colleague's" sincerity, it was at least satisfying to see him mouth the words. I could have lodged a complaint with the New South Wales Anti-Discrimination Board on the grounds of discrimination on the basis of sexual orientation, which is illegal in my state, but chose not to, as the DEO experience had been stressful enough. In retrospect, I wish I had.

Worn out by this harassment, I returned home to Darwin, where I got a job teaching in a private religious school. I decided I wanted a rest from lesbian visibility issues and used the school's religious affiliation as a reason to stay closeted. Being closeted turned out to be far worse than getting harassed had been. I desperately avoided any conversation not based on school issues, and succeeded so well that a song in the faculty's year-end "review" mentioned me as the teacher about whom the least was known. My isolation and loneliness grew, and after two years, I tired of spending all of my energy in avoidance and hiding. I decided to return to Sydney.

In Sydney, I decided to tackle the issue of lesbian visibility head-on the first time it presented itself. I didn't have to wait long. Soon after starting my job there, I was with a group of seven students who had been excluded from my class because they had not handed in their reports. One boy called another one a "poofter." The conversation then focused on homosexuality as a topic, with comments ranging from "They're disgusting" to "I hate lesbians and gays" to "Lesbians must have penises." My challenge to these comments was answered by a student with the question "Are you a lesbian then?" I replied, "Yes," feeling a quick shot of adrenaline rushing through me as I did so.

A barrage of questions followed. Julie asked, "Don't you think you should change?" to which I answered, "No." Karen followed with "Do you like men?" which I answered with "Yes, I like men as people." Julie then asked, "What makes people that way?" By now I was tense, wondering what other sorts of questions they were going to fire at me, and replied that I wanted to finish my marking and would answer questions about my sexuality some other time. A couple of minutes later (to my relief), the bell rang. A twenty-minute recess gave me time to calm down before I had to teach my next lesson.

It took the school grapevine about a week to circulate this piece of news about me. A few days later I was walking toward the main assembly hall when I heard "lesbian" being said in a loud voice. I went around to see where it was coming from, and confronted some year-11 boys I had overheard making comments about lesbians and "poofters" in the hall a few days earlier. I asked them who had just said "lesbian," but no one would admit to it. I then asked one of them to report to the science staffroom, where I had the following chat with him.

ME: "What were you saying?"

STUDENT: "Pardon?"

ME: "What were you saying?"

STUDENT: "Talking about lesbians."

ME: "In what regard?"

STUDENT: "I don't know how we got onto the conversation. Joe started saying something about it and it went from there."

ME: "What were you saying with regard to lesbians?"

STUDENT: (Silence) "Same as I think about homosexuals and faggots."

ME: "Which was?"

STUDENT: "Well, it's up to them if they want to do it, but I can't agree with it."

ME: "And that's the only thing you said?"

STUDENT: "Both of us didn't agree with it and that's the only thing we said, talking about that, and that's it."

ME: "Were you the person who called out 'lesbian' as I passed by?"

STUDENT: "No, it wasn't me."

ME: "You can tell your friends that, if they want to talk about homosexuality, they're quite welcome to, but if they want to say something to me, say it to my face — not when my back is turned. To me that shows rather a lack of courage. So, if you want to speak to me about lesbianism, you're quite free to, now that I'm facing you and looking at you."

STUDENT: "I was told about how you admitted to being a lesbian."

ME: "I didn't admit, I got asked a question."

STUDENT: "You got asked a question...?"

ME: "To me, 'admit' sounds like a sense of guilt. Usually, it's to do with criminals."

STUDENT: "Someone in the class asked if you were a lesbian and you said yes. How come you told everybody?"

ME: "Well, I got asked a question. If you were asked a question, if you were heterosexual, would you answer no?"

STUDENT: "Yeah, I would."

ME: "Do you know what a heterosexual is?"

STUDENT: "*Oh*, I thought you were talking about ... I mean..."

ME: "Well, would you answer no if someone asked you?"

STUDENT: "No."

ME: "Well, then, you answered my question."

STUDENT: "But there's nothing wrong with being ... I mean, I don't, you don't, see anything wrong with being a lesbian?"

ME: "That's right."

STUDENT: "Well, it's two different opinions, that's all it is."

ME: "Right, okay, that's fair enough. But if you want to say something about lesbians, say it to my face, not when my back is turned."

I had no further problems with him. The conversation was very important to me, because, for the first time in my teaching career, I felt I had dealt with homophobic harassment in a way that made clear that I was not going to put up with it.

I had the next three out of four days off from school and I sat on my verandah, thinking, "What have I let myself in for?" It was more like a state of numbness, trying to reassure myself that it would be all right.

My first day back to school things began reasonably enough. But early in the day, some year-7 students wanted to verify that I was a lesbian, and I then realized that the school grapevine was working efficiently. I started to get a bit anxious. The next day I met my class at the door and a girl asked me, "Are you pregnant and involved with artificial insemination?" I said no, and added that this was a strange question. It turned out that a television special on a lesbian couple using artificial insemination had run the previous night. Later a male student walked me out of the building at the end of the day and asked to know if what he had heard from the others was true. I said it was, and he replied, "Well, that's your personal life — as long as you keep it out of the classroom." I was flabbergasted at hearing that coming out of the mouth of a twelve-year-old, and wondered if he had discussed it with his parents and was merely parroting their comments. As he walked off he said to his friend, "I saw two of them kissing on TV last week" — presumably referring to the infamous "lesbian kiss" episode from *L.A. Law,* which had just aired here.

I knew then that the lesbian questions and possible harassment had only just begun, and that I had a long haul ahead of me. I remember feeling reasonably confident of being able to deal with it, but also aware that I had no desire to cope with the increased stress levels it would bring.

The next day was a real treat, as I didn't hear the word lesbian once. But over the next three weeks I recorded twenty-two incidents in which the lesbian issue was raised, ranging from kids wanting to verify that I was indeed a lesbian, to insults like "I like lemon juice" being whispered as I passed, to mere hissing of the word *leso*. In one incident a female student refused to sit down, saying, "My mother is going to write a long letter as she's heard rumors about you." I replied, "The rumors aren't rumors, they're true." I sent her off to my head teacher later for further rudeness. During that time there was a parent-teacher night and I was dreading it, as I expected the worst. To my surprise, the parents came and talked about their children as they would normally do.

I then left for the United States for a vacation, when I attended the Michigan Womyn's Music Festival. There, I participated in a lesbian teachers empowerment workshop run by the Lesbian Teachers Network, which was just what I needed at this point to recover. My attitude in returning to Sydney was bolstered by the knowledge that each lesbian teacher who had attended the workshop had pledged to do something, however small, to improve the system for lesbian teachers and students. I knew that I was not alone, but was part of a movement of women fighting for change.

When I returned I began substitute teaching at an inner-city high school in Sydney, and enjoyed a string of pleasant "lesbian-free days." Then I appeared for a few brief seconds on a television program entitled *Sex: The Series,* with the Gay and Lesbian Teachers and Students Association (GaLTaS). The next day, as I walked into school, I didn't even reach my classroom before I heard "lesbian" yelled out from three floors above.

For the remaining nine months, I faced an average of two incidents a day. In a year-9 class I was writing on the blackboard when a male voice called out, "There's a leso." I turned around to a group of four boys, where the voice had come from, and leaned over their desks, asking if it was supposed to be an insult. There was no reply. I further said that, if they wanted to say something to me, they were welcome to do so now that I was looking at them, but not when my back was turned. No further comments were made. The next day one of the boys said, "We've heard you're a lesbian. Are you?" I nodded and said, "Yes, that's why I was on TV." The boy asked, "Do you have sex with women?" to which I replied that I don't ask my students such personal questions and that I don't expect them to be asked of me, either. Another boy said, "Do you find being called that offensive?" I replied, "No," trying to look as incredulous as possible at the very question. He went on to say, "Do lesbians have sex with ladies?" I replied, "That's the definition in the dictionary." The bell then rang and, as he went out, he said, "I don't have anything against it, anyway." A few months later, a boy in the same class said, "Are you still a lesbian?" "Are you still a boy?" I answered. He looked surprised and said yes. "That's good," I replied. I was getting exasperated, as if I were the token lesbian on a dissecting table for the entire school to probe.

The first day I started teaching my year-11 class, I was writing on the blackboard and, within the first five minutes, I heard, "Show us your crack," repeated three times, followed by a breast comment, and then a lesbian comment. I turned around and said, "If I wanted to say something to someone, I'd say it to their face, rather than act like a coward." I then turned around to complete my sentence when two science corks landed on the blackboard, one missing my ear by a millimeter. I turned back around and said, "Someone's a gutless wonder."

As I took them to the library shortly after, one boy said, "I've seen you before." He said it was on TV, and I asked him when. "On the sex show," he replied. I said, "Yes, it was when I was representing the Gay and Lesbian Teachers and Students Group." In the library he then came up with some naked diagrams of men and women together and said, "Isn't this a disaster?" (We were doing a unit on natural disasters at the time.) I looked at him with the most bored expression I could muster and said, "Are you in grade 7 or 11?"

I felt quite angry, and was determined that these boys were not going to win this little battle. A few days later, I caught the boy who had thrown the cork at me, in the act of attempting to do so again, and reported him to the head teacher and principal. He was placed on disciplinary probation, and didn't bother me after that. At last things settled down. While one boy continued to make negative comments about lesbians and gays, another became quite curious, and frequently asked in a respectful way what I thought of various news stories involving this battle. That interaction did a lot for my confidence, and I felt I could face whatever came my way involving gay issues.

At about the same time, I was umpiring volleyball during sport and being rather lazy, sitting on a milk crate rather than standing up. I called a ball out. A male student disputed it, saying, "How can you see it from there?" I replied, "I have X-ray vision." He retorted, "I didn't know lesbians had X-ray vision." "Well, now you know. We are very multitalented," I answered.

At the break, a group of them surrounded me and fired questions at me. One asked again if I were a lesbian, which I affirmed. After a moment of silence, she said, "Well, it's natural, anyway," and walked off, with the others following her. I felt, however briefly, the glimmerings of hope.

My favorite conversation about the "L" word arose when a year-7 boy, who had been misbehaving the whole lesson, said, "You're a leso." "Yes," I replied, to which he said, "I might be a leso, too." "You can't be a lesbian," I told him. "Why not?" "Because you're a boy!" As he walked off, he said, with a cheeky smile, "Well, I'll be a transvestite, then!" The exchange showed me how younger children use derogatory terms without even understanding their meanings. For once, he didn't use these terms in an abusive manner, but rather to show off how much he knew.

Visibility for lesbian and gay teachers is the crucial element in starting to change attitudes among teachers and students in the school system. While I didn't see a major shift in attitudes after I came out, this was in part because I was relief teaching and didn't have a chance to work with students over a long period of time. They at least learned, after one or two incidents, that lesbians did not have to put up with harassment. That was an important lesson in itself.

To be inspired that things can change, I have only to look at Derek Williams and Marg Edwards, openly gay teachers who have worked in Sydney for seven and seventeen years, respectively. Derek has led anti-homophobia workshops at his schools and even appeared, along with some of his students, on the national television show *Attitude* to discuss how to fight homophobia in schools. Marg incorporates gay and lesbian issues into her Society and Culture class and has won support for anti-homophobia work from students and administrators.

Their example teaches that an individual gay or lesbian teacher can make a huge difference.

Gay and lesbian students desperately need role models to validate their existence and to feel okay about themselves in a homophobic and lesbophobic world. They can also take action to change those attitudes themselves. GaLTaS was founded by Derek Williams in conjunction with a year-12 student named Jennifer Glass. Along with two other students named Claudine Moutou and Duncan Kirkland, Jennifer took a same-sex date to her graduation, and even appeared in the *Sydney Morning Herald* (our biggest mainstream newspaper) to speak out against homophobia. Their examples inspire both students and teachers to work to make Sydney's schools gay-positive.

While I have found that being "out" is difficult at times, I have noticed that my confidence in dealing with harassment has improved enormously. I am much more comfortable talking about lesbian and gay issues with students in a matter-of-fact way. I must say, though, that I am looking forward to the day when a student asks me, "Are you a lesbian?" and, when I say, "Yes," someone else will pipe up and say, "So?"

On Being Out in the Classroom: Dilemma or Duty?

Raymond Saint Pierre

English as a Second Language Teacher
William Howard Taft High School
Bronx, New York

I teach English as a Second Language (ESL) in a New York City public high school in the West Bronx. Our "little" school of four thousand students, four floors, no athletic fields, over two hundred rooms, and forty stairwells, runs twelve periods a day on a split session. For most of the winter of 1993, my school was mentioned daily as the most violent school in the Bronx, even surpassing the reputation of the neighboring South Bronx. The sheer desperation of most of my students' lives cannot be expressed or encapsulated within one essay.

Yet some still strike at my memory. Virtually all of my students are immigrants, and most are Hispanic. I remember individuals whose stories stand out among the many extraordinary ones I encounter daily: the 24-year-old mother of three, who used false papers to get into the school to learn English, not knowing that by law I couldn't report her, and wouldn't have, anyway; the two brothers and their sister, who came to school every day in white shirts and black slacks or skirts, until one day they came in with their clothes dirty, an occurrence I only understood after reading that day's *New York Times* and learning that their father had stabbed their mother and pregnant sister to death in a fight for crack money, while the children, my students, hid under their beds until morning when it felt safe to go to school; and a gay student, whose father beat him and threw him out of the house at two a.m. with only a t-shirt on his back. And then I remember that these are the survivors. Being a teacher in New York

City demands more than our teacher education courses planned for or even conceptualized.

I have always been out, at least since the midsixties, and have dealt with bias incidents most of my life. Why, then, do I write now? Students need to know we are out there and we care. The children who attend our school bring with them very traditional cultural biases. Combine this with a faculty and an administration that is no less racist or homophobic, and the battle lines are pretty clearly drawn. Yet my openness is both a defense for me and an offense to some others. Being both out and tenured, I am now somewhat protected from the accusations and discrimination that is sometimes directed against me. But I am still, in many ways, both lightning rod and flash point, neither role one which I relish at times.

Yet I chose to be out before the security of tenure. Why? Partly out of my personal philosophy and political stance, but also because I teach in the center of a maelstrom of homophobia expressed in the media, society, and, consequently, in my classroom. Incidents in my classroom which provoked or concerned me were both an opportunity and a necessity, pedagogically and personally, to correct misinformation or temper injustice and intolerance. This is, after all, what I became a teacher to do. It would be hypocritical to ignore or subsume such issues without using their educational potential.

My classroom has posters on HIV and AIDS, the Gay Games, careers in the military, cats, student poetry, and gay, lesbian, and bisexual youth. Students know; I spent eight years working in two neighboring high schools, and the older brothers, sisters, cousins, and friends of my current students have passed the word. So I expect them to know. This has led to some comic moments. When a new student suddenly comes to the realization that I am gay and questions me on it, the other students wait like famished ferrets for my response. These responses are contingent on the situation, but "Can we talk?" "Why are you so interested?" "Why do you want to know?" and "You're not as smart as I thought you were!" fairly cover the quick and acerbic tenor. These usually create a somewhat dissonant, but openly comic and playful banter, which contributes to a healthy discussion.

Another student's comment about Roseanne Arnold's kissing Mariel Hemingway on her TV show led my class into a discussion of values. Was it better to see two women kissing, or watch countless murders on TV? The import of that student's judgment and the class's reactions have since led us into topics such as sexual harassment (both male and female), homophobia, racism, and others. Since I'm a language teacher, these of course become compositions, journal entries, debates, and stories — all impeccable means by which to learn English. By writing about something that matters to them, my students acquire the skills that I am charged with imparting to them, and learn other important lessons on the way.

Then there are the confrontational scenes within the classroom. These demand a careful response, which is not easy at times. When a hostile or intolerant student shouts out, "We should kill the faggots to stop AIDS," during a state- or city-mandated class on AIDS prevention, how does one respond? Not confronting the student immediately will only accede to the perception or implicit threat. My standard response is to say, "Then you had better start with me." Since most students are still silent from the previous outburst, my response is heard by all. The immediate personalization strikes the conscience of the class as a whole. Those students "in the know," and those who have just joined that group, make responses that are both value-based and personally informed. One Haitian student quoted me and stated that often people say Haitians caused AIDS, but that it wasn't true. Another told the class that her uncle had AIDS, as did his wife and their child. By using the information they have learned in my classes, my students learn the value of tolerance, and develop the English skills to express and defend it effectively.

Other scenes in the hallways and staircases of my school are meant to be direct personal harassment, and I deal with those verbally. Students who scream, *"Faggot!"* or, *"Maricon!"* get short shrift from me. Being able to answer in English, Spanish, or French helps to quell such incidents quickly and, at times, congenially. It also has stopped other remarks. Gym coaches no longer tell students to "Stop being a sissy" or "Be a man, not a girl" — especially after students have complained to me and I went to these teachers directly, or to their superiors, when necessary. Fortunately, New York City law forbids discrimination on the basis of sexual orientation. There are also Board of Education policies that explicitly address such discrimination. These are the "big sticks" I wave in confronting unprofessional behavior, when vocal suasion is not enough.

Yet even with my openness and advocacy, there continue to be incidents from entering classes and the administration, sometimes openly, mostly not. And some students, a minority of them to be sure, can become confused and intimidated by discussions about a topic that has traditionally been taboo. They can react in threatening ways other than mere verbal commentary. I have been accused of molestation, assault (not sexual), and other actions. Once a student who had dropped his pants and "mooned" me from the back of the class created a story of me fondling him at the blackboard. Yet in each case my students, and only they, have provided the proof of my innocence, often despite administrative maneuverings to try to prove the contrary.

It has recently become necessary for me to take a more political and activist stance in light of New York City's current ideological battles over condom distribution and, later, over the "Children of the Rainbow" curriculum, a 700-plus teachers' resource guide for the first grade that included approximately ten mentions of the words "gay" or "lesbian" in reference to parental partners, with no sexual or pictorial content whatsoever.

So when my turn came to speak at the New York City Board of Education on October 11, 1993, my first sentences broadcast on the local news were "I am an openly gay teacher at William Howard Taft High School in the Bronx. I will not permit one student in my care to die because of intolerance or ignorance concerning issues which are meaningless in the face of a public health crisis that is decimating your — and our — children." The rebroadcast of these remarks on local news stations created great excitement from and among my students as well as in the school at large. Those gay students I knew of smiled extra brightly that week. For them it was more important that I spoke for their rights than it was that I had announced my own sexual orientation.

I have spoken out and have learned that, for myself and my students, this is what I must do. I must be as honest with them as they are with me. This is not always one hundred percent effective, but the reality is overwhelmingly positive in my classroom. The day my beginning third-month ESL class heard that Sergeant Joseph Zuniga of the United States Third Army had been named "Soldier of the Year," they were ecstatic — especially a young Mexican student who shared the surname Zuniga. Six months later, when Sergeant Zuniga was dismissed for admitting he was gay, these same students realized the unfairness of what was happening, and wrote letters to Congress and the Joint Chiefs of Staff to protest. A small connection had been made — a connection that creates lifelong lessons in equality and tolerance. It is a connection that is only possible when the teacher is "out" and open to the possibility and challenge that such an action brings with it.

Say It to My Face

Leslie Brtek

History Teacher
"Del Mar High School"
"Zuma, California"

I have been a teacher for over twenty years, teaching all grades from seventh through twelfth. For the past ten years I've been at a public high school of about two thousand students in coastal Southern California.

For the first half of my career I was very much afraid of being "found out" as a lesbian. During that time I can't say I felt proud of my sexuality; embarrassed was probably more accurate. There were times that I even felt ashamed of my affection toward other women. But this constant state of shame and fear eventually became intolerable to me, and I sought ways to combat those emotions and replace them with healthier ones. Today, although I have not made any announcements at work that I am a lesbian and do not claim that I am "totally out," I no longer attempt to hide my sexuality or to ignore the homophobia I witness constantly. Judging from information shared by friendly colleagues and students, I am certain that a significant number of people on campus correctly assume that I am a lesbian.

One young man made an important contribution to my personal growth as a lesbian teacher. Jake was in my eleventh-grade history class in 1985. He was one of the lucky ones among his peers: a handsome and poised teenager, about five feet seven, with dark wavy hair and a good sense of humor. He was quite popular among both students and teachers, performed well academically, and smiled often. He contributed frequently in class, and acted as if he genuinely liked me, so I was grateful that he was there. I didn't see much of him during his senior year, but whenever we passed in the hall, he made a point of saying hello. After he left high school, however, I did not hear from him.

Years after he graduated, I happened to be standing outside a local queer club one Saturday evening waiting for friends when I heard someone shout enthusiastically, "Ms. Brtek!" I'm not accustomed to being addressed that way when out socializing, and as I looked toward the voice, I recognized Jake immediately, even though six years had passed since I had last seen him. He gave me a big hug, which I returned without hesitation. Jake was surprised that I remembered his name. For me, recalling his name and even seeing him there didn't seem unusual. I realized that for some reason, perhaps that infamous "gaydar," I had always sensed that he might be gay. Because of that, I felt open and trusting toward him.

In the brief discussion that followed our chance meeting, Jake shared a high school memory. He had looked forward to my class each day, and confided, "I loved your class. I knew you were a lesbian and I would get to your room and think, 'Ah, I'm safe in Brtek's room. Now I can relax.'"

Although I was flattered by Jake's words, I was also distressed to know that a student did not feel safe at school because of fear of others' ignorance and judgments about sexuality. I was certainly aware of the common use of the epithet "fag" on school campuses, and of gay-bashing by teenagers, but until I ran into Jake I was not forced to associate that type of homophobia with a student whom I actually knew. I wonder what other young lesbians and gays must be experiencing, especially those who do not fit in as well as Jake did.

Jake's revelation has had an important effect on me. Our conversation spurred me to become more active in efforts to help gay and lesbian youth. I joined our local lesbian and gay resource center's youth planning committee. We help plan activities for young people involved in a weekly youth rap group, and are forming a mentor program for youth who would like to have access to a lesbian or gay adult "big sister" or "big brother." In addition, I am involved with another organization that offers college scholarships to gay, lesbian, and bisexual students. These activities have brought me into contact with some outstanding and committed members of the lesbian and gay community, and have provided me an avenue to contribute in a way that is especially fulfilling to me as an educator working with young people. As I become more involved I find my sense of pride and personal strength increasing, my identity as a lesbian acknowledged, and my circle of friends growing.

Another change is that I am increasingly less closeted at work. This has resulted in another wonderful reward: in recent years, several high school students have come out to me. I have gained tremendous personal satisfaction from knowing that they trust me enough to confide in me. But even more important is my understanding of *why* these students have turned to me. They know I will listen and offer them encouragement, as I would for all students. But the key factor, I believe, is that they sense that I, like them, am not straight. In years past I would have been fearful of this recognition, but today that fear is gone because Jake clearly confirmed that it was precisely because I am a *lesbian* teacher that I made a positive difference in his life. And it is because of Jake that I will continue to welcome opportunities to make contributions for lesbian and gay people. Last year, for example, I was able to provide a supportive ear for a self-identified lesbian who eventually became the first student to attend our senior prom with a date of the same sex. I listened to her plan, offered a little advice, and later received thanks from both the student and her mother for "being there." Happily, she reported that the dance chaperones and almost all of the students were as gracious and welcoming to the female pair as they were to the other couples at the event.

Sometimes, opportunities to contribute positively present themselves in unexpected and even uncomfortable ways. For example, I remember that one day last year, as I was walking down a very crowded hall, I heard a word spoken in my ear as someone passed. I did not see who it was, and could not tell as I turned to look. I thought the muttered word I heard was "dyke," but within a second I began to deny it, thinking I was "just being paranoid." In any case, I was in a rush to accomplish some mundane daily task and soon forgot the incident. But as I walked down an almost empty hall a week or two later, a young man who looked familiar (but was not one of my students) passed me. As he did, he clearly and undeniably growled, "Dyke!" I turned immediately and followed him to his locker, where he had paused. There was absolutely no question that he had said it and that his intention was to harass and intimidate me. Without a second thought, I purposely positioned myself close to him. He was only a couple of inches taller than me, so I said directly into his face, "Did you say something to me?" Looking astounded and nervous, he stammered one word, "No!" I added, "Well, if you *do* have something to say, then say it to my face." He did not speak. I then turned and continued on my way. There was not another person in the hall, and as I walked away I was aware that the boy and a friend who stood with him were dead silent. I did not look back at them.

I continued to the teachers' workroom, my original destination. Once there I felt a little unsteady and my hands were shaking. Fortunately, I had some time to spare before I had to return to class and no one was in the workroom, so I had a moment or two of solitude and a chance to calm myself. I must admit that I wondered if he would retaliate, perhaps by vandalizing my car or some such action, but in a matter of a few minutes my fears and nervousness were replaced, it seemed miraculously, by a sense of victory and empowerment. I even caught myself smiling! For the rest of the day my classes went smoothly and I went home eager to tell my story to friends, who offered congratulations and support.

I am sure that the student never expected to be confronted on his cowardly and mean-spirited actions. I would like to believe that he was shocked into realizing that there are many of us who will not accept or permit such behavior. I have seen him two or three times since then, and I have not been harassed in any way. Although I will never know his personal reaction to my words, it is not important. What is significant is that I gained an invaluable sense of self-esteem from being able to confront a person whose homophobic actions were completely wrong. As a result, I feel more confident than ever that I am capable of asserting my right to be treated with as much dignity and respect as any other person. And as a teacher, I feel more adept at modeling that type of self-assurance for my students. In fact, at a recent October "Coming-Out Day" rally in town, I was put to the test. While there, I spotted my school's student body president. At six feet six, he couldn't be missed! Years earlier, I probably would have fled the scene in a panic. But this time, although I admit to being a bit nervous, I decided to approach and greet him. I was resolved that I did not want to behave as if I was uncomfortable being there or being seen. Of course, I was also curious to know why he was at the rally. He returned my greeting with a gentle hug, and I learned he was there to support a friend. We spent some time chatting, and he seemed flattered that I had taken the time to talk with him. After we parted I found myself elated by the experience as I enthusiastically described to my friends what had happened. At times I had wondered what I would do in such a situation, but until it actually happened I never dreamed it would leave me feeling so positive.

My experiences have made me believe that direct exchanges between individuals are extremely important. They can validate a person's sexual orientation, curb anonymous harassment, and increase understanding by those who are quick to judge out of ignorance. Through personal conversations, and sometimes confrontations, education and acceptance of diversity can be made more possible in our society.

Get Over It

Karen Keough

Physical Education Teacher and Coach
Milton Academy
Milton, Massachusetts

*U*ntil I was about eleven, I played every sport with the boys and girls in my neighborhood. I could throw harder, run faster, hit the ball just as far, and score more touchdowns than any of the boys or girls I played with. I would pitch the ball until my right arm got tired and then start throwing with my left, switching my glove and wearing it backwards. I knew it bothered some of the boys that I was better than them, but I also felt their grudging respect. Nevertheless, it made me feel different even then, as if I had crossed some imaginary line and needed to retreat.

I was not supported or encouraged in athletics until my next-door neighbor, who was coaching a team in the town softball league, asked me to play for his team when I was in sixth grade. Most of the players were in seventh or eighth grade, but I wasn't intimidated, at least not at first. I was the pitcher for our team, which won every game and eventually the championship. I was proud of my efforts and of our team's success, but was very aware of the resentment by other girls, even by some of my own teammates. One parent complained that I shouldn't be a pitcher, because I was striking everyone out, which wasn't fair for the other girls. Sure enough, I was put on a different team the next year with a new coach, who put me at catcher. I was never given an explanation, but I was definitely "put in my place."

Sometimes I see the same type of things happening to the girls I coach. I hear stories from other coaches about the lack of support and the intimidation other women coaches and athletes face daily. I have seen aggressive players actually stop their efforts when the boys show up to watch, because they're afraid of being labeled "dyke." And I have seen in my own career how homophobia can be used to attack women who refuse to conform to society's expectations of proper feminine behavior.

My interest in sports continued in high school and college. During my freshman year in college I decided that I wanted to teach and be involved in athletics in some capacity. I switched majors and ended up in education. After graduating, I began coaching and teaching at the high school and college levels. While I was teaching at Lincoln-Sudbury High School and coaching part-time at Wellesley College, a full-time position at Milton Academy became available. I applied and have been teaching and coaching at Milton since 1987.

During this time, my coming-out process had moved along slowly. I had come out to friends and family but not to anyone at work. During my fourth year at Milton, a faculty member came out to the entire school. Soon after that, I began meeting with a group of faculty and students who wanted to form a support group. From those meetings emerged our Gay-Straight Alliance and the beginning of my coming out at Milton. I gradually started coming out in my classes, beginning with a Human Relationships and Sexuality class I team-taught. By 1990, I was out to the entire community.

During the 1992–1993 school year, I heard that an "anonymous" parent had been in to complain that I should be removed from my coaching position because I am a lesbian. This was after I had been coaching at Milton Academy for five years without ever hearing a complaint about my coaching. When it was explained to this parent that my orientation had nothing to do with my coaching ability, the targeting went more underground. All of a sudden my performance was being questioned, even though my teams have been successful and no one has ever quit a team I have coached. In fact, to this day, I am the only coach who has taken both a soccer and a basketball team to the New England championship tournaments.

I learned of this targeting from a sympathetic adult who told me that a couple of other parents had been calling other parents and getting kids involved as well. During the season I had known some-thing was wrong, because the good communication I had enjoyed with previous teams simply wasn't there and I couldn't figure out why. What disturbed me most was that I was never informed as to what was happening and why until it was too late. It damaged the rapport I had had with the team and left me disgusted with some of these parents as well as some colleagues, whom I found were targeting me as well. I even had one faculty member tell me that, based on a conversation with one parent, she definitely felt that their attempts to get rid of me were rooted in homophobia. When she had pressed this parent as to what I was doing wrong in my coaching, he could not give her an answer.

The positive part of this story is that I did fight back, and I won. I was told I could come back as coach — under certain conditions. These conditions included that I would "co-coach." I would not have an assistant but would share the head coach role. At the time it was explained to me that this was a model that they would like to see other teams use. But, to this day, the head and assistant assignments exist in all of our programs.

I knew that the next year was going to be rough, and after much thought and consideration, I decided not to return to coach that particular team. My reasons had nothing to do with the parents, the kids, or the administration. I had explained to my boss that I might be moving off campus to live with my spouse, whom I was marrying during the summer. If I moved off campus, I had to give up coaching on the varsity level.

My spouse, Christine Huff, was not allowed to retain her position at the private school she worked for if I lived there, so she left her job and moved to Milton. (Chris subsequently filed a discrimination complaint, on which we are still awaiting results.) Chris had supported me through a very difficult time and had suffered along with me. I felt it was time to support her, our relationship, and our marriage.

During this time, my boss had been asking if I would help out with the field hockey program, since I had coached field hockey for many years before coming to Milton. I agreed to coach the JV team during the upcoming season. It was the best decision I ever made. I was able to start with a new group of students who were willing to learn and who accepted me as their coach.

And did they learn! We won every game in our league but, most importantly, the kids had a good time and appreciated my coaching. The parents were wonderful. I had been so worried that they would judge me on my sexual orientation and not on my ability to coach their daughters. Instead, they were wholly appreciative of my efforts. I didn't really do anything different than I had the year before, but I sure felt a lot less pressure. Maybe that was the most important thing I learned — to keep it all in perspective. I realize now that I am not going to change every homophobic parent I come across, but neither am I going to let them run my life. As for those who choose to target me, they have their consciences to live with — if they have any.

The greatest lesson I learned is that you cannot fight these battles alone. I got advice from other coaches who had experienced similar targeting. I received several notes from rival coaches who had heard what was going on and wanted to write letters of support for me. Having the support of other adults at Milton, both gay and straight, was extremely important. I cannot thank those people enough for the advice, friendship, and support they provided. They say that in every cloud there is a silver lining ... and that certainly was the case for me. I found strength I didn't know I had, and found that being married changed my life for the better. If I were to say why I have changed, it has been because of Chris and our relationship.

Coaching has always been an important part of my life but it does not define me. I would describe myself as a happily married lesbian who is a good teacher and coach, likes to read and write poetry, lives a healthy lifestyle, and is a good role model. Presently I teach full-time, coach JV field hockey, run our aerobics program, and coach varsity lacrosse. I guess, as the old saying goes, you can't keep a good woman down.

Insisting on Ignorance: The Paradox of Withholding Knowledge in Our Schools

———David Bruton

English Teacher
Chapel Hill High School
Chapel Hill, North Carolina

"**Y**ou're crazy," said some of my friends.

"Do you really want to give *more* of your life to this school?" asked a colleague.

"Well," sighed a supportive but apprehensive administrator, "if you must do this, be careful; be discreet."

"I'm very proud of you," replied Duff, my life partner of twenty-three years, even though he knew I would have even less time for him after starting a support group for gay and lesbian students at Chapel Hill High School, where I teach American literature.

So, in late November 1992, as discreetly as is possible using a microphone at a total school assembly, this middle-aged, balding, bearded, apparently crazy English teacher began the Support Group for Gays, Lesbians, and Friends, which we now call the Chapel Hill High School Gay-Straight Alliance, one of a very few on-campus high school support groups in the country.

The story of the CHHS Support Group actually begins in the late 1950s and early 1960s with my own emotional and social development. I knew that I was gay from an early age, but I had absolutely no one to turn to for affirmation and nowhere to go for information — except the library. I knew all the terms and the prevailing theories, but I knew that *I* wasn't as the books described homosexuals to be. I also knew from the playground, locker room, and library that it was of no use to try to convince peers, family, church, and state of that.

I couldn't defend myself against such overwhelming condemnation, so silence was my defense. My choices were to tell nothing and be dishonest with myself, or tell the truth and be condemned by others. I was in a kind of limbo: I couldn't be the heterosexual man society accepted, but neither could I find the courage to say, "I am gay, I am a good person, and I accept *myself*."

I was wasting so much energy trying to be what society said I was supposed to be that I couldn't be who I was — until I met Duff Coburn in 1971. Duff, a fellow student at the University of North Carolina at Chapel Hill, was a freshman, and I, trying to "find myself," had drifted into the "Never-Never Land" of the professional student. Duff made me whole. From the day we met, he taught me to feel good about myself, he made me happy, he showed me the meaning of friendship and of love, and he is the best teacher I've ever had. We grew up together, and I'm looking forward to growing old with him. When Duff decided to be a teacher, my own love of learning, coupled with the ever-present memory of my adolescent despair, prodded me to become a teacher as well. I began to believe that perhaps I could help others avoid what had been such a struggle for me.

However, I discovered that things looked different from the teacher's side of the desk. Reason argued that my role was to teach the subject I was hired to teach without commentary from personal experience. Wisdom argued that continued employment required that I be silent about myself as a real person whose life included many gay and not-gay people. Prudence argued that I hide the reality that a gay man could have a stable life and be an exemplary role model for his students, both gay and not gay. Consequently, I settled for the notion that if I saw a youngster struggling with his or her sexual identity, then I might be able to help quietly from the sidelines. Very discreetly. Anonymously, if possible.

I would, however, in the context of studying writers or literary movements, point out and discuss that Whitman's *Calamus* poems are quite homoerotic, that a number of Shakespeare's sonnets are addressed to a young man, that many important figures of the Harlem Renaissance were homosexual, that the works of Baldwin, Auden, Williams, Stein, Sarton, Forster, Ginsberg, Cheever, Coward, and many other notable literary figures reveal what today is so mockingly called alternative lifestyles. This, I rationalized, would provide gay and lesbian students in my classes something of an affirmation without violating that strange boundary marking what I may teach from what I must never mention.

These best-laid plans went awry in the fall of 1991 when a student wrote a letter to the faculty advisory committee of another CHHS student group I co-advise, Cultural Awareness Sensitivity Educators (CASE), literally begging us to discuss sexual orientation. He said he probably wouldn't have tried to commit suicide the year before if he had been able to talk to someone about being gay. Other faculty advisors didn't think such a topic warranted discussion, and *certainly* not for impressionable high school students.

It was exactly there, with that kid's letter, that reality shattered theory, and the wall marking the boundary between what may and may not be discussed in school fell in fragments around my feet. I was incensed that adults — teachers, of all people — could be so ignorant and so insensitive to a human cry for help. I politely insisted that one of the monthly CASE discussions deal with gay and lesbian teens. Now I *could* offer a defense against gratuitous condemnation. So, after I presented the facts and the statistics and the real-life examples, the opposition lapsed into an embarrassed silence.

Posters announcing the discussion went up in halls and classrooms around campus. Of course, many were defaced or torn down, but we replaced them, and the discussion about gay and lesbian teens on February 28, 1992, was an unprecedented success. A mother and son from P-FLAG described how each had felt when the son struggled with his sexual orientation and came out to his mother. An OutRight! spokesperson discussed the confusion and frustration lesbian and gay teenagers face as they try to accept themselves and be accepted by friends and family. About seventy-five students and a dozen teachers attended the optional noon-hour discussion and asked questions ranging from how to help a friend trying to determine his sexual identity to how lesbians and gays could ignore the standard Biblical arguments against homosexuality. Those who asked questions or made comments repeatedly expressed open admiration for the courage the panelists demonstrated by discussing the impact homosexuality and homophobia had on their lives.

In addition to the natural empathy of youth for any person or group enduring irrational discrimination, adolescents very much want to talk about homosexuality with knowledgeable people. They see it as something that directly affects them, so the discussion of gay and lesbian teens generated supportive articles, editorials, and letters about the difficulties facing sexual minority youth in the next three issues of the school newspaper; however, there were also negative consequences. Vandals began their work around the same time as the CASE discussion in late February, and they continued through July of 1992.

I was the object of a series of virulent, homophobic attacks generated, I assumed, because I was the CASE advisor sponsoring the discussion of gay and lesbian teens. My classroom windows were shot out and broken with stones and pop bottles several times, and on one occasion, a dead 'possum was thrown through the broken window. *Bruton's a faggot. Fire Bruton!* was spray-painted on buildings, parking lots, sidewalks, and ten school buses that made their rounds with the graffiti intact. Several small buildings and a truck were set afire and burned.

These attacks occurred, always including my name painted on some nearby surface, at the high school and at three schools in Chapel Hill where Duff has taught. Ultimately some Chapel Hill Public Safety officers set some bait, staked it out, and caught three of my students in the act. One of them, it is sad to say, felt compelled to participate to deflect suspicion about his own masculine image.

It was an unbelievably stressful time for both Duff and me, but I found it relatively easy to maintain a calm, upbeat demeanor at school: young gay students were watching from the safety of silence, and I refused to let them think they could be diminished as a person by ignorant gay-bashers. I wanted them to get the message that to a *real* gay man, such attacks were nothing more than silly pranks by stupid, insecure boys.

This is not a happy story, but it has a happy ending. The administration at the high school supported me. The faculty was shocked and outraged, but stumped about what to do. This was a problem generally glossed over in schools of education, but one of my colleagues, a well-respected, dignified, and very proper English teacher suggested that the faculty have an old-fashioned, sixties-style protest demonstration. Although I have trouble thinking of the sixties as an old-fashioned era, her idea was enthusiastically accepted, the date set, and the entire day planned to have discussions in every class about the vandalism and its attendant intolerance.

The reaction of eighteen hundred students watching their teachers walk out of class, form a large circle in the courtyard, hold hands, and stand in symbolic protest against intolerance was as unexpected as it was astounding. Students poured out of the buildings and joined the circle, its diameter expanding as more students joined hands with the faculty, and we soon had such a large circle that the buildings defining the courtyard prevented it from getting any larger. Students formed another circle within the one they had just swelled to capacity, and in a short time most of the faculty and a large number of students stood together in support of tolerance and understanding.

Throughout the remainder of the day, students, many of whom I didn't know, came to me expressing sympathy for me and disgust for people who would harass another because of, as several students said, "being who you are." For the remainder of that year and the whole of the 1992–1993 school year, several very impressive athletes — all my students or former students — seemed to be hanging around by turns wherever I was, and one, in a burst of passion, vowed to "take care of" anybody making my life difficult if I'd just give the word. Students, parents, and total strangers wrote and telephoned with messages of support and encouragement. Some parents wrote angry letters to newspapers criticizing the press for persistently identifying me as an "openly gay" teacher; they feared my reputation was being gratuitously damaged by such a label. I was totally unprepared for this outpouring of human compassion, generosity, and love.

The 1992–1993 school year began with something else no teacher is prepared for, an event I felt as a very personal tragedy: one of the finest young men I've known, a former student, committed suicide just days before our scheduled meeting to discuss some problems he was having. He was nineteen. I have never done anything harder than speak at his memorial service. Six weeks after his death, Duff and I went to Washington to see the Quilt. We weren't prepared for that, either, but what devastated me even more than seeing the panels of our friends was seeing the number of very young men sitting alone on the soggy ground beside panels and weeping uncontrollably.

A simple act of human compassion and love caught my attention. A grandmotherly woman, making her way deliberately around a square of the quilt, bent down and held a young man who was weeping beside a panel. It was a small, simple thing to do, but it was definite, public, and selfless.

That woman's act of compassion, coupled with the profound pain of dealing with loss upon loss, made me realize that I had been wrong to consider my sexual orientation incidental to "who I am," that I had been wrong to believe that my sexual orientation has no place in my classroom, and that I had been wrong not to speak up and become visible to our youth. I resolved at that moment that I had to do something definite, not at all discreet, and if it cost me more than I anticipated — then so be it. Reason, Wisdom, and Prudence would have to take a backseat to Action.

When Duff and I returned home, I asked Mary Gratch-Abrams, a "straight but not narrow" guidance counselor at Chapel Hill High School, if she'd be willing to co-sponsor a support group for gay and lesbian students. She agreed with no hesitation, so at a total school assembly sponsored by CASE, I talked to the student body and faculty about the need for such a group and announced its formation. I decided we'd be discreet after they knew we existed. The students were quite attentive.

We began with two advisors and almost immediately two more teachers asked to help. Soon we added nine more CHHS personnel to our list of advisors. We put up posters in classrooms of supportive teachers listing the advisors and telling how to become involved in the Support Group. This worked very well. We began with one person, then four, soon six, and by midsemester the Support Group had twenty-five student participants representing all four grade levels. Our purpose, stated on our posters, is to make sure our gay, lesbian, and bisexual students at Chapel Hill High School can be *affirmed* as good people; *appreciated* for who they truly are; *empowered* to be themselves — fully and completely; *free* of self-hatred, fear, and shame; and *proud* of themselves.

Immediately after we began meeting we discovered a problem. Because our Support Group welcomed friends and supporters of gays and lesbians, students who identified as gay or lesbian expressed some difficulty in being as open as they would like to be.

Consequently, at the beginning of the 1993–1994 school year we changed our name to the Chapel Hill High School Gay-Straight Alliance and made the Support Group an additional, private arena for discussions or activities exclusively for students who identify as gay or lesbian. We also began meeting weekly to be as accessible as possible.

One definite, public step we took was to raise the awareness of the student body about a rather basic social situation taken for granted by heterosexuals. We wrote a letter to the junior class describing the feeling of exclusion that sexual minority youth feel at the junior-senior prom. In response to our letter, the prom committee extended the same considerations to gay and lesbian couples as to heterosexual couples.

So, not wanting to miss the festivities, the Alliance had a pre-prom party at a member's house and then went to the prom more or less together. One member admitted, while fussing with the dress she was unaccustomed to wearing, that under no other circumstance would she be going to the prom. She couldn't see any point to it. As the evening wore on she slid up beside me, and with eyes twinkling and an impish smile spread across her face, she slipped her arm through mine and almost breathlessly told me the clearly awesome news: she had danced with a girl she really wanted to dance with. Her bright eyes and broad smile lasted for weeks.

Activities for gay and lesbian teens sponsored by public schools catch the attention of news reporters. I had communicated with teachers from California to Massachusetts who had developed support programs, so with the benefit of their experience, I devised an effective strategy for dealing with the media. Since sound bites can so easily be placed in a context that distorts the intended meaning, I wouldn't speak with radio or television reporters. I agreed to talk with newspaper reporters if they would come to my classroom and talk face-to-face with me. Well, I'm a teacher, and here were some people who needed educating. Several hours of note taking later, consistently accurate, informative, and supportive stories appeared in local and state papers. This after-hours tutoring produced some superb advocates for our mission to help gay and lesbian youth.

We are fortunate to have strong support from our school system office and our board of education. In 1991, members of the board discussed including sexual orientation in the system's multicultural curriculum. They felt then that they didn't have enough information to see the necessity to do so. When the vandals and I provided them with the information they needed, they immediately passed a resolution denouncing intolerance in the school system, specifically mentioning sexual orientation. In less than a year, the board approved a revised Multicultural Education Action Plan which included addressing issues of prejudice toward and intolerance of both students and staff because of their sexual orientation.

Some people, however, can't bear to have lesbians and gay males affirmed as whole, loving people who have a right to full and open lives. The town fathers like to promote Chapel Hill as the Southern Part of Heaven, an appellation that must have attracted the attention of a few outspoken bigots who recently moved into our community. These authoritarian personalities quickly found a small coterie of like-minded people who didn't have a leader until they arrived or a particular focus until the board of education included sexual orientation as part of its systemwide Multicultural Education Action Plan.

Suddenly the right-wing bigots had a cause, and they thought they had a patsy. The vandalism and hate graffiti directed at me in the first half of 1992 generated quite a bit of publicity in the news media, but I apparently had been doing more things right as a teacher than not; the community at large had expressed outrage that I was being abused and bashed. This was both a blessing and a curse for bigots: here was one of those dangerous perverts teaching vulnerable children in our own local high school; however, everyone seemed to like him. This didn't exactly square with the picture they wanted to present of a homosexual menace infiltrating the public schools.

Since July of 1993, when this right-wing group incorporated (its catchy name proclaiming it to have only the best interest of children at heart) and began its harangues, I have regularly listened to its members address the board. Speakers regularly intoned a monotonous theme and variation: "I'm not prejudiced, but..."; "I'm all for respect, but..."; "I'm for tolerance, but..."; "I'm not a bigot, but..."; "I'm not homophobic, but..."; "I don't hate, but..." These and other disclaimers prefaced misinformed comments about homosexuality, fear that their children would be recruited into a "lifestyle" by hearing about or seeing gays and lesbians, or blatant hatred thinly veiled by outrageously false information designed to do nothing but perpetuate hatred. All these claims of fairness and tolerance possessed one common denominator: ignorance of any real knowledge about homosexuality.

If ignorance is *not* at work here, the alternative explanation is that a deliberate distortion of the truth is at work, and that is an even more insidious evil than ignorance. These right-wing zealots were incensed that the board had compromised their "moral beliefs." Those who addressed the board were intelligent, well-educated people; thus, bigotry is the least damning charge that can be brought to bear against people who continue to tout their "moral values" as justification for deliberately disregarding copious evidence that homosexuality is a natural human variation.

Refusing to relinquish prejudiced beliefs is an exercise in irrational behavior, so I found it interesting to note how speakers representing this right-wing group altered their focus and their rhetoric as the weeks passed. They originally claimed that the board of education had secretly furthered its own agenda without informing the community, the majority of which, so they claimed, felt its moral values to be compromised by the board's action. They merely wanted, they said, for the board to reflect the values and act on the wishes of the voting citizens of the community.

Their second claim, since the board wouldn't agree that it had ignored the citizenry, was that sexual orientation was not a culture; it was, the bigots claimed, a *choice*, a *behavior*, and had no part in any plan that purported to address multicultural issues. Some ranted that this godless plan was designed to teach their children how to be homosexual and that the next step would be teaching pedophilia, necrophilia, and bestiality in our schools.

When this right-wing group realized that the board wouldn't quickly and quietly capitulate to their demands to remove the sexual orientation component altogether, they badgered and intimidated the board into suspending the implementation of it until a communitywide ad hoc committee could be formed to make recommendations they believed would more accurately reflect community values.

Early in the game these bigots acknowledged the "homosexual club" at the high school and said that it was okay for homosexuals to have a place to be together, but as time passed and they weren't getting their way, the CHHS Gay-Straight Alliance became the third menace, and the bigots tried to characterize it as an affront to the board's decision to suspend discussion of sexual orientation in the schools until they had had input through the ad hoc committee. They failed, however, to sway anyone to their conviction that the Alliance violated the board's intentions.

When people who reject reason and accept misinformation get desperate, they get personal. I became the fourth menace these benighted people targeted. Not only was I a problem because I am gay, which they were always careful to say really wasn't the issue, but I now was revealed to be an idiot, who deprived his students of the best of American literature. Instead, these bigots claimed, I taught them drivel written by people whose only claim to literary merit lay in their membership in some multicultural group. What was especially repugnant, it seemed, was that I was teaching feminist as well as gay and lesbian literature. I was amazed and fascinated to hear about what and how I teach my classes from the lips of people who have never even been inside my classroom. Things were moving rapidly from simple ignorance to blatant lies.

The 1993–1994 school year marked the third year I've had my American literature students do a year-long independent-study multicultural literature project, which *they* teach at the end of the year, in addition to the regular canon-based curriculum which *I* teach. Students choose (*choose* is the operative word here) to study one group from among the following seven: Native Americans, African-Americans, American feminists, Jewish Americans, Hispanic Americans, Asian-Americans, and American gays and lesbians. High school juniors have a tremendously heavy academic load in addition to extracurricular and social activities, so I tried to point them in the direction of *American* writers of the specific cultural group they were studying by compiling a 46-page bibliography of over two thousand titles, which they could use or ignore as they chose. I also gave the students a fourteen-page description of the project that included the reason for doing it, suggestions for approaching the task, and specific directions for presenting their topic to the class and their final paper to me.

At the beginning of the year, the entire CHHS English Department discussed my project in view of the right-wing opposition, and I received unanimous support to continue. Not only did my project have intrinsic merit, but it also was begun prior to the system-level multicultural initiative and was, in fact, totally independent of the Multicultural Education Action Plan. In addition to the support of my colleagues, I received a letter at the beginning of September from a former student named Geoff. He included a paper he'd written on a multicultural theme, and he said, "You inspired me to write this paper. When I look back on doing the research project, I realize what a great effect it has had on my life. That project was the best thing I have gotten out of high school."

Imagine my surprise when, a week after I'd read Geoff's letter, reporters called with the news that the mother of one of my students was incensed that I was *making* her daughter study gays and lesbians and *forcing* her to read *assigned* books on a list of gay and lesbian writers. This was, indeed, news to me.

I arrived at the next board meeting to discover that the right-wing bigots had photocopied my project description and list of gay and lesbian authors and were passing them around as conclusive evidence that their children were being corrupted and that I should be "disciplined" because I was scoffing at the board decision to suspend the inclusion of sexual orientation in the Multicultural Education Action Plan. As further evidence that they were not targeting me as a gay teacher but only as an incompetent idiot, they took great offense at my "insensitivity" in referring to WASPS (white Anglo-Saxon Protestants) as the group against which we would be comparing and contrasting the seven groups in the project. That almost all writers studied in the typical high school American literature programs *are* WASPS is a fact that escapes these unhappy people.

My principal, the superintendent, and the board supported my right to continue the project. They agreed that in no way was I violating board decisions, and they refused to move the student out of my class. The mother withdrew her daughter from school, gave her a new car, and enrolled her in another school system. The right-wing radicals launched another volley of harangues against the board and me and then lapsed into relative silence for a few weeks.

One week before the school board election, the news reporters called me again and informed me of the fifth assault. It seems the mother whose values would be so compromised if her daughter had to read books by gay writers (or even hear about them) had busily combed the area libraries and book stores for books on my list until she found one or two containing passages that offended her.

This mother, whose daughter was now in another school system, made hundreds of copies of the material she so diligently sought out, and wrote a cover page in the best supermarket-tabloid style warning the unsuspecting reader that this was disgusting, pornographic stuff. She named me as the teacher who had *assigned* these books to my students at the high school, sent copies of her packet to the media, to school personnel, and to every public official she could find an address for, then passed out copies to anyone who stuck out a hand, including high school students, at the next board meeting.

By this time my students were beginning to take offense at both the tactics and the comments of those bigots who claimed to be protecting the welfare of students. Letters of support from my students kept appearing for weeks on my desk and in my mailbox; it was some of the best writing I've seen in years. Several of my students wrote letters to the newspapers. Many began attending board meetings and spoke in support of me as a person and as a teacher. Many got their parents to write letters and speak out against intolerance and censorship. Annalee, one of my students, concluded an eloquent letter to the editor this way: "By reading and listening to very educated people speak so closed-mindedly on this subject, I am able to see clearly their ignorance on the subject. In many ways the students at CHHS are handling the subject more maturely and open-mindedly than many of the adults." Another student, Erica, wrote, "I don't know, I guess I'm just so sick of these ignorant people who think if we ignore homosexuality then it will just disappear! Everyone deserves the right to live without fear and to be respected as an individual, despite any differences."

A particularly telling indication of the real agenda of this right-wing group was the total lack of regard for the beliefs and comments of the high school students who have spoken at the board meetings. Students were ignored or heckled while speaking and were then lectured to afterward by those persons who profess only a concern for youngsters as their mission. It was perhaps the most hideous display of hypocrisy and self-righteousness I've ever seen. Some of the students who tried to clarify what my course was really about were motivated to join the Alliance after they saw this irrational fear, hatred, and bigotry at work.

Finally the bigots wore the board down by expending extraordinary efforts to discredit me and distort my multicultural literature project. They didn't succeed in getting me "disciplined," but they did manage to get the gay and lesbian portion of my project suspended until the board can create guidelines for teachers to use in compiling bibliographies.

That only the gay and lesbian list was suspended has created quite a controversy and has attracted the attention and involvement of the National Coalition against Censorship and People for the American Way in letter-writing campaigns and in co-sponsoring a forum held on the CHHS campus about censorship and gay and lesbian writing. Working with these national organizations, two recently formed local groups invited Susan E. Johnson (author of *Staying Power*, which was banned at CHHS), Perry Deane Young (author of *The David Kopay Story*), and the Reverend W.W. Finlator (retired Southern Baptist minister and longtime civil rights advocate). These three spoke eloquently about the harm done to all of us when some people try to restrict information, withhold knowledge, perpetuate misinformation, and insist on ignorance about the sexual orientation of human beings.

Almost exactly one year after my former student's suicide, a friend and classmate of his also took his own life. On the evening after his death, when Duff and I went to offer our condolences, his younger brother asked to speak with me privately. I couldn't tell if his discomfort was more from grief or from embarrassment at being so forward, but with apologetic urgency he said that because of all the "things that had happened" at school, he "knew" about me, and with a direct purposefulness indicative of much thought about the issue, he asked me if his brother could have been gay. I had no answer that would have helped, but it broke my heart that this was the first thing he wanted to know. We talked, trying to make some sense where none existed, until some of his friends arrived, but just before they got close enough to hear us, he put his hand on my arm and looked directly at me, his eyes filled with more pain than a seventeen-year-old ought to have to bear, and he begged me to keep on with the support group. "No matter what," he said, "don't stop."

The efforts of the Alliance make discussion of homosexuality possible; it is no longer a topic spoken of only in whispers or in derisive language at Chapel Hill High School. Students from all grade levels come to me asking for information about homosexuality for projects in other classes. Earlier this semester a sophomore whizzed into my room between classes to thank me for helping him defeat the irrational arguments that anti–gay rights advocates had trotted out in the debate his team had just won. We didn't know each other prior to his project, but now he goes out of his way to speak whenever he sees me. I am continually amazed by the large number of students, most of whom I don't know, who now smile and speak to me on campus and around town. The topic is out of the closet, but we still have gay and lesbian students and staff waiting to see if it is really safe to be whole people.

I have discovered what doing nothing costs, and I have paid a far greater price than I realized was possible for the folly of believing that I didn't need to acknowledge my sexual orientation, that it wasn't important. It is *very* important. It is a significant part of who I am, and it is relevant in my teaching because it shapes my perceptions, it informs my responses to my subject and my students, and it is a significant part of my being as a whole person — teacher, colleague, friend, life partner, role model, human being.

My students sometimes teach me as much as I teach them; sometimes they teach me more. They have taught me that to be whole, to be real, requires that I be honest with them about who I am. They have taught me how easy it is to give of myself when I don't have to fumble around behind a mask. They have taught me what trust and respect and compassion really feel like. They have taught me about friendship. But above all, they have taught me how important it is to continue to stand up for the rights of people who can't yet stand up for themselves. Students tell me they think I'm brave because of that. They say they admire my courage, that they respect me for standing up for what I believe in. I can see they don't really understand it when I tell them that whatever bravery or courage I might demonstrate is possible only because I believe in them.

In the middle of the frustrations of the attempt to portray me as a purveyor of pornography, a postcard arrived from Beijing, China, from Geremy and Kerr, CHHS Class of '88. Each had written me a note on the card, but Kerr said, "Once you told me that in times of doubt I should remember those who support me, and I want you to know that, likewise, we support you and wish you only the best." Even though he really didn't *need* my encouragement back in 1988, I wanted him to know that I had noticed him, that I believed in him and respected him. I had no idea that in 1993 he would return those words of support and encouragement to me when I *did* need them.

I attempt to teach my students about American literature, but they have succeeded in teaching me about the strength of love, about the healing power of speaking openly from the heart, about the vitally necessary freedom to be a complete human being by *being* "who I am." And for these lessons I am very grateful.

Part Four:

Victories

"We must continue the education that began
in this campaign.
We must destroy the myths once and for all,
shatter them.
And, most important of all:
Every gay person must come out.
You must tell your family.
You must tell your friends, if they are truly your friends.
You must tell the people in the stores you shop in.
You must tell the people you work with ...
And, when you do,
you will feel so much better."

—HARVEY MILK, _____
on the night of the defeat of the "Briggs Initiative,"
which would have banned the employment of gay and lesbian
teachers in the California public school system,
November 1978

Private
Conversations

Patty Smith
Middle School French Teacher
The Pike School
North Andover, Massachusetts _____

"*L*et's focus on the *positive* aspects of being out in our schools," we said, "instead of always talking about the difficulties we face, or the problems we cause." *We* were the steering committee, planning the third annual GLSTN (Gay and Lesbian School Teachers' Network) Conference, in Milton, Massachusetts. "Celebration and Challenge," we were calling it. I volunteered to be one of four teachers who would speak at the opening plenary, "Celebration: The Contributions of Lesbian and Gay Teachers."

"I'll do it," I said. "If you need someone else."

A woman. Elementary school. "Okay," the others approved.

But I felt like an imposter.

At Pike, I came out slowly. To my friends there first. And to the administration under difficult circumstances.

I am not one of the brave ones.

I have not changed curriculum or come out at an all-school assembly. There is no gay-straight alliance at my school. No new policies that recognize same-sex spouses. We do not celebrate National Coming-Out Day.

"What'd I get myself into?" I moaned. "What'll I say?"

"You'll do fine," Cindy told me. My girlfriend, she is not even a little objective.

"But the other three," I say. "They're practically *famous!* I've done nothing compared to them!"

For weeks, I think about my positive contributions. I even ask my head of school for advice. My influence, I finally decide, has been with individuals. With administrators and faculty. In private conversations.

———

"You are," my headmaster told me, "a valuable member of this faculty. You are," he said, " a good French teacher."

"Your greatest contribution to this school," he continued, "is in your role as French teacher."

What I heard was: being a lesbian is not important.

"Wait a minute," I wanted to say. "I don't think you understand. What you get is a package deal."

A former student had confided in me about an abusive parent. She ran away from home and called me in the middle of the night.

"But the other thing is," I had said to my headmaster, "you need to know I'm a lesbian."

I had come out to this student.

I wanted the administration to know in case the school was contacted by the girl's parents.

The call never came.

———

The French teacher–lesbian sits in a faculty meeting.

"She is becoming so much more feminine," a colleague says. "Isn't that wonderful?"

We are speaking about one of our students.

"It could be," I say. "It depends." Is it *better* to be feminine? Our dress code would suggest that. We are sending our girls a message.

———

I move onto safer terrain — my French class.

"That's so gay," I hear one student say with disgust to his buddy. "I hate that."

I don't know what they are talking about.

"What do you mean, 'It's gay'?" I ask.

"You know — *gay,* " he says, as if the hidden meaning is blatantly clear.

Students are filing in. They whisper to each other about what has happened. They look at me and wait.

"Didn't he know? Ms. Smith hates when you use that word," I hear one of them say.

"Why do you use the word *gay?*" I ask. The kids roll their eyes. They have heard this one so many times now. "What is it that you mean? What were you talking about?"

A picture. A movie. Something that has happened at recess. It doesn't matter. It is dismissed as gay.

By now, class has begun. But the lesbian–French teacher can't yet launch into her *"Bonjour! ça va?"* She is a precise user of language, after all. Just what does *gay* mean to her students?

————

"That's funny," a colleague says at lunch when I retell the story. "I never notice them saying that."

"They do," I say. *Gay. Fag.* "But from me, they get a talk each time."

"They're just words," another offers. "The kids don't know what they mean."

"Like *nigger?* It's a word, too. Once upon a time, we didn't know what it meant."

"Hmmmm," they say.

————

A year later, I hardly hear the words *gay* and *fag* anymore. It gives me courage.

————

I go back to the headmaster. I tell him I want to come out to the kids. We should be proactive, I say.

Faculty first, he says. He wants to go slowly. I am restless, but I agree.

"You know," he says, "if I had known seven years ago that you were a lesbian, I'm not sure I would have hired you."

He likes me, though, in spite of himself. I sense the fear of what he doesn't understand. I hear his internal struggle. *I like her. What if the parents find out? She* is *a good teacher.*

"But it isn't right," I say, "to run a school based on fear."

————

I bring Cindy to the holiday party. I am awkward with the trustees, but not with the faculty, many of whom have met her already. I want to quell any lingering doubt that I am single.

"But whose business is it anyway if you're a lesbian?" I am asked by colleagues, the well-meaning ones.

"I look at it another way," I say. "Don't your students know you are married? They even know you have kids. Do you hide it from them? Why? Because there is nothing to hide." It's the package deal.

———

It is suggested by some that I reconsider teaching at Pike. That I find a school that more closely suits my needs.

I am depressed. I feel like a burden. Just one person, I think. I am unreasonable to assume the school would change only for me.

What about the students, then? I think of the girls who confide in me. The ones who tell me they don't fit in with the others. I think of the ones who wonder silently.

"In Human Sexuality, is homosexuality discussed?" I ask.

Not much, I am told. It depends on who is teaching it.

"So the gay and lesbian kids don't hear anything that rings true to them? Where is their validation?"

———

"Have you heard of GLSTN?" I ask my headmaster. "The Gay and Lesbian School Teachers Network?" I know the conference information was mailed to the school, but it is not posted anywhere. I tell him I want to attend.

If you go, he says, people might see you there. They might talk, mention your name.

I don't mind, I say. I am not asking for permission.

I also want to announce at a full faculty meeting that I am a member of GLSTN and that anyone who would like information could seek me out.

Somehow, I am still nervous to announce it. Introducing Cindy to people is one thing. Just saying the word *lesbian* in front of everyone is another.

Nobody asks for information.

Three administrators come to the conference, though.

Afterwards, the headmaster calls me to his office, says something about "damage control." Word will get out, he says. Parents might call. We need a strategy.

I am furious. I leave his office and cry in a friend's classroom.

"I can't work here," I say. "Not when he thinks of me as a liability."

"I know it's hard to believe," my friend says, "but I think he *meant* well. He wants to protect you."

"He might have chosen better words," I say.

———

The head of the Upper School, my immediate boss, says he enjoyed the conference.

"I learned a lot," he says. He tells me about the changes he has made in his Human Sexuality class, about the matter-of-fact way he broaches homosexuality.

Good, I think. But there is still literature, math, science, history...

———

"I think I need to leave Pike," I say to my head of school. "I feel too much like a liability."

We talk some more, agree to discuss my situation further with the headmaster.

———

"It's one thing if we were a secondary school," my headmaster says. "But elementary school children don't need to hear about this."

"So, nobody should tell the kids if they are married or not, then? Is that what you mean?" I ask. "What about the kids who have gay parents? Or siblings?"

"I hadn't thought of it that way," he says.

———

At the end-of-year meetings, I push for a diversity workshop. Gay and lesbian issues must be included, I say.

We begin the year with a half-day workshop. The first one ever. We focus mainly on racism, but the words *gay* and *lesbian* are brought up over and over. The school brims with talk of diversity. People begin to explore what Pike is like, what it could be like. We are not a complacent bunch. We talk with optimism.

———

"I have a sense," the headmaster says, "that the kids are aware of your situation and they don't mind."

I agree. "I know they know," I say. "It just isn't a big deal for them."

———

This year, the headmaster announces the GLSTN conference himself at a full faculty meeting. He says that it is important. He encourages people to attend. The conference bulletin is posted on the faculty room door. Six or seven people say they are interested. All of them come.

My head of school says: I want my own children to grow up without the fears I have. The kids at Pike would profit from the realization that the teacher who inspired them to enjoy French, who was funny, and caring, and fair, was also gay. They should know that.

I am told that whatever I do, I have the support of the school.

———

A full year later, the headmaster says to me: At the board meeting last night, one of the trustees asked me if I would hire a gay teacher.

What did you say? I ask.

I told him all things being equal, sure. Then I said: You mean would I ever hire *another* gay teacher?

He smiles and walks off.

———

Two of my sixth-graders hang around in my classroom after lit class one day. I know what they want to talk to me about.

"Ms. Smith," one of them begins. "We were just wondering ... not that it's any of our business or anything ... but who was that woman at the medieval banquet with you?"

I know they are wondering about Cindy. For the first time, I have brought her to the annual sixth-grade medieval banquet. We dress as peasants and sit among the kings, jesters, and knights who otherwise are my sixth-grade students. These two girls have noticed our identical rings and have asked another teacher whether or not I am a lesbian.

"Her name is Cindy," I say. "I guess you noticed our rings?"

They look relieved, nod.

"We had a ceremony," I say. "Like a wedding."

"Oh," one of them says, the braver one. "We were just wondering. We heard rumors, you know?"

"Well, they're true," I say. "Did the rumors bother you?"

"Oh, no," they both shake their heads. "No one said anything *bad* or anything, just like, you know, when you're getting the dirt on your new teachers."

"Well, thanks for telling us," they say, and head off to lunch.

I wait for the fallout. There isn't any.

———

Cindy and I go to the school fair. We bring my toddler nephew, and the three of us definitely get some interested looks. Mostly, the students rush past, yell hello. Some stop.

"Oh, isn't he cute?" they say.

A mother of one of my seventh-graders waves from across the field.

"I've been wanting to talk with you," she says. "My daughter jumped in the car the other day. 'Guess what?' she said, excited. 'I think Ms. Smith is a lesbian!' *I'm* a lesbian, too, and my daughter was so relieved that someone else she knew and liked besides me and my friends is a lesbian. She knows the other kids like you, so maybe they won't be horrified if they find out about me. Anyway, I just wanted to let you know that this is one family that is happy you are here."

———

In January, when I return to school after the holidays, I find a white envelope in my mailbox in the faculty room.

"Happy Anniversary," the card reads when I open it.

I smile and begin to feel at home in the fabric of daily life at school.

Telling Our Stories, Winning Our Freedom

Rodney Wilson

History Teacher
Mehlville High School
Saint Louis, Missouri _____

I have known I was gay since I was seven. Seventeen years later, after much effort to become straight as well as hundreds of prayers pleading for a dispensation of straightness, I came to understand that I was simply meant to be gay and that the God and Parent of us all was not concerned about the issue.

Then, at age twenty-four, I began my journey from the closet toward freedom. I made contact with the Gay and Lesbian Student Association at Southeast Missouri State and began to come out to my friends. When I moved to Saint Louis in August 1990 to teach at Mehlville High School, I became more deeply involved in the gay community through the Metropolitan Community Church, volunteering at Saint Louis University's AIDS Vaccine evaluation unit, and civil rights work. By mid-1991, I was out to my family (from grandma to cousins) and all of my friends.

The only place where I was still closeted was at work. However, in the fall of 1991, a classroom exercise prompted me to seriously consider coming out to my students. In class, we debated various civil rights issues, including whether or not a lesbian couple should be allowed to adopt children. I was taken aback by the students' overwhelmingly negative response. Some proclaimed that they would burn down the house of any lesbian couple who moved near them. I felt it was my duty at the time to tell my students that I was gay: they needed a human face behind the word *homosexual*. I thought of the following analogy: if I were an African-American in Montgomery in 1956, teaching blind white students who did not know my racial heritage, I would be morally compelled to reveal my blackness to help them overcome their prejudice. Similarly, I felt compelled to tell my "blind" students in 1991 that I was gay, but could not.

As a second-year, nontenured teacher, I felt that to reveal my true identity would have put my job in jeopardy. I had a choice: honesty or bread. At that point, I chose bread. However, I needed an outlet for my frustration. After the class ended, I bumped into the school's wellness counselor, Joanna Van Der Tuin, in the cafeteria. I came out to her amidst the clamor and chaos of five hundred hungry students. Her support was a key element in keeping me going in the years to come.

As my second year in teaching gave way to my third and then my fourth, I became more convinced that I needed to come out to my students. But I found it hard to take that final step out of the closet at work, although I was, by my fourth year, out to about a third of my colleagues on the faculty.

After all this, a single question must be answered: why, then, did I choose to come out on Tuesday, March 22, 1994?

To begin with, I had returned that Sunday night from Washington, where I had attended a National Education Association conference entitled "Affording Equal Opportunity to Lesbian and Gay Students through Teaching and Counseling." I had taken time off from school to attend the conference, and had always in the past informed my students about the reason for such absences, whether it was a Teenage Health Consultant training, my mother's hospitalization, or a history conference. The only reason I would not explain the reason for this absence would be homophobia, I realized, and I simply could not participate in my own oppression one more time. I decided to be honest with my students. I had bought many items in D.C. that I wanted to share with my students, partly as a way of coming out to them. During our class "Show and Tell" period on Monday, a student asked where I had been the previous Friday. I answered that I would tell them the next day.

During my absence, I had asked my substitute to show the film *Escape from Sobibor*. An engrossing account of the only successful mass escape from a Nazi death camp, the film captures and holds the students' interest. I was aware that, during my stay in D.C., they were watching a film about one of the most horrific chapters in human history, one that took place because one group of people felt justified in hating another group — a group that included gays who had perished by the thousands in the Nazi-led Holocaust.

While in D.C., I had visited the Holocaust Museum. There I purchased a poster that illustrated the different patches worn by camp inmates — including yellow Stars of David for Jews, purple triangles for Jehovah's Witnesses, black triangles for gypsies, and pink triangles for homosexuals. I brought the poster to class on Tuesday, with the intent of discussing it as part of the concluding lesson for the film.

We began class by watching the final fifteen minutes of the film. Afterwards, I pulled my chair to the front of the room to begin discussion. I began to talk about crimes against humanity. I noted the different groups that the Nazis had persecuted, using the poster as my visual aid. The room was absolutely silent. Then I pointed to the pink triangle and said, "If I had been in Europe during World War II, I would have been forced to wear this, and I would have been gassed to death." And so I came out to my students.

I went on to tell them that thousands of gays had been killed in the Holocaust by the Nazis. I switched my focus to today and told them about Allen Schindler, a navy sailor who was beaten to death by a Missourian because he was gay. I told them about Harvey Milk, the courageous San Francisco politician who was assassinated because of his homosexuality. I told them about Bobby Griffith, a gay teenager who jumped off a bridge to his death because society would not accept that he was gay. I told them that thirty percent of adolescent suicides in our country are by gay teens driven to despair. I tried to give them a sense of the oppression we still face in this land of the free and home of the brave.

I waited nervously for their reaction. Absolutely none of them responded negatively. M. raised his hand and said, "I respect you a lot for having the courage to say what you just said." J. followed with "You are really brave to do what you just did," and began to clap. Almost everyone in the room joined in. Moved, I told them about how risky this could be, that by coming out I had placed myself at risk for various forms of discrimination that are still legal in our state. Astounded, C. asked, "Why would they have the right to fire you?" J. chimed in with, "Well, I think you would have a lot more students on your side than against you."

Others followed with more personal questions: "Do your parents know?" "Do they allow your boyfriend to come to their house?"

"How did you know you were gay?" "How did your being gay affect your growing up?" I answered as best I could. Three female students began to cry: the tears, I learned, came from the level of emotion in the room, not from anger or prejudice.

As the end of the hour neared, I told them, "You may do with this information as you wish. Keep it to yourself, or tell everyone. But I am not going to tell my other classes at this time." S., who had been crying, replied, "You have to tell your other students. My whole outlook has changed because of what you said." With that, the class came to a consensus that I should tell my other classes, nodding their heads unanimously when I asked them if they agreed with S. As the class ended, two students came up to shake my hand and express their approval. One young man said, "That took a lot of balls to tell us." "Perhaps that's one way to put it," I replied.

As the exhausting hour came to an end, I felt at peace with my decision. The moral universe had opened a window through which I had just traveled, and the students had applauded my journey. The feeling that this was the right thing to do swept over me, just as it had when I came out to my mother over the phone on May 22, 1991. As Jesus put it, "You shall know the truth, and the truth shall set you free." Finally, the truth was known, and I felt freer than ever before.

Another student was still crying quite a bit. I approached her and asked what was wrong. She answered that she had a gay cousin who had been persecuted for being gay, and she was now worried for me. I expressed my hope that everything would turn out well, handed her some tissues, and hugged her good-bye. Later that day, she returned and handed me the following note:

Mr. Wilson,
  I'm sitting here in my class and cannot stop thinking about the things you told us today. So many things came to my mind and I wanted to tell you all of them, but I could only cry. I don't even know why. Perhaps because my cousin is gay and he has a very unhappy life, because his family and all his previous friends think he is a pig or perverted or whatever ... A lot of people think, "This poor woman or man is homosexual. What a horrible life they must have." I don't think these people realize their behavior is as bad as the behavior of people who hate homosexuals. Even I have a tendency to react like that. I know it's wrong, and I wish I could stop being so influenced by society.

Mr. Wilson, I always liked you as a teacher, because you liked your subject so much. You weren't prejudiced against anybody and that takes a lot of character strength. I think you should know that a lot of people look up to you because you were brave enough to tell them about yourself.

Mr. Wilson, I'm happy that I got to know you and I'm sure I will never forget you, your class, and this special day: March 22, 1994. I'm looking forward to our next hour. Good luck.

Another young woman in my third-hour class sent me this letter:

Mr. Wilson,

I am sitting here thinking about what you said in your class today. Mr. Wilson, I have always had respect for you. But after today's class, I have seen a different side of you. I see the courage, bravery, and valiance that you deserve.

Today's class made me understand some things I've never had to think about. Mr. Wilson, you are a great role model for anyone, Black, White, Gay, or Straight. Your extreme talents to teach should not be based on your sexual preference.

I just wanted to drop you a line in case you are feeling alone. Don't ever feel alone. You will always have a friend.

I was only going to tell my third-hour class, but, because of their encouragement, I told my fourth-hour (another junior-year American History class) as well. Their response was positive but quite different. After a couple of questions, they returned their attention to more prosaic matters, asking, "When are we going to get our tests back?" They seemed not at all concerned about the matter. By fifth hour, word was making its way around the school of two thousand students. I heard students talking, with one telling another, "Mr. Wilson told his third- and fourth-hour classes he was gay; I bet he does it in this class, too." I did tell my freshmen Introduction to Social Studies class about the conference but did not "come out." I'd had enough for one day.

The next day began with an early-morning letter. A. wrote:

Mr. Wilson,

I don't want to forget this so I'm writing. I accepted you long ago as a person. I held a great deal of respect for you and was proud that you thought so highly of me. I still feel the same way...

Know that I will be the first to defend you to the hilt, if the need should arise ... I am also honored that you would choose to tell us personally of your decision...

As J. (the young man who had commenced the hand-clapping the day before) entered my room for third hour, he reached out and patted my arm in a "we're still on your side" way. I discovered a folded piece of paper on the floor at the beginning of class, however. It had been pushed into the room by an unknown student. I opened it. It had one word written on it: "Fag." I whispered to myself, "And so it begins." But then we began class, and nothing further was said on the matter.

The day passed largely without incident. At one point, two female students I did not know came into my room, looked at me, and walked out. I got the idea that they wanted to see for themselves what a "real gay person" looked like. After school, B. (a teacher with whom I had discussed events) told me that one of his students had told him that some of his friends were going to "get me." According to B., this student, whom I had taught last year, was concerned about me.

I had heard a similar report from another student. I took the reports seriously, but was not afraid. Other teachers warned me, "Watch your back — don't remain alone at school into the evening." As I did not fully share their fears, I understood for the first time what Martin Luther King, Jr., said the night before his death: "I'm not worrying about anything: I'm not fearing any man." I felt at peace with my decision, largely as a result of the strength my students' positive responses had given me.

By Thursday (two days after the event), it seemed safe to say that nearly every one of our two thousand students knew about the "gay teacher." However, I had yet to formally explain the situation to my freshmen. One outspoken young woman in that class burst out with "Don't you just hate rumors?" I realized this was my cue to talk to them. I replied, "Sometimes rumors are true; sometimes they are false. Do we need to talk about rumors?" She nodded her head yes. After giving a test, I talked with the class and received yet another positive reaction.

During my fifth-hour class that day, Mr. Dulin, my department chair and a veteran teacher who began his career in the late fifties, came to my door. He said that Mr. Brandenburg, the assistant principal, wanted to "see you now." Mr. Dulin took over my class and I headed for the office. When I reached his office, Mr. Brandenburg was seated in the office of Mr. Jones, the principal. Together, they asked me to come in, close the door, and have a seat. I asked if this was about the "gay issue." They said yes, and I asked to have MCTA (Mehlville County Teacher Association) representation at the meeting. It so happened that the chair of MCTA's Grievance Committee, Gail Egelston, was on conference that hour. I asked her to attend the meeting with me, and she agreed. I did not feel threatened by the meeting, partly because I had expected it to come at some point. I simply listened to their questions and answered them.

The meeting lasted most of an hour, with Mr. Brandenburg doing all of the talking. His tone was pleasant and unthreatening. He asked me to confirm or deny various rumors. I gladly told him the entire story and gave him a five-page report I had written documenting the events. He voiced concern for the rights of an individual versus the rights of institutions, but also praised my classroom work and my teaching ability. He did not criticize my decision to use my being gay as a teachable moment. As the meeting concluded, I thanked Mr. Jones and Mr. Brandenburg for their past support, and told them that if they had any further questions, I would be happy to answer them.

Returning to my fifth-hour class with about ten minutes left in the period, I decided to tell them about what had happened. I asked how many had heard rumors about my coming out, and all of them raised their hands. I told them the story. They then asked some questions, to which I responded as thoughtfully as I could. As class ended, two students came up to shake my hand and to show their approval. Sixth hour was much the same: the same confirmation of the rumor's spread, the same thoughtful questions, the same positive response. One student gave me a letter after class that read:

> It takes a lot of guts to announce a sexual preference. I'm not against it whatsoever. I think you are a well-rounded, well-adjusted person, and I don't think any less of you. Regardless of however you are, you're a great person, and I think that is something everyone can respect, and is something you can be proud of.

Many colleagues have been supportive as well. One came to me out of "professional courtesy" to tell me that one of his students had reported in his class about my coming out. I shared my five-page account of these events with him, which he returned to me with a note attached:

Rodney —

While our convictions are very different, I appreciate a lot of things about you. Maybe some time we can talk.

The remainder of the story has yet to occur. I expect some negative flak. However, I feel that freedom is ours and we have only to take it. Gay and lesbian teachers have worked for hundreds of years in fear that the wrong person would learn our story and expose us to public ridicule and economic deprivation. We must now take the offensive by throwing open the closet door and telling our stories, so that our colleagues, our supervisors, and our students can know us for who we truly are: great teachers who happen to be gay or lesbian. Martin Luther King, Jr., once said, "Freedom is never *given* to anybody." He was right. Freedom will *never* be given to us. We, as out and proud gay and lesbian educators, must reach out and take it. Our time has come.

Building a GLOBE
in Nebraska

——John Heineman
Language Arts Teacher
Lincoln High School
Lincoln, Nebraska _____

*H*ow is it possible for an openly gay teacher to be sponsoring a gay and lesbian support group in the middle of Nebraska? It starts with the word "No."

It was October of 1992 and I had just returned from a year's sabbatical leave to my seventh year of secondary school teaching at Lincoln High School in Lincoln, Nebraska. I had taken the sabbatical leave because I was burning out in my classroom. Although I had many success stories to tell, my commitment to teaching was beginning to fade.

I went off to graduate school at the University of Northern Iowa where I learned about the tragic suicide and runaway rates among gay and lesbian teenagers. It was this knowledge alone that brought back the fire to my teaching. I knew there was still work for me to do.

The other significant event happening for me at this time was finally coming out to my parents. My younger brother had come out to them several years before. By the time I told them about myself, my mother responded with a smile: "We thought so!"

I now knew it was time to make a difference with my teaching. I had to find support for gay and lesbian students at Lincoln High. My first chance for change was National Coming-Out Day. Although I was not ready to come out of the classroom closet, I did want to put an announcement in the daily school bulletin about NCOD. This kind of announcement was common with other cultural and gender issues at my school. There were always announcements about Black History Month and Women's History Month.

The announcement I submitted dealt with the tragedy of suicide and runaway rates among gay and lesbian teenagers. It assured the students that if they were dealing with sexual-orientation issues, there were supportive teachers, counselors, and administrators who cared about them. I knew this announcement would be controversial, so I submitted it directly to one of the assistant principals for approval several days early. She brought it to the whole administration and the answer came back, "No."

She explained, "Only announcements coming from a specific group can be read as part of the daily bulletin." She had even gone back over the previous month's announcements to see if there were any exceptions. There weren't. I then asked, "So if I had a gay and lesbian group, I could put this announcement in the bulletin?" My assistant principal grinned and said, "I guess so."

I ran up to my room, copied my original announcement, and added these words: "If you are interested in starting a gay and lesbian support group, please put your name in my box in the main office." I then resubmitted my announcement to the administration and after a deep breath they said, "Yes."

Announcements at Lincoln High are read every day by any teacher with a fourth-period class. The announcement was read on a Friday and by Monday I had a note in my box from an interested student. I clearly remember being blown away by the first note. The student was a senior and had discovered his sexuality two years earlier. He had come out to his mother at age sixteen and was excited about starting the group. I knew then the challenges ahead would be many. Was I qualified to help students who were out to their parents when it took over thirty years for me to do it? Would I be able to fulfill their expectations of the group? I didn't have long to contemplate these questions, because by the end of the week I had five interested students and we set a date for our first meeting.

I was also delighted that several teachers and counselors approached me to say how very pleased they were that our gay and lesbian students would be getting the attention they needed. One teacher who taught human sexuality commented on how she felt she could never do enough in the regular classroom for gay and lesbian students. She and several others offered their time and support to the success of the group.

The first meeting was exciting. It reminded me of my first day of teaching, when I wasn't sure if I had what it took to be an educator. I was also nervous because we had decided to announce the meeting in the daily bulletin, meaning anyone, including the homophobes, could walk through the door.

When we started the meeting, there were several students attending whom I didn't know. I laid out a few ground rules. First, our group was not going to be a place where we would out each other. If anyone wanted to share their sexual orientation, it was going to be their choice. Only one student objected; she had just moved to Lincoln and was hoping to find a date. The second ground rule was that the leadership and direction of the group were to come from the students. There were no objections.

To be an official group or club at my school there are two basic guidelines: groups must have a name and they must have a constitution stating the mission of the group and stating that the group is open to all students. Our first order of business was to work on the name and the constitution. After much brainstorming and lots of acronyms we settled on GLOBE, the Gay and Lesbian Organization for the Betterment of Everyone. We wrote the constitution, submitted it, and started meeting on a regular basis.

A lesbian teacher, along with two counselors, helps sponsor the group. The typical meeting consists of talking about the latest gay and lesbian issue in the news, keeping a file of newspaper and magazine articles for students' and teachers' use, designing and ordering t-shirts for the group, and watching the latest issues of *Network Q*. It was also not uncommon for us to write our governmental officials about both national and local issues. We were fortunate to have the media's daily coverage of President Clinton's "gays in the military" policy. This gave us the opportunity for many lively discussions and letter-writing campaigns to our congressional representatives.

When April rolled around, I had saved several special-leave days so I could go to the March on Washington. The local TV station came and filmed one of our GLOBE meetings, which they used as a follow-up to the coverage of the march. The reporter outed me on the ten-o'clock news, but it was all right, because I was also quoted in the local newspaper in a story about Nebraskans who were in the march. When the newspaper reporter asked if he could use my name, I said, "Yes." How else could I be a role model for my students about the importance of being out and proud?

Coming home from the March on Washington was just as empowering for me as the march itself had been. Returning to school, I was met by the members of GLOBE, who wanted to know every detail of the march and to talk about my being on the ten-o'clock news. Some had watched the march on C-SPAN and the national news, and all had their opinions and questions about it. I felt honored that I was the one getting to hear their ideas and to answer their questions.

One week later, when my pictures had come back from the developer, the excitement was back. I had intentionally tried to capture the wonderful diversity of the march. I wanted to be sure that my Nebraskan students knew of the endless possibilities and life choices gay men and lesbians had. Each picture brought a wide range of reactions from my students. Some were impressed with the carnival elements of the march, while many wanted to know the stories of each couple that appeared in the pictures. What was clear from their reactions was the lifting of limitations to their personal possibilities. They could see their hopes and dreams lived out in other gays and lesbians, something often missing from their lives in Nebraska.

At the next several meetings we watched the videotape of the march. The students saw many things they wanted to discuss, but most importantly, they saw gay and lesbian people fighting for their rights. I will always be proud that I was there and proud that I could bring part of the march back to my students.

The group is still going strong. We now meet every Monday after school, and students from the other three high schools in town have also been coming to the meetings. I have received lots of support from my colleagues and I feel good about the fact that many teachers and counselors refer students to the group.

I have been fortunate that my being out has not caused me any serious problems at school. I did overhear one of my sophomores refer to me as *the* gay teacher. I laughed when I realized this student could not imagine more than one gay teacher in the world, but I also smiled, knowing the whispers of a student about my sexual orientation were not a secret but a statement I was proud to make.

Out and Outcome

Jan Smith

Elementary School Teacher
Sands Montessori School
Cincinnati, Ohio

"*an Smith's principal knows. Her fellow teacher at Sands Montessori know. But many parents of her grade school students don't know. What they don't know — until now — is that Smith is a lesbian.*"

These were the opening lines of an article entitled "Coming Out" in the *Cincinnati Enquirer*'s Sunday "Tempo" section on March 26, 1993. For weeks I had known the article was coming, but when I saw those words in print I prayed the phone wouldn't ring. I had just outed myself to thousands of people. To a small-town Ohio girl (now middle-aged), daughter of an English teacher and a school superintendent, this was a very public display of what my parents would have seen as dirty linen and would have "tsked" about at the dinner table. Many years ago I had moved to Cincinnati to go to college. I married, had two children, divorced, remarried, divorced again, and then found a satisfying, even exciting, relationship with a woman with whom I have now lived for seven years. Why did I, a respectable gray-haired teacher, risk my image, hold up my "good name" for public scrutiny? What would the families of my students think?

In some ways I felt safe in coming out. The Cincinnati public school system has a policy forbidding discrimination based on sexual orientation. In addition, I have taught in the system for nineteen years and have tenure. I also know that people who send their children to Sands, the first public Montessori school in Cincinnati, are mostly educated, liberal parents who did not flee to the suburbs in the eighties, but stayed in the city and are working hard to make the magnet school system attractive to others like themselves. On the other hand, as a Montessori teacher, I teach the same children for three years in a self-contained classroom and I depend on the goodwill and respect of the parents for this long-term connection. If they don't like me, it can be three very long years. That was one of the reasons I was nervous about coming out.

Cincinnati's ultraconservative reputation was another reason I was uncomfortable. Our sheriff tried to close down the Mapplethorpe exhibit. He also jailed a gay man for jaywalking, escalating the charge to attempted murder when the man claimed to have AIDS and then spit on a police officer. The city council passed a human rights ordinance in November of 1992 protecting gays and lesbians, but many people were working to rescind it. I had some reason to worry.

I knew when the reporter, John Johnston, called me to get references for the article that I would agree to speak out and put myself in the public eye. I am quiet, even shy in public, but I believe strongly in human rights, and I will act on my beliefs. I believe that if we all stay in the closet, bigots will go on voicing their fears and lesbian and gay young people will think they are alone, so I felt I had to come out. Nevertheless, I still cringed over the decision, and decided at the last minute not to be photographed for the article, for fear the children in my class would bring in the article with my picture on it and ask, "Ms. Smith, what is a lesbian?"

As it turned out, I "came out" to my class of six- to nine-year-olds the next day anyway, despite my misgivings about parental response. By the time the children all arrived at 9:30, I knew some of them had read about me in the paper. One parent came in with her son and talked with me about the article, and another parent sent me a note in support of my coming out publicly. I knew others would hear remarks on the bus that afternoon about their teacher's sexual orientation, and that it could be confusing and upsetting to them. So, in a brief explanation, I told the class about the article, and that, yes, I am a lesbian: I am a woman who loves another woman, we live together, and we are raising a teenager together. One child asked what I thought about the contemporary "gays in the military" debate, and I answered that it made me sad that some people discriminate against gays and lesbians. I said that I am the same person today I was before the article, and that I still care about them very much. But then the class discussion quickly turned to a news article about the birth of quadruplets and why there are Siamese twins — questions that interested these young people more than "What is a lesbian?"

The next day I found two notes in my box at school. The first, from an instructional assistant, read: "Be strong, Jan, my support has always been with you. Love, K." The second, from a fellow teacher, said:

"Thanks for your courage. You are an inspiration to me. Sands is lucky to have you and I am lucky to count you as a friend. G." I also received a brief visit from another instructional assistant, whose niece T. I was teaching at the time, who said she had read the article and called T.'s mother. They wanted me to know that they both thought I was doing a great job with T., and that they supported me one hundred percent.

But the letter I found in my mailbox at lunchtime, from the parents of one of my students, took my breath away:

> We are upset over what we have been told occurred in class yesterday. The brief details we have come from a conversation with another parent and then a brief conversation with A. Our understanding is that yesterday in class you told your students: you were gay; it was OK for a woman to love another woman; it was OK for a man to love another man; gays should be allowed in the military. We already had some understanding of the strong feelings you have about homosexuality and understand your need to be open and honest about your own homosexuality. However, you were wrong to introduce this topic to your classroom of grades 1–3 children in the manner you chose.
>
> We feel strongly that parents should have been informed before yesterday's event occurred and certainly afterwards, but you did neither. This is something you knew we would feel strongly about.
>
> We request two things of you: do not continue to discuss homosexuality in class; inform parents exactly what you told their children about your homosexuality and homosexuality in general.
>
> If you are unable to meet these two requests, we would like you to arrange a timely meeting with parents of children in your classroom, the principal S. [the school principal], and yourself.
>
> Sincerely,
> Mr. and Mrs. ———

I was shaken by this letter. I had known this family would be more upset than any other. (I had been on two committees with the mother: the Sex Ed and Family Life Committee, which reviews videos that might be used in the Cincinnati public school system, and the ad hoc committee that was assigned the task of updating the STD and AIDS portion of the Cincinnati public schools' health curriculum. She had been the loudest voice for stressing abstinence and for not mentioning condoms.) I didn't know to what lengths this family would go: whether they would try to get their child moved to another classroom, or write letters to the local paper, or try to get me transferred out of Sands.

Even though my principal knew about the *Enquirer* article in advance, she was out of town for a conference during the few days when the news was the hottest. I hoped to avoid her when she came back, because I knew I would have to come face-to-face with the uproar I had caused, but that was impossible. She, too, had received the letter from A.'s parents, and called me into the office. "There were a lot of phone calls while I was gone," she said, with a funny look on her face, "and now there's an angry letter. I think we need to talk." I felt my face turning red, and I said, "Can it wait until I get back from my trip?" (I was leaving for a three-day weekend with my partner, who had a conference in California.) So we made plans to sit down for a long talk when I returned.

After I got back, I was able to be a little more relaxed when the principal and I talked in her office. She was pretty reassuring, even though she had had to talk to a number of people who had called her office. The principal didn't think I had done anything wrong and *she* assured me that she would respond to the angry family who had written the above letter. She wanted me to talk to the Equal Opportunities Officer from the Board of Education (which I'm sure was a directive from a downtown administrator), but she said it was just a formality.

A few days later, when I talked with the EEO, she was cordial and asked me why I came out to my class. When I explained that I wanted the kids from my class to hear a nonbiased explanation from me, rather than teasing from other kids on the bus, she merely advised me that if I did it again, I should tell "my" parents ahead of time so they could be prepared to talk with their children at home. The implication was that then the parents could have the first opportunity to deliver any moral judgments which they might want to impart to their children rather than the children possibly getting the impression from me that homosexuality was okay. I agreed and felt very relieved when the meeting ended. I didn't know what power she had over me, or how much grief I had caused "downtown," so I was apprehensive. (I think I am still too much the superintendent's daughter.) But fortunately my fears were groundless and I was never reprimanded in any way by the administration. Since that time, I have thought about her request and have realized that it is up to me to decide if and how I will come out to my students, as I know that this is a process that continues.

Over the next few weeks I became aware of solid support for coming out in the newspaper. I received tons of support from other teachers in GLUE (Gays and Lesbians United for Education), a local group made up of educators, some of whom were quoted in the same article. My singing sisters in MUSE, Cincinnati's Women's Choir, gave me a lot of encouragement. I wouldn't have had the courage to be so forthright if it weren't for these friends.

I also got many letters of support. A retired teacher wrote, "I want to applaud you ... It's not only a testimonial to your courage but to the quality of your teaching. We look forward to a time when 'coming out' is as old-fashioned as corsets..." I got a note from a nun who teaches at another school: "I was glad you were willing to be open and up-front about your experience. I'm sure this will mean a lot to a lot of people." Another friend sent a letter: "Thank you for coming out. It has to start somewhere. People must see that gays and lesbians are not 'them' — they aren't strangers or ogres — they are people — just people everywhere in our lives. This is the only way to start the process of the stereotypes being questioned. Thank you, thank you." A neighbor and former teacher wrote, "I have young adult children aged twenty-seven and twenty-four, and I wish they had been able to have gay and lesbian teachers who were comfortable with their sexuality and able to be a presence to others who might be fearful or questioning." People I didn't even know sent the following note: "My husband and I read the article in the Sunday *Enquirer* in which you were featured. I'm sure there are many reasons why this was a difficult and frightening interview to give. We want you to know that we are Sands parents who appreciate your honesty and courage." In fact, most of the mail I received was positive.

I did, however, get two thoughtfully critical responses from parents:

The father of one of my second-grade girls wrote me a three-page letter explaining that he had talked to the principal about the situation before writing me a letter. He stated that he had already known that I was a lesbian but had hoped I could keep the controversial aspects of my personal life to myself. His seven-year-old daughter wasn't fazed by the classroom discussion, but when confronted by her father (after another parent tipped him off), she said that maybe *she* was a lesbian, because she loved her mother and her sisters, and she lived with them. And then she asked her father, "What about the two nuns who live together down the street? Are they lesbians?" (He didn't tell me how he handled that question!) His dilemma was that I had presented my "lifestyle" as value-neutral, while he wanted it presented as wrong. He ended by saying that "perhaps this can be a growing experience for us all." Nine months later, she is still in my class, and the parents have not mentioned any problems related to this situation since the original letter.

The father of a third-grade girl called me (I give him credit for talking to me directly) and said he didn't feel that his eight-year-old daughter was ready to understand lesbianism. He didn't say anything about moral values, but just that he felt uncomfortable explaining homosexuality to her. I asked him if his family watched the news on TV, and if his daughter saw any of the gay controversies that were being shown practically every night. He admitted that she probably saw these controversies, but he didn't think they meant anything to her. I wanted to say, "Now they will," but I didn't want to seem arrogant.

No parents in my room asked to have their children removed from my class. I had a short conversation with the principal a few weeks later in which we discussed the possibility that parents whose kindergartners were assigned to come into my room as new first-graders next fall might want another teacher for their children. The principal was clear that she would not capitulate to any form of discrimination. As it turned out, the only letter I got from the parents of an incoming first-grader was totally supportive. The irony of this unexpected letter was that it came from a man whose wife had recently left him for another woman! More pleasant fallout came from a third-grader in my room, who was about to move, and was having a going-away party. He offered this invitation: "My Suzuki [a music-teaching method] teacher is bringing her husband, would you like to bring...?" When I supplied the name of my partner, Deb, he said, "Yeah, bring Deb, too."

If I had the whole ordeal to do over again, I think I might write a note to the parents on the Friday before the article came out, suggesting that they read and discuss the article with their children. I think this preparation would defuse the situation, and give parents a chance to talk with their children if they chose to. I think the few angry parents felt I had usurped their prerogative in the sex education arena; perhaps I could have been more sensitive in anticipating these concerns.

I now feel free and ready to move on. I am happy that I no longer have to hide an important part of who I am. Not long ago one of the girls in my class asked me, "Ms. Smith, are you gay?" and before I could answer, a boy standing nearby supplied, "No, she's not gay, she's a lesbian." I had to smile. April 1993 was a scary time in my life, but now I feel confident that nothing is going to happen. I just hope my openness will be of value to other lesbians and gay men who might be thinking of coming out, to young people wondering who they are, and to people who thought they didn't know any of us.

We Don't Have a Problem Here

―――――― Robert Parlin

History Teacher
Newton South High School
Newton, Massachusetts ―――――――――――――

"You know, I don't think this school is ready to deal with homophobia. Newton may be a fairly liberal suburb, but I don't think the parents will approve of this type of work."

"Perhaps we need to discuss this issue more amongst ourselves. The timing just doesn't seem right to me."

"This is so divisive, I'm afraid we'll do more harm than good if we try to talk about gay and lesbian issues here at school."

"Sexual orientation seems like an issue that is more appropriate for discussion at the college level. High school is too soon."

"I've been a guidance counselor at this school for more than twenty years, and I don't ever recall a student coming to me and telling me that he or she was a homosexual. I don't think we have any gay kids here."

"I'm actually not that certain that having a program on homosexuality is that relevant to us here. Maybe communities in other parts of the country — say in California — are struggling with this, but we don't have a problem here."

The time was May of 1991. The occasion was a meeting of the Newton South High School Committee on Human Differences, a faculty committee meeting once a month to discuss issues of diversity and how they affect our school community. The committee had been in existence for three years, and over the years we had discussed a wide range of topics, looking at anti-Semitism, racism, sexism, and class issues, and attitudes toward foreign students. This year for the first time, we had raised the issue of homophobia, reading a number of articles about the negative impact of a homophobic environment upon gay and lesbian students. At our last meeting, we had agreed that it was time to take action with the entire faculty. As a school we had ignored this issue for too long, and we had an obligation as educators to confront bigotry and promote tolerance and understanding.

I had been teaching history at the school for four years, but I was "out" only to a few colleagues who were close friends. It was therefore with particular excitement and anticipation that I participated in this discussion. For the first time, I began to hope that I could come out to the whole school, and that we could all work together to create a place where gay and lesbian teachers and students felt comfortable, welcome, and valued. It now appeared, however, that my hopes were about to be shattered.

The May meeting of the committee was reserved for planning. We would combat homophobia in the next academic year. Unfortunately, I arrived fifteen minutes late to the meeting, and as I sat listening to the conversation, I realized with growing dismay that our consensus to take action had crumbled. Fear had taken over.

Looking around the room, I saw nothing but anxious faces. My department chair was also the chair of the committee, and she had led the discussion all year. Now, however, she sat silently listening, clearly bothered by the turn of the discussion, but uncertain as to whether she should intervene. After all, the members were simply sharing their thoughts. Likewise, the principal of the school was sitting quietly with a concerned look on his face. I knew him to be a strong ally, and he looked quite upset now, but he said nothing. In the midst of all this, my closest friend on the committee passed me a note that read, "I don't know what's happening here. Everyone seems to be moving backward. This is awful!" I looked up at her, and she appeared to be close to tears. Something had gone terribly wrong, I realized, and a golden opportunity was slipping away.

As I sat in that room, absorbing what was happening, I came to appreciate that I was also filled with fear about confronting homophobia at my school. After all, I might be putting my job on the line if I came out as part of this process. I knew that the Massachusetts gay rights law made it illegal for me to be fired, but with no seniority in my department, job security was a major concern. I feared coming under attack from all sides, helpless to stop responses ranging from hurtful comments to malicious destruction of my property. I anticipated outraged calls from parents, who would demand the removal of their children from my classes. I imagined students running by my room yelling, "Faggot," through the open doorway. I expected to one day find my car in the faculty parking lot with its tires slashed. Even worse, I feared losing my effectiveness as a teacher, with my relations with students becoming awkward and difficult as they avoided looking at me or responding to my questions with sincerity. Was it worth it?

It was the final comment — that we didn't have a problem with homophobia at this school — that prompted me to speak out. I knew that it was simply not true, and my anger allowed me to overcome my fears. "Let me tell you why we *do* have a problem," I began. "I am gay and I have never felt truly welcome here at this school." My colleagues sat at rapt attention as I opened the floodgates of personal experience, sharing with them what it had been like to grow up gay and feeling profoundly alone and isolated. I told them what it was like to feel that who you were was sick and disgusting, and how I was taught to hate myself. I described how the pain nearly drove me to take my life the summer after my first year in college, because I could not envision a life in which I could be happy and whole. I shared the tremendous pressure of being closeted at work, afraid that one day I might let something slip, feeling that I could never be fully honest with the people around me. As I spoke I could feel the fear slipping away, being replaced by a sense of self-confidence that I had never before known. It was a turning point in my life, and a turning point in the life of my school.

When I finished talking, I looked around the room to discover that everyone was crying. I particularly will never forget the look on the face of my principal as he gazed at me sadly with tears streaming down his face. Clearly, my words had made an impact. Afterward, many of the faculty came up to me and hugged me. One colleague even told me, "I felt like standing up and saying: 'And I am a lesbian!' — But I'm not." What happened in that room that day was that fear was replaced by hope. The good intentions and sincere goodwill that had always been present were given the chance to rise to the surface and overcome the fears, anxieties, and denials that our society had forced upon us. We have never looked back.

It didn't take long to build a consensus that we should go forward with our program, beginning with an anti-homophobia training for the entire faculty at the first faculty meeting of the following year. At that meeting I came out to the entire faculty and shared my willingness to be a resource on gay and lesbian issues. It was the Committee on Human Differences, however, that led the effort to make Newton

South High School a place where all gay and lesbian students and faculty feel safe, welcome, and valued. Together, we began a process that continues today, building a truly inclusive school community.

After a series of faculty meetings dealing with various aspects of homophobia in the school, the committee organized an anti-homophobia training for the PTSA (the Parent, Teacher, and Student Association) that was attended by more than seventy-five parents. In the spring, a series of student programs on homophobia were begun. We ended the year by forming the first public school gay-straight alliance in Massachusetts, an organization open to all members of the school community, meeting to discuss issues of sexual orientation, to provide support for gay and lesbian students and faculty, and to continue the work of fighting homophobia in our school.

As Newton South moved forward on fighting homophobia, my personal odyssey also continued. When I came out to the entire faculty in September, I announced my plans to come out to my students soon. How exactly to do this, however, eluded me, and I procrastinated for several months. My hand was forced in late November when my principal arrived in the middle of class with an urgent question. He was teaching a group of seniors a lesson on the Japanese economy. He had just asked the class why they thought the Japanese were doing so well when a girl raised her hand. Anticipating a response to his question, he was therefore hard-pressed to respond when she asked, "Is Mr. Parlin gay?" He told me that he had not known how to answer the question, so he said, "Give me a minute," to his students and left the room to find me. As he related this series of events to me in the hallway, all I could think was that his students thought that he had left to find the answer to the question. The comic nature of the situation was not lost on either of us, but the principal was still left with the tricky issue of how to respond. I told him to say, "Yes," but then to ask why she wanted to know, and to try to discuss with the class the potential ramifications of my coming out of the closet. The principal later told me that the ensuing conversation was remarkably sensitive and thoughtful, and that the students had reacted very positively for the most part.

Of more immediate concern to me, however, was my desire to talk to my classes before rumors spread around the school. The next day I bit the bullet and announced to each of my classes that I had something serious to discuss with them. I explained that I wanted to be honest with them, that I wanted to help fight ignorance about homosexuality, that I wanted to challenge the predominantly negative and harmful stereotypes of gay people, and that I wanted to provide them with a role model of a gay person who was happy, healthy, and successful. It was a frightening day, but also an exhilarating one. My students did not let me down. They reacted with thoughtful curiosity, compassion, and sincere respect. "Do you want to have children someday?" "Do you have a boyfriend?" "How did your parents react when you told them?" Their questions revealed an open, caring attitude that I have now witnessed in young people around the state. Many came up to me after class and later that week to tell me how much they admired what I had done. It had changed their way of thinking about gay people. Some even hugged me. The reverse of my fears occurred. I actually became closer to my classes as a result. From that day onward, the level of thoughtful participation in class discussions was noticeably deeper. Students began to take risks and share personal concerns that had a remarkable impact on their classmates and their own lives. Again, one small step led to leaps that are continuing today.

Even the parents of my students did not live up to my fears. When I arrived at school the next day and found seven calls from parents waiting for me, I automatically anticipated trouble. But the parents were not calling to complain. They were calling to thank me. One told me that my announcement had sparked one of the best dinner-table conversations her family had ever had. Another told me that he felt that my coming-out talk had been the single biggest learning experience in his son's life. Each parent wanted me to know that they appreciated how much courage it took to come out, and that they fully supported me. Since that day I have certainly heard murmurings of discontent from some people in the city, but I have continued to receive expressions of support from students, parents, former students, and alums who are grateful that finally the school is beginning to fight the homophobia that made their adolescent years so miserable.

I am not naive enough to presume that none of my fears will never become reality, but as I look back on the path I have traveled I am certain of one thing. I will never let those fears rule my life. In the spring of 1992, after a momentous year at Newton South, I was invited by the senior class to attend the senior prom with my partner. As we slow-danced on the dance floor that night, surrounded by hundreds of heterosexual couples and one other gay couple (two amazingly courageous young men who had also overcome their fears), I wondered why there was so little reaction to our presence. I realized that the students truly did not care. They were there to celebrate their school years. Fears and hatred had no place in such a celebration. The barriers that divided us were, at least temporarily, dissolved. For one brief night, I had a glimpse of a world where being gay could be valued, and where fear was not welcome. This vision will always guide my teaching as I work together with my students and colleagues to build a world in which gay and lesbian young people will want to live.

What's a Girl to Do?

————————Gretchen Hildebrand Coburn

Primary School Teacher
Andover Elementary School
Andover, New Hampshire _____

*I*t's the end of the eighties in beautiful, pastoral Andover, New Hampshire. There's a t-shirt sold at the corner store bearing a motif that pretty well sums up the town this way:

ANDOVER, NEW HAMPSHIRE
population ... 1883
deer ... 486
moose ... 29
covered bridges ... 3

In the broader spectrum, however, Andover is a community of contrasts. Fourth-generation natives and diverse foreigners, millionaires, farmers, teachers, airline pilots, and blue-collar tradespeople all live side by side and pay taxes.

Most everyone who lives here seems to want to live here. Some people work right in town, but most travel forty-five minutes or more to go to work. Many say they moved from other places because they heard what a nice town it is, and they are not disappointed.

I am an Andover resident who works right in town. I moved here from Massachusetts. And I have not been disappointed.

But what's a girl to do ... if she teaches little kids, is married to the chairman of the school board (who is also her boss), and finds she has fallen in love with the school's bus driver, who just happens to be a woman?

1. She could deny all that she feels and thinks, and carry on as if nothing happened.

2. She could shake hands with her new love and say, "Nice to meet you, but I've gotta go now."

3. She could live a life of illicit liaisons.

4. Or, she could do the *unthinkable* and risk losing her two children, her career, her community, her family, and her friends.

I could never imagine living my life as a lie, so I acted on the only choice acceptable to me. I came out of the closet, divorced my husband, and began life anew with my partner and our combined family of four children.

I did not turn the knob of my closet door and walk out quietly or gently; rather, I kicked the door open, with motions ranging from justified rage to the joy of freedom in my heart and soul.

And, you may ask, what repercussions did this action create?

For starters, my decision scored about an eight on the Richter scale of our community shock level. My partner, who by this time had quit being a bus driver and had become a full-time member of the school community, was fired by my ex-husband. Her car was vandalized at school. Hate notes were stuck on her door, foul messages were left on her answering machine, and false rumors were spread by certain hostile staff members. She changed the dead bolts on her house doors.

My job as a thirteen-year tenured teacher was threatened. I was blackmailed by my ex-husband during our divorce process. His lawyer told my lawyer that I could probably keep my job *if* I agreed to certain custody and financial stipulations. Furthermore, my school principal kept nervously warning me about the spreading of hostile sentiments among a few townspeople. I walked on eggshells, wondering if and when the attack from students' parents and the administration would come.

I stopped going into the teachers' room for about two years. Why did I decide to do this? Anytime I walked into the room the conversation ceased. My allies let me know that I was the brunt of disdainful remarks. Most of the staff chose to be cool and distant when I passed them in the halls. And, after all, there is nothing like being stared at in silence to aid in one's digestion!

I purposely removed myself from my circle of close friends and faculty for a period of several months. I was unable to answer the many questions and hurt, searching eyes that were upon me every day. This was primarily because of the time and space I needed to deal with many horrendous personal struggles. My child custody battle, rejection by my own parents, and sexual assault were just a few I faced at the time.

But, four years later (although it seems like twenty), I am here in Andover, New Hampshire, teaching and helping to raise my family.

Because Andover is such a small, close community and *because* it has such a small school, and *because* I have been there for so long and *because* I am so intimately involved with our four children daily at school, I have no choice but to be completely out everywhere I go.

The only openly shared ramifications of my outness are positive.

I never lost or left my career in teaching. The attack from parents and the administration never came. In fact, the administration and school board have left me alone.

Parents in the community choose to be either supportive or quietly let me live my personal life. I still get requests for students to be in my class. Some parents sense that I am a "safe" person to talk to privately about painful issues, such as AIDS or abuse. Occasionally, I receive an awkward verbal "okay" from even the most private, conservative New Hampshire natives.

The teachers' room is now a welcoming place. The hostile, critical, unhappy staff persons have moved on and in their places are open, caring teachers and new building administrators.

All of this positive feedback has enabled me to be a stronger advocate for diversity and change. I am also a better teacher. I have become a more able, influential part of my school based on what I have become rather than who I was. My peers have told me I am now a person of courage, not afraid to face adversity.

Of those friends and faculty worried and hurt with my silence and distance, all but a very few are closer to me. By sharing in my daily life and in my life with my partner and our family, they have had to grow within themselves. They have been forced to make a choice. They have either had to choose openness and understanding, or accept their responsibility for the loss of a solid friendship, knowing full well that their ignorance and arrogance would be the cause.

Looking back at the past four years, at times through eager, fiery eyes, and at other times through the clouded mist of not-yet-exhausted tears, I must say that — for me — truth is better than fiction. I must live honestly, albeit dangerously, rather than in a cocoon or a web of deceptions. I know who my friends are. And I can hopefully do the most important thing: teach my schoolchildren and my own children, by my example, to be caring, decent, honest individuals, no matter what the price.

It's Who You Are That Counts

Bob Zimmerman

Biology Teacher
R.A. Taft High School
Cincinnati, Ohio

"**A**re you a fag, Mr. Z?" That came right from LaTasha and it was a question that I could tell was going to come up sooner or later ... building up like molten lava under a long-dormant volcano. Like geologists studying the swellings, escaping steam, and minor tremors around the peak, I too was feeling the pressure from my students as they sought a way to bring the question to the surface. Not that I was trying to hide anything. Not anymore. After all, marching in a gay pride parade on a hot summer day carrying a banner that read, "Gays and Lesbians United for Education," through the city in which one teaches was bound to elicit some response from someone. I was open about my sexual orientation at school. My partner Bill comes to school functions and faculty parties. Those teachers whom I had not told quickly figured it out for themselves or were clued in by their more-astute co-workers. But it was not something I had yet shared with my students.

I was teaching in a special summer enrichment class and after the parade I had expected at least one of my students to say, "I saw you in a parade last week," or, "Saw you on TV last night." (Was it our striking banner or just the idea of a bunch of teachers actually marching in such an event that caught the media eye?) But no. What emerged was a chorus of "We're here, we're queer..." in small voices and giggles in the hallway, as they entered the classroom. Nothing to begin a discussion about ... just some steam escaping from a small crack.

Not until the fall, when some of my students from the summer program showed up in my regular classes, did the pressure begin to build again. Our high school is located in the heart of the projects, about 80 percent African-American, 20 percent Appalachian whites, and almost 100 percent on some form of public assistance. Under their tough skin are some fragile interiors. Many are leading adult lives without first having had the luxury of a normal childhood. Working with such students requires honesty and a certain standard on the part of the teacher. Critiquing students' work or their behavior can be a sensitive issue, as the notion of who they are is so wrapped up in what they do. As a teacher, you invade their space, and teenagers have many ways of maintaining the space about them, protecting themselves from intrusion by peers and authority figures. In a world where attitude is everything, defensive tactics are employed when someone gets too close, physically or psychologically. Most just tune out, flash an evil eye, or mutter something under their breath as a response to teachers' comments. But the bold and the brazen go for more. LaTasha had told her friends of her "discovery" over the summer and it was obvious that they were going to try to use this as a sort of psychological blackmail to keep me away from them. One girl began muttering, "Fag," as I tried to encourage her to do better on her classwork. I took her aside and told her that those kinds of comments were unacceptable in my classroom. More steam escaping from the vent.

A week later, LaTasha came late to class with no excuse, and as I reminded her of the consequence (a thirty-minute detention), she retaliated with "Why did you get a divorce?" in a tone that was clearly confrontational. There was steam, smoke, and the smell of brimstone in that remark. I had already given my classes the usual personal introduction, stopping short of the details that led to my divorce after almost twenty years of marriage — details that included counseling, dealing with my homosexuality, coming out, my relationship with another man, telling my wife and two teenaged sons, more counseling, a separation, moving in with "the other man," and ultimately divorce by mutual consent. These missing details made my students wonder, and made for great speculation. "We had our differences" was all I felt like saying to LaTasha, but that was not enough. LaTasha went for the big guns and let it all out. "Are you a fag?"

The class was silent. LaTasha had said it. She really had. What was Mr. Z going to do? "Are you asking me if I'm gay?" I replied. She nodded her head, and I simply said yes. This was it. I had said it. "Let's talk," I offered, and for the next thirty minutes I related my story and answered questions from my students, so many questions. "When did you know you were gay?" "What do your kids think about you being gay?" "Does the principal know?" "Are there other gay teachers at this school?" "How do you and your partner 'do it'?" "Do you ever wish you weren't gay?" "What are your parties like?" "Are you afraid of AIDS?" For the most part, the questions were an honest attempt to get some real answers. I was candid with them, but drew a line at privacy, my own and that of others. To questions of a sexual nature, I told them that those were personal, but that what goes on between two people of the same sex is not unlike a heterosexual couple. The important thing, I explained to them, is the love and caring that exists between the two individuals. The bell rang. It was over. In came my next class, the last one of the day. Word had traveled fast. "Mr. Z, did LaTasha really ask you if you were gay?" And so it went. Similar questions. The same desire to discuss the issue. One student talked about an uncle who had died of AIDS. Another had a cousin who was gay. Tony wanted to know if I knew a good friend of his who was gay, and I did. All of a sudden, there was a link between us, a part of me he could relate to.

The year went on as usual. Students had their problems. I had my share of frustrations and small triumphs along with them. Some of my students were successful and passed their courses to become tenth-graders. Many did not. Shortly after this incident, LaTasha went off on the principal and got suspended. She never returned to my class-room. There were no repercussions from parents or other students. Occasionally, a student would ask me a question about a gay-related issue in a matter-of-fact way. Then we'd go on to other things. And so the year ended.

At the beginning of the next school year, with all new students, I wondered if this experience would repeat itself. Should I start the year off with full disclosure, or let it come out on its own? I was sure that by now most of the students knew I was gay. I decided not to make an issue of it and to deal with it as it came along.

Well, it didn't take long. This time it was a group of boys. The same tensions in the class were building up. The school had settled into a routine. There were certain expectations to be met and consequences to be faced if they were not. The students realized that we were serious about education. Most importantly, they realized that summer was indeed over. It was Andre who took the first shot. "Saw you at the

Court Street and Plum [a local gay bar]." "You mean the gay bar?" I answered. "Yeah. What were you doing there?" he asked. "Well, I guess I was going in to have a beer!" The class laughed, everyone relaxed, and we began our discussion. Same questions. Same desire to discuss the issue. Antonio said I was cool to level with them. And that was all. No big thing.

But it *was* a big thing. It was a big thing for me to realize that I could be out with my students; that they were capable of keen insight on the adults around them, and could respect us when we try to be as honest as we can with them.

It has not been without some negative moments, however. One day I was held up with a parent conference and could not get to my room in time to open it up for the next class. A homophobic security guard was sent to unlock my door and complained to the group of students in the hallway that the "faggot teacher" should have had the door unlocked to begin with. The students were able to tell me about this and we discussed the levels of prejudice in our society and ways of dealing with it. Dontonio, six feet four and dark-skinned, told me how the clerks at the department stores watch him so closely as he walks by their counters that he can feel their eyes on his back. Greg told me how awkward he felt being the only white student in the class. Then there were the stories the students couldn't come out with: Roger, who had to endure the taunts of some of the other students because he had no hot water at home and hadn't bathed in a week; Barbara, who felt so ashamed because both her mother and father are crack heads and she didn't want anyone to find out. As it turned out, we had a good discussion. Latonia pretty much summed it up when she proclaimed, "You know, it's not what you are, but who you are, that counts."

After spending years in the classroom hiding a secret that, as I have since found out, many students had suspected all along, I am out, happier, and much more relaxed.

Teaching and Learning

―――――Eric Temple

English Teacher
Crystal Springs Upland School
Hillsborough, California _____

Three years ago I taught a seminar in Modern and Contemporary Drama to sophomores. Along with Ibsen, Shaw, and Fugard, next to Beckett and Williams, Ntozake Shange and Larry Kramer raised their urgent voices, and the students listened with such intimacy and interest I was taken by surprise. Certainly the canon spoke loudly, but an interesting change in my teaching emerged when I found myself discussing date rape, racial prejudice, gay rights, and AIDS. Perhaps more importantly, I found myself changing as well. As I gained confidence speaking about my experience, my journey, at first as a closeted teacher and then as an openly gay educator, I realized the value of my story and the importance of all stories.

I read Shange's *For Colored Girls Who Have Considered Suicide When the Rainbow Is Enuf* in my junior year at Woodlands High School in Greenburg, New York. The school was about 40 percent African-American. The halls rang with rhythm as I shared my lunch with Felice and Janet and joked with Robin. I dreamed of having the strength of these black women. Indeed, I stereotyped the ability of these women to face their world. But Shange's play is about the search for voice and, as a closeted youth, I desperately wanted a voice to express the pain of isolation. I identified with my women friends and in particular my African-American women friends. In their struggle against sexism and racism, I recognized my struggle against stereotyping and assumed heterosexuality.

However, I didn't really understand these women. One day I realized I saw my African-American friends only at school. At the end of the day I went home to the middle-class, tree-lined streets of

Hartsdale, and many of these young women returned to the Greenburg public housing projects. I felt our difference and I wanted them to be more like me. I couldn't understand some of their jokes and thoughts and I especially wanted them to work harder in school. I wanted them to "help" themselves. I remember coming home one afternoon and sitting with my mother on the front steps. It must have been spring, for the large crab apple tree in the front yard was blooming and everywhere the world looked remarkably pink. I asked my mom, "Why don't they work to get good grades?" as if "they" were not my friends at all but an "other," an aberration to middle-class Jewish expectations. I distinctly recall my mother's response. She said with a look of profound sadness, "You don't know their experience." But I thought I did know their experience, for I thought it was my own. In truth, I had just became aware of the need for my own journey and the singular nature of alienation.

It was Ntozake Shange's choreo poem that helped me piece together the naivete of my question on that spring afternoon. Shange's play describes the spiritual growth of seven women of color. Seven: seven days, seven virtues, seven deadly sins, the seven colors of the rainbow. Shange sees the ways American culture separates minorities, pits them against each other in a frantic desire to be accepted into the norm. But for a woman of color and, I began to note, for a gay man, acceptance is not the goal (for it assumes there is something to accept) but rather strength is the goal. I *must* understand others' experience as best I can, for through understanding experience comes a unique power; the ability to face the world, indeed face history and then stand up to its judgments. When Shange's Lady in Brown says, "its hysterical/ the melody-less-ness of her dance/ don't tell nobody don't tell a soul/ she's dancin on beer cans & shingles." *I* began to understand. I, too, each day, danced around the eggshells of expected masculine behavior. I held my schoolbooks with an extended arm and not against my chest as the girls did. I pretended to date. I talked about drinking and went so far as to guzzle Jack Daniel's until I got sick to prove my virility. I still remember swinging the bathroom door closed on laughing faces and wondering where my peace could be found. This play echoed throughout my adolescence and into my adult teaching life. I knew that as I struggled to truly understand my own experience I would begin to understand others. I wanted to help my students do the same.

Crystal Springs Uplands School, where I now teach, is nestled in the green hills of Hillsborough, California, offering vistas of the San Francisco Bay. Curiously missing from view, however, are South San Francisco and East Palo Alto, both lower-income areas, though both are only ten minutes away by car. In my first year at Crystal, I knew it was important to teach Shange, to teach the process of understanding others, to counter the insulation of the school's limited exposure. I wondered, could Shange's play reach across the economic and emotional boundaries manifested by a ten-thousand-dollar tuition and a 3 percent African-American presence on campus? Yes, partially it can and did.

Each day, the students sifted through Shange's poetry and uncovered a universe of emotion. After reading a section of the play about date rape they wrote their feelings on the board: closed down, scared, shame, ashamed, powerless, hurt. And then the search for why. Why are women raped? Are they responsible — ever? The students and I struggled. "Yes," they said, "at times the woman is to blame. That short skirt, that seductive walk and talk, that last drink? She should know better." We butted heads as young women and men admitted to their own phobias and prejudices. They questioned me as I had questioned my mother. I asked, *"What are a person's rights?"* How can anyone force another person to have sex against their will? Silently I thought, how can a society force a sexual identity on a young person against their will? Silence, then a deluge of responses and accusations, until Shange cried, "cuz it turns out the nature of rape has changed/ we can now meet them in circles we frequent for companionship." Rape can happen anywhere with anyone. Betrayal, anger, outrage, fear. Internally I noted how close these emotions paralleled many of my feelings as a gay adolescent. Which students in this room could also feel these stings, for whatever reason?

The boys sat silent and the girls looked at each other and finally — the answers aren't so easy and the cause is not so clear. What did become clear during the two weeks we read the choreo poem is that emotion is universal. Though experience may not be easily understood, we are all betrayed in various ways by our world and we know it and we feel it. By enabling and asking students to search themselves to feel what a person beyond view feels; to understand they too can feel as though they are "dancin on beer cans and shingles" opened a new and mysterious chapter in teaching for me. So why not push the boundaries?

The only time I can remember the word *faggot* used in high school was to put a student down. Though I knew I fit this definition cruelly assigned to others, I kept silent behind my smile and grades. Silence does equal death, not only physically, but spiritually and emotionally as well. Besides my posturing and attempts to fit in, I was mostly silent. A classmate whispered to me about one of my friends, "Don't invite him along, he's a fag." No, I'm the fag, I thought, but I only nodded. I betrayed even my own friends with silence. Elie Weisel says: "Take sides. Neutrality helps the oppressor, never the victim. Silence encourages the tormentor, never the tormented," and Ned Weeks in Larry Kramer's *The Normal Heart* echoes, "Yes, everyone has a million excuses for not getting involved. But aren't there moral obligations, moral commandments to try everything possible?"

When I decided to teach Larry Kramer's *The Normal Heart* to this group of sophomores, they were perhaps not quite as ready to discard silence, and discussing homosexuality was difficult for some. Kramer's play documents the beginning of the AIDS epidemic in New York City, concentrating on the gay community's response. It is both a diatribe against the insensitivity of a dominant culture that allows the deaths of its citizens, and a plea for understanding. After reading Act One I came into class and faced an angry barrage. "Why are we reading this?" "This makes me sick." I shook my head sadly and one student noted later that she thought I was going to cry. I was disappointed that Shange had not prepared them for Kramer.

However, disappointment is often followed by discovery. As my students learned about the troubles faced by gay youth, as they began to understand the injustices faced by people with HIV and AIDS, they became more human, and they, too, began to understand. The students thought back to the first play of the semester, Ibsen's *An Enemy of the People*. Ibsen's Dr. Stockman had ultimately prepared them well for Kramer's Ned Weeks. Both characters are absolutely unwilling to compromise their truths, no matter how many people they anger. The students saw in Ned a continuum of protest against an intolerant society and applauded his determination. Some cried when his lover, Felix, died of AIDS. Almost all, however, saw for the first time a positive depiction of gay people. One student wrote:

> I never understood what being gay could mean, or how two people of
> the same sex can possibly be intimate with each other. My family is

against this sexual orientation and I believe that I often agreed because I didn't have the security to think on my own ... When we read this book, I ascertained a completely different perspective of gay people. There are as many aspects to gay relationships as there are with men and woman relationships ... I have stopped and realized just what this disease can do and how I can't ignore it. Most of all I really have a more positive attitude toward homosexuals."

I was both enthralled and frightened by this young woman's response. I was enthralled that she challenged the teaching of her family to forge a very different belief. I was enthralled that she felt she couldn't ignore the scourge of AIDS. Yet, I was frightened too. Was I responsible for this independence of thought? Certainly, this is what I had wanted. But all of a sudden, I undeniably understood how much influence a teacher has. As Shange had done for me many years earlier, Kramer did for these students. They knew that their own way of seeing the world needed to be broadened.

Teaching *The Normal Heart* was a turning point in my career and in my personal journey to understanding. While discussing gay rights, my students often said, "But, Mr. Temple, we don't know any gay people," while once again I sat silent. This time, though, I refused to betray myself and especially any gay students who perhaps were hiding behind their own silence. I came out to this group of students, and this year, as seniors, I am teaching them Tony Kushner's *Angels in America*. They enjoyed *Millenium Approaches* (Part One) so much they demanded I order and teach *Perestroika* (Part Two). I am continuously amazed at their level of understanding. They have certainly gone beyond my ability as a junior at Woodlands High School to actually see and hear the "other." For some, they are no longer just accepting the other but instead are nurturing differences. They have embarked on their own journey to understand themselves, through understanding others.

We like to think we influence our students, but when the evidence is unveiled, it is disconcerting and exciting. To dispense a new fact can be empowering, but to challenge a belief, to question an emotion and motive, in essence to try to get to who we really are: this is a journey I only vaguely expected to navigate with my students. Indeed, my own journey always seems to curiously coincide with theirs. I am reminded constantly of William Carlos Williams's words in Robert Coles's *The Call of Stories*. Williams says to the recently spiritually awakened

Coles, "Their story, yours, mine — it's what we all carry with us on this trip we take, and we owe it to each other to respect our stories and learn from them." I knew I respected Shange's and Kramer's stories and I have gleaned from them ways of being that have contributed to whole chapters in my life. But my students have now taught me to value my own story, and it is with this tale that I am now becoming firmly acquainted.

Among Friends

—————— Todd Morman

Math and Science Teacher
Carolina Friends School
*Durham, North Carolina*_____

I hated Mr. Duncan, my eleventh-grade history teacher. Little things about him — the effeminate way he held his hands, the way he walked, the pastel sweaters he tied around his neck — evoked fear and anger in me. It was 1980, in a big Ohio city, and somehow word got passed around to each successive class that he was gay. I don't remember anyone ever talking about it; we all just knew that the word applied to him.

I certainly didn't think it applied to me, even as I fumbled at sex with my peers and felt a powerful desire for intimacy with other boys. To me, "gay" meant the stereotype Mr. Duncan seemed to fit, and I made sure I treated him with contempt once in a while so everyone would know I wasn't like him.

I wonder now if he knew I was struggling. As I think back on the period from 1990 to 1993 when I was an openly gay high school teacher, I flash on the faces of adolescents who might have been labeled lesbian or gay, and ask myself if any of them disliked me as much as I disliked Mr. Duncan. Did they see me as a representative of something they weren't? Did they feel that, if they were gay or lesbian, they had to be like me? Did I do any good by being an example of a gay man to them?

————

Of course, a major difference between Mr. Duncan's situation and my own was that I was able to be out and still hold onto my job. In fact, not only did Carolina Friends School tolerate the fact that I was gay, they thought it was actually a bonus to have an openly gay teacher on their staff, since they knew of past gay and lesbian students who had struggled, and were smart enough to know they would have them again in the future.

You have to know a little about Carolina Friends School to understand my experience as a gay teacher there. It's a small school, with a high school enrollment of about 130 students, and is affiliated with the Society of Friends — that is, the Quakers. The underlying philosophy of Quaker education is one of mutual respect, cooperation, nonviolence, and community. Everyone at the school is on a first-name basis; there are few rules; and discipline is maintained by fostering an atmosphere of trust, honesty, and dialogue. Freedom of speech is encouraged, as is careful listening. This atmosphere made Carolina Friends School a unique place to teach and learn.

During my first few months at CFS, I thought often about my homosexuality and its relationship to my work there. As October 11, National Coming-Out Day, approached, I became more and more uncomfortable with word "just getting out" to students that I was gay. I knew some students were already wondering. Honesty was the heart of the issue. I could easily have said nothing and relied on subtle cues that implied I was gay, hoping the more savvy students would pick up on it and spread the news around. I then remembered the uncertainty I had felt around Mr. Duncan; the air of shame that lingered around the issue of his homosexuality hadn't helped me come to grips with my adolescent sexuality. I become convinced that being honest was the most positive example I could set for my students.

I soon realized, however, I didn't have a clue about how to broach this subject. My first step was to go to the guidance counselor, a wonderful woman who'd been at CFS since the sixties. I entered her office and asked if she had a minute to talk, feeling the same knot of anxiety in my stomach I've felt every time I've come out to someone. When I said, "I don't know if you know this, but I'm gay, and I'd like to be out as a role model for our students," she paused for only a second and replied, "That's a great idea. The kids really need it and I'm glad you want to do it." I slowly let my breath out and we began to talk over how to actually do it. We decided it would be better for me to first come out to the staff and then use the opportunity of "silent meeting" to come out to students. Grounded in Quaker tradition, "silent meeting" brought together everyone in the high school weekly for a 25-minute period to meditate, worship, share thoughts, or just sit quietly for a while. Revealing this side of myself seemed appropriate to the time and place, following in a tradition of sharing that was already well established. Before I left her office, the counselor looked at me and said, "You know, Todd, if we can't teach from the strength of who we are, what are we doing here?" I went back to work feeling valued and supported, feelings affirmed by the positive reactions I received from colleagues when I announced my "coming out" plans at the next staff meeting.

The next Tuesday morning, as the high school came together in the main room for silent meeting, I went over in my head what I was going to say: "There's something I want to tell you. I'm gay, and I'm very comfortable with being gay. I didn't want to hide it because I think it's important to be out. There's a lot of discrimination and negative stereotyping out there, and I want you to know that you know at least one openly gay person. It's not the only important thing about me, or the most important thing. I just wanted you to know. If you ever have any questions or just want to talk about it, feel free to ask."

I stumbled nervously a couple of times, but I said what I wanted to say. There was silence for a few minutes, and then a female student broke it by saying, "I think it's really great that Todd could say that." After the meeting a few other students (all women) came up to express their support, as did more of the staff. I spent the rest of the day on a nervous high, trying not to think about how tomorrow might be different because of what I had done.

I needn't have worried. The next day was no different, partly because I tried hard to be the same person I had been before I came out, and partly because sexuality just doesn't come up that often in algebra. In fact, I was surprised at how normal everything was, at how little it seemed to matter that they all knew I was gay. Classes met, students and teachers taught and learned, and the year went on as before, except the high school now had an openly gay teacher on its staff.

On some occasions, my openness became a useful adjunct to my teaching. During my second year, the neurologist Simon LeVay reported on brain differences between homosexuals and heterosexuals, generating an intense debate among political groups who tried to put their own spin on the subject. I'd always encouraged my students to bring in news articles related to science, so, when they asked what I thought about this issue, we decided to spend some time investigating the evidence.

As we examined LeVay's hypothesis, it was clear the students were waiting for my own biases to appear. I encouraged them to be scientists, to use skepticism, and to read critically, to get them to see for themselves the constant debate underlying science. We talked of the goal of objectivity, the value of careful analysis, and the need to set aside prejudices as much as possible. They learned an enormous amount about science in that short unit.

I can only imagine what dealing with the subject would have been like if I'd been closeted. Fear of saying the wrong thing and giving myself away might have led me to avoid the topic entirely, and a rich, teachable moment would have slipped through my fingers. In this case, it was clear that being out made me a much more effective teacher than I could ever have been while in the closet.

Another teachable moment arose when I was asked, along with a lesbian friend, to join the school's Human Sexuality class for a question-and-answer session. We emphasized to students that we were there to present our opinions and experiences, not to force them to accept "the truth." We encouraged them to listen critically and decide for themselves where they stood on the issue of homosexuality. Every time we visited, the students were extremely curious, and asked intelligent questions. Over and over, I saw adolescents grappling with strong emotions and complex issues in amazingly adult ways. Given respect and encouraged to share their opinions, they demonstrated sharp insight into mass media portrayals of gays and lesbians, the use of sex as an advertising tool, and the evasiveness of many adults in response to their honest questions about sexuality. The thoughtful, positive reaction of these young people to an open conversation about sex and sexuality confirmed for me the value of being out and reinforced my faith that, unless they're aggressively taught otherwise, few people have objections to homosexuality.

A few students did have clearly negative responses. These served to sharpen my sense of the responsibilities involved in opening up this kind of debate, as well as my commitment to allowing students the space to strongly disagree. I wanted it to be okay for a student to say, "The thought of two men together disgusts me," or "I get really uncomfortable around lesbians," reasoning that little long-term good would come of a student pretending to be accepting if that weren't really the case. It seemed to me that the best way to encourage tolerance was to model it myself. When objections were raised, I praised the speaker's honesty and spoke of the importance of living respectfully in a democracy where people often seriously disagree with one another. This seemed to work: at least, I never ruined a teaching relationship with a student because he or she didn't share my conviction that the world is a better place because there are lesbians and gay men in it.

————

One day, after class, a student asked if he could speak with me for a second and then surprised me with some news. "I just wanted to tell you that I appreciate you being out and all. I'm not gay, but my mother's a lesbian, and only one of my friends knows, 'cause they'd give me shit for it." We talked for a while but, when he left, I just stood there, amazed that I hadn't even considered the likelihood that some of our straight students would have homosexual parents. The next day, I asked a longtime staff member if she knew of any gay or lesbian parents in the school and watched as she silently counted off four students she already knew had gay parents. I later found out there were more. Denying the reality of homosexuality, I realized, clearly hurts more than the ten percent or so of the student body who are lesbian or gay; it also causes children, cousins, nieces, and grandchildren to suffer for their gay relatives.

————

That student was one of the few who ever took me aside and shared personal information relating to homosexuality during the three years I taught at the school. I must admit I was disappointed at first that more students didn't turn to me for support, but soon remembered that, when I was sixteen, approaching a teacher to discuss sexuality would have been the last thing on my mind. And so I contented myself, as most teachers do, with the faith that what I was doing was planting seeds of tolerance and self-acceptance, and that some would undoubt-edly bloom whether I was there to watch or not. I did get an occasional lift whenever the school counselor mentioned that a student who was struggling had told her I was a big help, just by being out and around, and I held tightly to those bits of positive feedback. For the most part, however, I sustained myself with the belief that I was doing a valuable thing.

————

Most of what I know about simultaneously being a teacher and a gay man I learned on the fly. I constantly felt that I was in strange territory with no map, testing strategies without knowing if they'd do any good. I spent nights agonizing over whether I was going about the business of being an openly gay teacher correctly. Most of the other gay or lesbian teachers I knew were of little help; they were far from out and reminded me of Mr. Duncan when they spoke of how their kids "just knew." They danced around the issue in their classrooms, in staff meetings, in their private lives. They often worked in schools far less supportive than CFS and faced a choice between openness and their love of teaching. They felt compelled to choose the latter, and I'd probably have done the same. I'm grateful I didn't have to make that choice. But often, the lack of a rulebook or role models often left me unsure if I was handling it all properly.

I'm convinced that I'm a better teacher precisely because I'm gay. Growing up with a profound sense of being different, searching constantly for role models, going through a difficult process of self-discovery, gaining tremendous strength from the support of friends, all helped refine in me the skills I used on a daily basis to communicate with students. It quickly became clear to me that as important as any information I might impart to them about DNA or quadratic functions was the message that each of my students was valuable, unique, slightly strange, and totally worthy of respect. Having fought all of my life against a culture which routinely denied me that message and, in fact, sent me one very much its opposite, I was particularly tuned in to the need for young people to hear it often. Over time I became convinced that students listen and learn more carefully if they know they are first valued as people, and I'm sure being gay helped me appreciate that lesson.

I tried hard not to be just "Todd, the gay teacher" to the students. I preferred to be "Todd, who gets impatient — and even angry — sometimes, but who really listens to what you have to say and respects you and is a good teacher whose classes are fun and interesting, and, oh yeah, did you know he's gay?"

Students can only benefit from that kind of honesty.

Working My Way Back Home

———Reggie Sellars

Spanish Teacher and Football Coach
Noble & Greenough School
Dedham, Massachusetts _____

*E*very time I do something like this, it brings up a lot that even I haven't processed. It is pointed out to me again and again and again that I am one of the only black teachers at my school, and the only openly gay teacher. Sometimes the tokenism smacks me right in the face. Writing this for a gay publication, but also knowing my story is "better" because I'm black ... well, I know it serves its purpose. Mainly, I do it because I hope it will help someone else. But we shall see.

I guess you could say I was born a poor black boy and now I'm a poor black man, but that's only in the financial sense. All of my life I have had loving care from my parents, my friends, and many of my teachers. Being the youngest of six children, I always had plenty of attention from my family. They were always there for me. My family always stayed together, and we're still very close. Another thing that added to the loving atmosphere in my family is that my father is a Baptist minister. Some people ask me if that wasn't an ordeal, growing up in a religion that is so opposed to homosexuality. I say no, because my father then and now doesn't preach against homosexuality. At the same time, within my own mind, was always that internal conversation about what my father might say or do if he knew his youngest son was gay. I was always afraid that if he found out about me, he would kick me out of the house. So, from early on, I learned to hide that side of myself from my family but especially from my father.

I was born in Winston-Salem, North Carolina, which is the fifth-largest city in North Carolina, but that doesn't make it a very large place. In the city you pretty much know everyone your own age, especially if you are an athlete. I played football since I was six years old. By doing well in football, I was able to garner a lot of support. I realized that, if I continued to do well in the sport, people would continue to like "me," quote unquote. Along the same lines, I also did well in my academics. I went to a school where, in my classes, only three students out of thirty-five were black. The vast majority were white. I learned early on that, to be a black person amongst a group of white people, you had to be "nice" — you had to smile at everything they said, you had to listen to their music, you had to do whatever you could to fit in because, as soon as you did something they didn't deem "appropriate," it was labeled as being a "black" thing.

My saving grace was that, whereas at school I might feel a little restricted to how I could be, whenever I went home I was free to be myself. I lived in an all-black neighborhood so, if I ever had problems at school, I could go home and talk to my parents and friends about the situation. That sustained me throughout my entire educational career. It also helped that, as an athlete, I was respected by the other students.

It was during these years, about fifth grade, that sexuality really made an imprint on my life. It wasn't homosexuality or heterosexuality, it was racial sexuality. Like all students that age, we would have sleepovers. I was always one of the students invited to the sleepovers. But when I went to the parties, which were coed, we would play the "kissing game." One of the rules was explained to me this way: "Hey, Reggie, you know you can't play, because you're black, and we can't kiss black people!" I learned that I had my limits to being accepted, even in the *straight* white world.

More and more, sexuality as well as race began to play a bigger role in my life. When I reached junior high school I met another black male student and we became good friends. In seventh and eighth grades we were always together. Since we spent so much time together, we began to call each other "cousins." Eventually it became a sexual relationship. We didn't call it homosexuality, we didn't say we were gay, we just said we really loved one another and cared for one another. Fitting all the norms I was supposed to, I still had my girlfriends, always girlfriends of color, of course, whom I really enjoyed being with as friends. But they always tended to be the best friends of my "cousin," so we could always be together. We would talk about what we would do when we got older. He would talk about his wife and how many kids they would have, and how he would name his first kid after me.

My scenario was that I never saw myself with a wife. I knew that I only wanted to be with him for the rest of my life.

About this time, I approached one of my guidance counselors to apply to a boarding school. I loved my school in North Carolina, I loved living with my family, but I also felt that I was missing something. In hindsight, I wanted to leave because I was ready to deal with my sexuality, but I wasn't able to deal with it in such a familiar setting where, if I wasn't accepted, I would be cast out. I applied to and was accepted to Phillips Exeter Academy. At age sixteen, I left for Exeter.

After I was accepted, the football coach contacted me when he learned I was interested in playing for the school. I got there a week before classes started, to attend football camp. I was one of two tenth-graders who eventually made the varsity team. Thus, coming into the school year, I already had a reputation. This helped me to be seen as a leader.

Initially at Exeter, one of my dreams was to have a boyfriend. But, due to my being on the football team, I instantly had a reputation, and everything that comes along with that reputation of being a football player. Then, sophomore year, a new student named Mark came in and was on the varsity diving team as a freshman. He and I hung out in the same crowd. The word got around that he was gay but didn't have a problem with it. I thought this was pretty intriguing so I resolved to get to know him. He was dealing with it in a more open way than I was ready to deal with it, though. One evening in the dorm he came over and closed my bedroom door. I totally freaked out: "What are people going to think? This guy has a reputation for being gay." I wasn't ready for people to think that about me. I threw open my door and ran out.

In my senior year, another player on the football team had become a little tired of Mark being openly gay. He found Mark and beat him up. Mark then came to me, seeking comfort, and when I saw him, I was outraged. I went out to find the other guy. I'm glad I didn't find him that night because I think I would have hurt him physically. I saw him the next day and told him that, if he felt he needed to show how much of a man he was by beating up homosexuals, he should start with me, because I was a homosexual. I screamed, "I'm gay! Why don't you try to fight me? You know you can't kick my ass!" He just laughed and said that I was just saying this — "You can't be gay. You're my friend. You're captain of the football team."

Toward the end of my senior year we had sexuality workshops. We did skits where a student would be homosexual, and I always volunteered to play that role. I felt that I could be myself. The health teacher always thanked me for doing this. She thought it was so great that the football captain, the track captain, the heralded student leader, would put himself in such a position. She said that my doing this would help some student who really *was* dealing with his sexuality. I just smiled and laughed to myself, only wishing that she knew that I wasn't role-playing, but was actually being myself.

In college, I decided to come out as a gay person and also go out for the football team. I made the freshman football team and resolved to tell my closest friend on the team I was gay. His response was that he had never really known a gay person before but that, since he now knew me, he realized that all the stereotypes about gay people weren't true. I was shocked, completely taken aback, because I had expected him to tell me to get out of his life. Instead he was telling me that he was willing to get to know me as a *gay* person. I could feel something being lifted from me. I was able to play football, I was able to be an openly gay person, I was able to be myself.

By the end of my senior year I decided I wanted to go into teaching, at least for a couple of years until I got a "real job," as my mother put it. I wanted to go back to an environment like Exeter and be a black role model. I wanted to go back to a school like Exeter, because I felt I understood what these students were going through in a way most of the other teachers didn't.

I went right into my first job that fall at Brewster Academy in Wolfeboro, New Hampshire. I was the only black teacher and, eventually, the only openly gay one as well. Coming in as a 22-year-old, I didn't realize what effect that would have on me. As a gay black man, I was never allowed the experience of being a young teacher. I found myself playing the role of spokesperson for two communities, while simultaneously trying to learn and understand what was still a new profession for me. Often, I would seek out a senior faculty member for advice on a basic educational issue and end up debating, explaining, or defending an unrelated topic dealing with racism or homophobia. Although the work was meaningful and rewarding, the stress that came with it was more than any beginning teacher should have to face.

The recurring thing I heard around the dorm, around the school, around the playing fields, was people constantly demeaning others with words like "faggot" or "dyke" or "cocksucker" or "lesbian."

Initially I would ask those students why they used those words, and they would say it was just teen slang. I would ask how they thought someone who was gay or lesbian would feel if they overheard, and they would reply that no one at our school *was* like that. I started answering their homophobic remarks by saying, "What if I were gay? That might offend me." They would say, "You can't be gay. You were a big football player at Yale and all the girls want you." I would then say, "Well, what if I was offended by that, even though I was straight?" I was walking the line between admitting I was gay and just being pro-gay.

I asked faculty members why they didn't stop such homophobic language. They said that, if they stopped it every time they heard it, they'd never have time to teach their classes. Another new faculty member at the school was attracted to me and I decided that I had to tell her I was gay. She was taken aback but then said that she respected that I could share that with her. She warned me that I'd better not tell anyone else, though, because I might get harassed or fired. I told more and more faculty after that, and always got that same response.

One situation that helped me to come out was when I noticed a student named Jean wearing a pink triangle. I asked if he knew what it stood for and he said, "Of course. It stands for gay rights." He was in one of my classes and, after this conversation, it sort of sparked him. He started paying attention and his grades started improving. He had been one of the problem students in the school, but the more he realized I supported his wearing the pink triangle, the more he began to turn around. Eventually we got into a conversation where we both personalized it — he was gay and I was gay. From then on, Jean blossomed academically. He started to shine in all his classes and began to try on some new activities.

While neither of us came out to the entire community, we did establish a relationship where we could talk about what was going on for us as gay people at the school. Not having any formal support system, we coordinated meetings with an administrator to whom we felt it would be safe to talk. Eventually, Jean felt comfortable enough to talk to his mother about his sexuality. Although I'd never advised him to do so (I would never advise a student to do that, as one never knows how a parent might react, and thus the student must make the final decision), he felt our conversations had given him enough confidence that he could deal with however his mother reacted. He felt she would be supportive, as there was already another openly gay relative in the family. He told me afterwards that she had been mildly shocked but had then told him that of course she still cared for him and loved him as her son. I was surprised, then, when she proceeded to call me and start screaming accusations: "You convinced my son to be gay" and "You had a relationship with my son that made him gay." After hanging up, I immediately headed over to the home of the administrator who had been helping us through this situation. She convinced me that I had nothing to worry about and that Jean's mother was simply taking out her frustration and shock on me. Just as importantly, she let me know that I had the school's support should this woman try to place any professional blame on me. Although still a little shaky, I was convinced I had handled the situation appropriately, and felt I would be all right, thanks to this administrator's support and the clear turnaround in Jean's academic and personal performance since we had begun our work together.

I continued to let more students know that I was gay. Initially some of them stopped talking to me. They didn't know how to deal with the situation, as they had never known an openly gay person before. Although I was initially hurt by this reaction, I held to my convictions.

One of the most painful initial rejections ended up being one of the most rewarding turnarounds. In my first year, a student named Sim was also beginning at the school. We instantly formed a strong student-teacher relationship. Although I was not his official advisor, he often came to me for personal and academic counseling. His parents wrote to me about the wonderful effect I was having on their son's life. They said he referred to me as the older brother he had always wanted but never had. They even extended an open invitation for me to visit them at their home.

Needless to say, when the time came for me to tell Sim I was gay, I was extremely anxious about what his reaction would be. At first, he seemed to have no problem with my gayness. He then proceeded to avoid me in every possible way for the next three weeks. I then got a message from his parents. Already saddened by Sim's reaction, I expected an even worse one from his parents. Instead, they were calling to convince me not to give up on their son, explaining that they thought he was just trying to adjust to a situation that was completely new to him and needed space and time to work it out. My biggest fear had always been the possible reaction of my students' parents; here, in one of my first encounters, they were encouraging me to hang in there and affirming my decision to come out! They closed by thanking me for being one of the best teachers and role models their son had ever had.

The headmaster was the last to know. The first time we ever had a conversation about it was when, as part of a "viewbook" featuring write-ups on teachers that the school was publishing, I told him I wanted to include the fact that I was a member of GLSTN, the Gay, Lesbian, and Straight Teachers Network. After all, other teachers were mentioning that they were part of women's teachers groups or people-of-color teachers groups. He told me I couldn't because this was a school publication, and I told him he was denying a part of me. Basically he said he was sorry, but he didn't want to leave a "bad mark" on the school. Even when I pointed out that, at one time, it would have been considered to be a "bad mark" to have a black teacher or a black students' support group at his school, he still refused to allow me to mention my affiliation with GLSTN. I felt enraged hearing my employer say he was willing to accept one part of me while so blatantly refusing to acknowledge another. Even though he admitted that he had been pleasantly surprised by the community's reaction to my coming out, he said he did not want to test how the general public might respond. He added that he had been so elated when he read my application folder: imagine, a black teaching candidate who went to Phillips Exeter Academy and Yale University, who wanted to work at his school! Without even being asked, he then volunteered that, if he had known then that I was gay, that my folder would have been "darkened." I will always remember that phrase because of his unintentional pun.

I worked for two years at Brewster trying to show people why it was important that people be able to be openly gay. We had workshops on why we needed to change our policies and curriculum, but the school steadfastly refused to do any of this. I decided I had to leave. I was saddened, because all of my relationships with students had turned out to be positive. Jean's mother had cornered me at his graduation, asking me to forgive her for the accusations she had made and insisting that I had probably saved her son's academic career as well as possibly his relationship with her; Sim and I had re-established our friendship in the last year, with him eventually calling me two years later to tell me of his own homosexuality. Nevertheless, I felt that, if I were to survive emotionally and professionally, I had to change workplaces.

When I came to my second school, Nobles, I planned to continue to speak out. While interviewing, I decided that I needed to find out if my identity and work would be supported by the school. I had set up my interview for the day following the GLSTN conference, which was held at a school only twenty minutes from Nobles, thinking I could save myself a four-hour round trip from New Hampshire by doing so. The interview went quite well. The headmaster, Mr. Baker, was impressed by my resume as well as my teaching experiences and philosophy. At one point, he casually asked how I had been able to come down in the middle of the week, on a school day. I realized that I could come out to him by telling about my participation in the GLSTN conference, or would have to make up some excuse while praying that he didn't find out I was gay before offering me a position. Since I was leaving Brewster because of the lack of professional and personal support for gay people there, I decided that now was the time to find out if Nobles was going to be different. I told him about the GLSTN conference and came out to him. Although it seemed that we were at the interview's end, we then proceeded to talk for another twenty minutes about my work as an openly gay teacher and what I would like to see happen on gay issues at Nobles. When we finished, I asked him what he thought of my candidacy now. He replied that it seemed that what we had discussed could only make me a better candidate and teacher. A few days later, I was offered a position as a Spanish teacher, dorm parent, and football coach. Having already felt pretty good about myself for having the courage to come out in the interview, I was elated to actually win a job after doing so.

At Nobles I coached football for the first time. Even though I had had a great time at Yale as an openly gay football player, I was still afraid of all the stereotypes the sport carried toward homosexuals. I wasn't sure how to deal with being an openly gay coach. Within the first few weeks, though, I felt the students had come to respect me as a coach and a player, and we had developed a very good relationship. I decided to first tell the captains that I was gay. When I approached them to tell them, they said they already knew from students who'd known me when I taught at the school the summer before. I asked how they felt. They said that initially they didn't know what to expect, but as the season went on, they had come to understand that I was a football coach who just happened to be gay and they had learned to respect that.

I then always wore a pink triangle, either on my whistle or on my cap, at practice. One day, the largest player on the team, who epitomized everything you could be afraid of, approached me, and asked what it stood for. I held my breath and said that it was a pin that stood for gay rights and that I wore it because, not only did I think that everyone should be treated equally, but also because I was gay. He said, "Oh, I thought so. I have a couple of pink triangles myself. My mother's a lesbian." That completely blew me away again, and taught me again the lesson that you have to trust people.

Recently I went to a people-of-color teachers conference. We had several workshops on how to deal with race in the school setting. But this was my third year there and I still didn't feel like I was a part of it. I had originally come just to be around other black teachers, but now I was wondering why I still didn't feel fulfilled by this conference. It really struck home with me at a breakfast for men of color that I attended. The men leading the workshop were telling us that we had to teach our boys to be strong black men, that we had to teach them to be aggressive, that we had to teach them "how to treat their women." It was these words that had helped me see why I had not felt at home in this conference, why I had not felt at home coming up all my life in the black community. I went up to the mike in the closing session and decided to address the entire group there. I didn't know what I was going to say but I knew what I wanted to get across. I was nervous, having never spoken up before at the conference because I had never wanted to risk being rejected by the crowd, my crowd, a crowd of people of color. I said that, until we learn to deal with the fact that not all men are going to be aggressive and that not all men are going to have relationships with women, we were not addressing the entire black community. I then told them that I was a black gay man, that I was a *proud* black gay man. I told them that, if this conference was to represent all people of color, it had to address the issue of sexuality within race, because it plays a huge part, especially within the black race. By the time I sat down I was so nervous that I was shaking and sweating. But the audience stood up and gave me a standing ovation. I left feeling I could come back to the conference with my head held up, seeing that we had taken the first step toward addressing the issue of sexuality within the black community.

It was only a summer ago that I told my father that I was gay. The previous fall he had been really sick, and while he made it through the winter, I realized that I didn't want him to die without really knowing his youngest son. When I was home that summer I sat him down and told him I was gay. He asked me why I had chosen to do that and I told him it wasn't a choice, it's the way I *am*. After my lecturing him for fifteen or twenty minutes, I asked what he thought as a Baptist minister, as a "man of God," about my being homosexual. He said, "As a minister, I can only follow what the Bible says, and it says homosexuality is a sin. If you don't change, you're going to hell because you will be judged. But as a man on this earth, I am a father first, and you're my son, and I love you no matter what. I will always pray that you will not be hurt in any way, just as I pray for all your brothers and sisters. Only God Himself can judge us — we as humans can only love one another. I want you to know that I will always love you."

My father taught me the ultimate lesson. You just have to trust people who care for you. They will try to understand you, and make you a part of their lives, if only you give them the chance.

Epilogue

The Question

Anne Osbaldeston

Director of the Extended Day Program
Bertschi School
Seattle, Washington

Are you married?
It was a question
I anticipated.
Yes.
Who are you married to?
Sonia.
Is that a boy or a girl?
A girl.
But you're a girl.
Girls can't marry girls.
Yes they can.
Nuh-uh.
Well I'm married to one.
Ewwww!
That's nasty.
No it's not.
It's nice.
Do you
LIVE together?
Yes.
Do you change your clothes in the
SAME room?
Yes.
Nah! You can't do that!
I'm gonna ask my mom.

Your mom may say
you can't
but I say
you can.
People have different ideas.
She shakes her head
and looks at me.

The next year
when she is five
she is overheard
correcting a boy
who asks
Does Anne have a husband?
Don't you know?
Her hand is on her hip.
She's married to a girl.
The boy looks at me
Shocked.
She sighs
exasperated
shakes her head
and looks at me.

Appendix A

A Legal Overview of the Rights of Gay, Lesbian, and Bisexual Teachers

Mary L. Bonauto

Gay & Lesbian Advocates & Defenders
P.O. Box 218, Boston, MA 02112[1]

I. INTRODUCTION[2]

These are charged and hopeful times for gay, lesbian, and bisexual people. Teachers work in the context of growing recognition of gay issues nationwide, including recognition of the existence and needs of gay, lesbian, and bisexual youth. Schools are not remote from this phenomenon; rather they are part of it. Indeed, in some areas, schools have become a battleground of sorts in which any school's movement toward acceptance of gay, lesbian, and bisexual teachers, or any curriculum content related to sexual orientation, is greeted with organized protest from those who want gay people to go back in the closet and stay there.

This essay addresses the major legal principles governing the employment of gay, lesbian, and bisexual teachers in public and private (but not religious) schools. Section 2 discusses the rights and protections afforded by the United States Constitution, particularly the First Amendment. Section 3 addresses the widely varying state law protections that may be available to gay, lesbian, and bisexual teachers. Section 4 addresses the role of unions and collective bargaining agreements for unionized employees. The Conclusion, at Section 5, sets out practical advice.

II. THE UNITED STATES CONSTITUTION

The United States Constitution[3] is a primary source of legal rights for public school gay, lesbian, and bisexual teachers. The Constitution and the amendments apply to government action, whether federal, state, or local (including school boards), rather than the acts of private individuals or organizations. Unfortunately then, these constitutional principles do not apply to truly private schools.[4]

At a minimum, the Constitution guarantees that when the government acts, it must act rationally and not capriciously.[5] While no government can be compelled to treat everyone in exactly the same way, the same basic rules that apply to the treatment of heterosexual teachers should be applied to gay, lesbian, and bisexual teachers.

A caveat is important here: while rights may exist, they are only real when the individuals asserting them encounter judges actually willing to uphold those rights by rendering decisions[6] interpreting the law to apply to gay, lesbian, and bisexual people.

A. Why a school board should not be able to fire or refuse to hire a teacher simply because the teacher is lesbian, gay, or bisexual

We have not yet arrived at the time when the presence of openly gay, lesbian, and bisexual teachers in the public schools is applauded as an expression of diversity that aids the educational process or that provides for role models to gay, lesbian, and bisexual students. However, even in those many places in which a gay presence is not welcomed, there is a legal bar to overt hostility from the government. The Fourteenth Amendment guarantees both "due process" before being deprived of life, liberty, or property, and "equal protection" of the laws. These clauses have been interpreted to mean that government actions must be rationally related to a legitimate government purpose. In other words, the government cannot act on whim, nor may its objectives be illegitimate (i.e., e.g., punitive, craven, or discriminatory). When applied to the rights of gay, lesbian, and bisexual people, it is clear that the courts have wide latitude in interpreting these principles.

In the 1969 case of *Norton v. Macy*,[7] these principles were used to require the reinstatement of a gay man to his federal job at the National Aeronautics and Space Administration. He succeeded because the government was not able to establish a rational relationship between Mr. Norton's sexual orientation and the efficiency of governmental operations, which the government claimed might be impaired by retaining Mr. Norton in his position. The important and enduring theme here is that the appropriateness of an employee for his or her position must be judged individually rather than on the supposed characteristics of all "homosexuals."

In 1969, the California Supreme Court applied the *Norton* principles in the case of *Morrison v. State Board of Education*,[8] involving a schoolteacher. The *Morrison* court adhered to the fundamental constitutional guarantee that teaching qualifications cannot be revoked because of homosexual conduct unless the school authorities could demonstrate "unfitness to teach." Critically, the Court also required specific factual evidence of fitness rather than mere speculation about immorality.[9]

Despite the analytic soundness of the decisions in *Norton* and *Morrison*, other courts have capitulated to anti-gay hysteria in cases involving gay and lesbian schoolteachers. For instance, in *Gaylord v. Tacoma School District No. 10*,[10] the Washington Supreme Court upheld the dismissal of a gay teacher on the grounds that his status as a "known homosexual" automatically impaired his efficiency as a teacher and, thus, justified his dismissal. A high school student who had sought Gaylord's advice outed him to the school principal. Ignorant about homosexuality, the Court resorted to encyclopedias, including the *New Catholic Encyclopedia*, for a definition. The Court then determined that homosexuality, which it deemed to include homosexual acts, was implicitly immoral, although the state sodomy law had been repealed by the time of trial. As an immoral person, Gaylord could not be trusted to instruct students in morality, nor did the school wish to be viewed as approving of Mr. Gaylord. Therefore, despite twelve years as a teacher in this school with positive performance evaluations, the Court ruled Gaylord's presence at the school would be inherently disruptive. In a popularity contest type of analysis, the Court based its conclusion on the testimony of one student and three teachers who objected to a known homosexual teaching at the school, and the opinion of the administration that his presence on the faculty "would create problems." No problems were actually demonstrated.[11]

One can only hope that decisions like these will soon be anachronistic. In the meantime, whether the law is "good" or "bad" in your area, a commonsense approach combined with an assessment of the support and backbone of your colleagues, the school administration, and school board is advisable.

B. Background on First Amendment rights of teachers

Teachers, as government employees, are scrutinized for what they say and do both in and out of class. In this context, their rights are governed by the First Amendment of the United States Constitution. In sweeping language, the United States Supreme Court has already ruled in *Tinker v. Des Moines Independent Community School District*,[12] "It can hardly be argued that either students or teachers shed their constitutional rights to freedom of speech or expression at the schoolhouse gate." Stated differently, teachers do not forfeit their basic constitutional rights when they accept a teaching job.

The question then becomes to what extent teachers may enjoy their First Amendment rights to freedom of speech, expression, and association. The short answer is that First Amendment rights in schools are not as extensive as First Amendment rights in other settings.[13] The reasons have to do with the uniqueness of the school setting. On the one hand, schools exist to inculcate morals and values, thus permitting school officials control over the content of what is said. On the other hand, our constitutional scheme values the rights of both teachers and students to speak and act without content control by a governmental entity. School boards may not "cast a pall of orthodoxy" over the classroom.[14] Neither the rights or interests of the school board or the teacher is absolute or paramount in every situation. Thus, in individual cases, courts balance the school's interests as educator and employer against the free speech interests of teachers and students.[15]

C. The teacher's right to associate

It is not uncommon for a school board, for example, in its zeal to hire only teachers who are morally exemplary, to inquire into the company a teacher keeps. While our right to enjoy the company of other like-minded individuals by joining groups or organizations is often taken for granted, it may be only because that right is secure. A teacher's right of "associational privacy" generally forbids the government from forcing an individual to disclose to what groups or organizations he or she belongs. However, in cases where the government has a compelling interest in discovering those associations, it may do so.[16]

In *Shelton v. Tucker,*[17] the Supreme Court ruled that school authorities may not require a teacher to disclose all of her memberships and affiliations as a condition of employment. However, historically at least, teachers have been in a classic "Catch-22" position. On the one hand, when asked, teachers are obligated to disclose those associations that may affect their effectiveness as a teacher. On the other hand, teachers may legitimately fear that if they are truthful about their membership in lesbian, gay, or bisexual organizations, they may be denied or removed from a job, particularly in states without civil rights laws protecting sexual orientation.

This Catch-22 was painfully illustrated in the case of *Ancafora v. Board of Education,*[18] decided by a federal appeals court in 1974. During the application process, Mr. Ancafora was asked both to state his membership in professional, service, and fraternal organizations and to list his extracurricular activities. He intentionally omitted his membership in an organization known as the "Homophiles of Penn State." He also certified that the information he submitted was accurate to the best of his knowledge. After he had secured his teaching job in Maryland, Pennsylvania officials inadvertently alerted the Maryland officials to Mr. Ancafora's sexual orientation. He was then transferred away from students to an administrative position pending further review.

The Court ruled that Ancafora's intentional misrepresentation was itself enough to justify his transfer and dismissal. He was never allowed to address the constitutionality of the county's policy against hiring gay teachers.

Not every school board will react to the announcement of an applicant's same-sex sexual orientation as did Maryland officials in 1973. However, given the possibility of job rejection for merely coming out and the penalties for lying (which in some cases can result in criminal penalties or civil liability), caution dictates that job applicants seek the advice of an attorney knowledgeable about the local community and laws.

D. The teacher's right to participate in the political process

Like other citizens in their communities, teachers may decide to become involved in political causes or the issues of the day. This sometimes attracts unfavorable notice from school officials, especially when the teacher's activities are viewed as controversial. Despite the consternation of school officials, however, teachers possess the right to express themselves as citizens about matters of public concern as long as they do it in a way that does not disturb the efficiency of the workplace. The leading case outlining this right of teachers to speak out in their communities is *Pickering v. Board of Education.*[19]

In *Pickering,* a teacher was terminated after he wrote a letter to a local newspaper criticizing a tax increase in light of how the school board raised revenues and the allocation of those revenues as between academic and extracurricular programs. Engaging in a balancing test of the teacher's rights as a citizen to comment upon matters of public concern and the school's right to regulate the speech of its employees, the Court found in favor of Mr. Pickering. In particular, the Court ruled that as long as Mr. Pickering's statements were not knowingly false or made with reckless disregard as to the truth, the school could restrict or punish his speech only if the speech harmed the school's ability to operate efficiently or inhibited the teacher's ability to carry out his duties.

The *Pickering* rule largely has been followed in cases involving a teacher's advocacy of civil rights for lesbians, gay men, and bisexuals. For example, in *Ancafora,* the Court determined that the press interviews Ancafora gave after his transfer urging acceptance of homosexuals were protected by the First Amendment and thus could not be used to justify either his transfer or his dismissal. In reaching that conclusion, the *Ancafora* court observed that the interviews neither disrupted the school nor substantially impaired his capacity as a teacher.[20]

A similar result was obtained in *National Gay Task Force v. Board of Education of City of Oklahoma City.*[21] This case, brought on behalf of gay and lesbian teachers in the Oklahoma City school system, targeted a state law permitting punishment for "public homosexual conduct." It defined conduct as

> advocating, soliciting, imposing, encouraging or promoting public or private homosexual activity in a manner that creates a substantial risk that such conduct will come to the attention of school children or school employees.

The Court ruled that "advocacy" is squarely within the protection of the First Amendment, and that this law's punishment of advocacy rendered it unconstitutional. The Court observed that the advocacy prohibition would extend to a teacher urging a mere change in the law, whether it be enactment of basic civil rights or the repeal of sodomy laws. Articulating a now-familiar rule, the Court opined that the state's right in regulating the speech of its employees overcomes the teacher's free speech rights only when the free speech results in a substantial or material interference or disruption in school activities, neither of which was demonstrated here.[22]

E. The right to raise homosexuality as a topic in class

No United States Supreme Court opinion has directly addressed the First Amendment rights of teachers in the classroom. Teachers share the province of the classroom with school boards, which have enormous discretion to make curriculum-related decisions.

While the case law on this subject is sketchy, there is some indication that classroom activity is protected by the First Amendment.[23] In *Keyishian v. Board of Regents of the State of New York,* a case overturning New York laws that forbade teachers from engaging in subversive activities and barring from employment teachers who belonged to subversive organizations, the United States Supreme Court observed that "academic freedom is of transcendent value ... and ... a special concern of the First Amendment."

While principles of academic freedom should apply to classroom discussions of homosexuality, a commonsense approach is advisable. Talking about the struggle for gay and lesbian civil rights, for example, is more appropriate to civics class than math class.[24] It is doubtful that a school could flatly prohibit discussion of a topic relevant to a subject being taught.[25]

It is important to note that academic freedom, like other rights grounded in the First Amendment, may be limited if its impact causes a material and substantial disruption to the school. In a Maine case,[26] a high school teacher organized a "Tolerance Day" program in response to the death by drowning of a young gay man named Charlie Howard who had been thrown off of a bridge by three high school students despite Mr. Howard's entreaties that he could not swim. The program was to consist of a mandatory assembly and two optional periods with representatives from twelve groups that had experienced prejudice, including an open lesbian. After the school received threats of pickets, bomb threats, and threats of sabotage of the school furnace, all in response to the lesbian's presence at the school, the school canceled the program.

The teacher and others sued after the program was canceled, claiming First Amendment violations, including infringements on academic freedom. The state's highest court concluded that the cancellation effected no violation of the teacher's academic freedom because the threatened disruptions would have resulted in the loss of an entire educational day. However, the Court was also careful to note that the school board did not prohibit this teacher from discussing "tolerance [of] or prejudice against homosexuals, whether in Solmitz's classes or otherwise within [the school]."[27]

Since there is no Supreme Court precedent directly addressing the scope of First Amendment rights in the classroom, it is entirely possible that a different standard will apply than the balancing test used in an academic freedom analysis. Two 1980s United States Supreme Court opinions constricting student free speech rights, *Hazelwood School District v. Kuhlmeier*,[28] and *Bethel School District No. 403 v. Fraser*,[29] may be ominous for teachers as well.

In *Hazelwood*, the Court allowed school officials to eliminate from a student newspaper articles about pregnancy and divorce. The Court ruled that the school could censor curricular speech that was "inconsistent with its basic educational mission," "so long as their actions are reasonably related to legitimate pedagogical concerns."[30]

In *Fraser*, a student was disciplined for his sexual imagery in a speech endorsing a classmate for school office. Among other things, he referred to the student as "firm in his convictions," as someone who "takes his point and pounds it in" and "who will go to the end — even the climax — for ... you." The Court agreed with the school that the disruption caused by these remarks justified a brief suspension and denial of certain privileges. Ominously, the Court added that school boards can punish vulgar and sexually offensive speech.[31]

There is hope that the United States Supreme Court will permit teachers' broad rights in the classroom when squarely confronted with such a case. This is particularly appropriate since, as the Court itself has observed:

> The classroom is peculiarly the "marketplace of ideas." The Nation's future depends upon leaders trained through wide exposure to that robust exchange of ideas which discovers truth "out of a multitude of tongues, [rather] than through any kind of authoritative selection."[32]

Of course, there is also no more effective way to teach the importance of constitutional freedoms than by example. The Supreme Court in *Fraser* re-affirmed this principle:

[S]chools must teach by example the shared values of a civilized social order. Consciously or otherwise, teachers — and indeed the older students — demonstrate the appropriate form of civil discourse and political expression by their conduct and deportment in and out of class.[33]

However, if the Court resorts to a *Hazelwood/Fraser* formulation of teachers' rights, then school boards will be able to regulate class content, particularly "vulgar" and "sexually explicit" speech, as long as the school's actions are reasonably related to legitimate pedagogical concerns. Thus, it is best to tread carefully in this area by making sure that any classroom discussion can be defended, if necessary, on legitimate pedagogical grounds.

F. The right to come out at school

While coming out, that is, a simple statement of identity, should be protected speech in schools and elsewhere, that is not yet the law.[34] At present, speech by government employees in the workplace must touch on a matter of "public concern" in order to merit First Amendment protection.[35] Whether the speech constitutes a matter of public concern depends on the content, form, and context of the statement.

In *Van Ootegehm v. Gray*,[36] a federal appeals court overturned the discharge of an assistant county treasurer who had informed his supervisor both that he was gay and intended to testify as a citizen before the county commissioners on the subject of civil rights for lesbians and gay men. In bold language, the Court stated:

It may be true that some treasury workers, or [the Treasurer] himself, found the prospect of an employee addressing the Commissioners Court on homosexual rights to be distressing. However, the ability of a member of a disfavored class to express his views on civil rights publicly and without hesitation — no matter how personally offensive to his employer or majority of his coemployees — lies at the core of the Free Speech Clause of the First Amendment.[37]

Even in *Ancafora*, discussed above, the teacher's statements to the press, which explicitly included his acknowledging his own sexual orientation, were held by a federal court not to be sufficient reasons for firing him.[38]

The nadir in coming-out cases involved a high school guidance counselor in an Ohio town.[39] Marjorie Rowland, on a one-year contract, confided to a school secretary that she was bisexual and had a female partner. Later, she disclosed her bisexuality to the school principal as well as several teacher friends. After being suspended and then re-assigned into a position with no student contact, her contract was not renewed at the end of the year. Relying on the public concern rule, the Court swiftly dispatched Rowland's First Amendment claim on the grounds that her speech was only personal, even though there was no evidence that her speech interfered with the performance of anyone's duties or the operation of the school.[40]

In conclusion, *Rowland* is reality in some communities, but not all. It is best to think strategically and consult with an attorney before coming out if you are in a more repressive community. The outlook is likely more bright in communities with specific gay civil rights laws, but it is still important to think strategically.

III. State laws that affect employment rights

State laws, whether crafted by a legislature or created through judicial decisions, generally apply to both public and private employers. Thus, this discussion is equally relevant to public school employees and teachers at private institutions.

The "at-will" rule generally governs employment relationships in the private sector.[41] Crudely stated, it provides that an employer may terminate an employee for a good reason, a bad reason, or no reason at all. There are several critical exceptions to this law, with federal and state anti-discrimination laws being the most prominent example. Nor can an employer terminate an employee in violation of a contract. In some areas of the country, terminations that are "wrongful" or contrary to "public policy" are also forbidden. Finally, labor laws and union contracts, discussed in more detail in section IV, also limit an employer's discretion to hire and fire at will.

A. Anti-Discrimination Laws

Anti-discrimination laws provide that an employee may not be terminated or treated differently from other similarly situated employees solely because of a characteristic like race, religion, or sexual orientation. No person is entitled to a job simply because she is African-American, or Catholic, or lesbian, or all three. Nor can an individual be deprived of a job solely for these reasons.

The federal Civil Rights Act of 1964[42] prohibits discrimination in employment on the basis of race, color, religion, sex, and national origin. Other federal laws forbid age[43] and disability[44] discrimination. No federal law prohibits sexual orientation discrimination in federal employment.[45]

In contrast to federal laws, eight states and more than a hundred cities and counties include sexual orientation as a prohibited basis for discrimination in their employment laws.[46] These laws vary tremendously in their scope, procedure, and remedies, so it is imperative to speak with an attorney knowledgeable about local law. These laws do not provide "special rights" to gay people, but rather forbid employers from making employment decisions solely on the basis of an individual's sexual orientation. Merit, the ability to follow rules, and other job-related criteria remain legitimate bases for evaluating all employees, including lesbians, gay men, and bisexuals.

While the scope of employment nondiscrimination laws varies, they generally forbid an employer,

> because of the ... sexual orientation ... of an individual to refuse to hire or employ or to bar or to discharge from employment such individual or to discriminate against such individual in compensation or in terms, conditions or privileges of employment...[47]

This means, for example, that an individual cannot be denied a job, be terminated from a job, be denied a promotion, be paid differently,[48] receive a demotion, receive different discipline, be harassed, or otherwise be treated differently on a job simply because of sexual orientation. Some local laws also prohibit employers from "retaliating" against employees who invoke the law to complain of discrimination to their employers.[49]

Typically, anti-discrimination laws apply to both public and private employers. Usually the employer must be of a certain size: federal law requires a workplace with fifteen or more employees while state laws require fewer employees. Some laws contain explicit exclusions for certain types of employers, particularly religious employers.[50]

Virtually all of the anti-discrimination laws require the individual aggrieved to file a complaint with a state or local administrative agency within a very short time of the last act of discrimination. These deadlines are strict and failure to follow through in time often forfeits any kind of legal claim. A person uncomfortable filing a complaint in his or her own name may request to file as "John Doe" or "Jane Doe" to protect his or her identity from the public. While the procedures at the agencies vary, the agencies are typically required to investigate the alleged discrimination, which includes speaking to the parties and examining relevant documents. The powers of the agencies also vary tremendously from state to state. It will always be the teacher's burden to demonstrate that the action complained about (e.g., firing, denial of promotion, harassment, unfair discipline) occurred because of sexual orientation. Upon a finding of unlawful discrimination, some can order any variety of reinstatement, back pay, emotional distress damages, interest, punitive damages (rare), and changes in employer policy and practice.

B. Common law claims

Much of the law is created by judges relying on past precedents. This "common law" varies widely from state to state. It is important, because such claims are another exception to the at-will rule, thereby permitting a teacher to challenge the legality of a harassing work environment or an unjust employment decision. Any potential claims should be evaluated with an attorney knowledgeable about local law.

A critical common law exception to the at-will rule is the fact that an employer may not lawfully terminate an employee in violation of a valid contract. Some contracts designate the term of employment or the permissible bases for discipline or discharge, either of which provisions an employer could violate. Some states permit contracts to be created orally rather than just in writing. Still other states allow handbooks, personnel manuals, and the like to form the basis of a contract. These may be especially helpful when they contain a clause forbidding discrimination on the basis of sexual orientation. Still others require the employer to deal fairly and act in good faith toward their employees.

In addition to possible contract claims, employees in some states and in some circumstances may be able to overcome the at-will rule and claim that their termination or other unjust treatment violated an important public policy of the state and thus should be redressed. These claims, too, vary widely from state to state. Some require the state legislature to have articulated the public policy that the employer allegedly violated. Others examine the totality of the circumstances on a case-by-case basis, creating new law along the way. In some states, this is a potent charge for teachers treated unjustly but who are not specifically included within the scope of anti-discrimination laws.

In sum, any number of claims are available to public and private school teachers depending on the law in your jurisdiction. See a lawyer about the feasibility of discrimination claims, contract or tort claims, wrongful termination, and any other claims that may be viable in your state.

IV. THE ROLE OF UNIONS

Employees who are unionized, whether in the public or private sector, have an additional tool to use in combatting unfair treatment on the job. Federal (and often state) laws regulate the collective bargaining process between an employer and the union as the employees' representative.[51]

A collective bargaining agreement, or union contract, may contain a nondiscrimination clause[52] or other standards defining when discipline and termination are permissible. Some provide that an employee may only be terminated for "just cause." It is difficult to imagine that one's mere status as a gay, lesbian, or bisexual person, without more, could be construed as just cause for termination.

What is more likely than a termination is the possibility that a teacher will be harassed or sexually harassed in violation of rule against such treatment. Incidents should be reported to the administration, or to whomever is designated in the contract or anti-harassment policy. Once the incidents are reported, the administration has the duty to investigate, and if warranted, to take appropriate remedial action. Administrative failure to investigate and/or remedy the situation may give rise to further contractual violations.

If an employer violates the contract standards, the employee may (and in many circumstances must) seek assistance from the union in "grieving" the personnel action as violative of a specific provision of the contract. Often the timelines for filing a grievance are short so the union should be consulted as soon as a problem arises. Typically the grievance procedure is a several-part process and can culminate in arbitration, at which an arbitrator makes a final decision in the matter, and can usually award back pay, reinstatement, and other appropriate relief.

While some may fear that their union may be hostile to them, unions have a legal duty of fair representation to all of the employees they represent, including lesbian, gay, and bisexual employees. A union that refuses to assist an employee solely because of his or her sexual orientation violates the law and gives the employee a claim against the union.

V. Conclusions and practical advice

Sometimes courts are beacons of justice illuminating principles of basic fairness; other times courts lag behind even what public opinion can tolerate. Many of the cases discussed here — admittedly grim — do not accurately reflect what would actually happen in a particular situation. Despair is not appropriate; thinking strategically is. The best thing to do before coming out at school or otherwise enjoying the First Amendment rights guaranteed by law is to speak to an attorney knowledgeable about the local legal and political landscape. Even then, for the sake of our own integrity, sometimes we take risks although enforcement of our legal rights is uncertain.

If you believe you have been or are being discriminated against, contact a lawyer immediately. These steps may also help you in recovering from the discrimination and determining whether or not you have a legal claim.

1. If you were fired, apply for unemployment. Often, employers don't bother to contest unemployment, but if they do it will give you a clue about their defenses to a discrimination claim.

2. Get emotional support, not only from friends, but also through a professional. This will both make you a better client and serve to document your distress.

3. Gather together all of the paperwork you can about your job, including contracts, offer letters, handbooks, policy and procedure manuals, and communications between you and your employer.

4. If you can do so in your state, request a copy of your personnel file. Keep it intact and keep a copy of the letter in which you requested the file. If your state only permits inspection of the file, do so and make a list of its contents.

5. Prepare a written chronology of your employment, including such information as: how you became known as gay, lesbian, or bisexual; how you feel you are being treated differently from others; and why you believe it is your sexual orientation that has caused the unjust treatment. Make sure to indicate negative comments as well as any peculiarities in the timing of the decision (a blatant example being that you come out and are "laid off" two weeks later). Keep track of where incidents occurred, exactly what was said, who witnessed the incident, when, how, and to whom you reported it, and the nature of the response. Never give a copy of your chronology or the only copy of a document (e.g., harassing letter) to the administration.

6. Avoid signing resignation letters, negative evaluations, or written warnings until you have seen an attorney.

7. If you have been fired, look for a job. You have an obligation to reduce your back-pay damages. Keep copies of letters you send out and responses received, and keep a log of telephone contacts and job interviews.

NOTES

1. The author's comments are hers alone, and do not reflect the opinions of Gay & Lesbian Advocates & Defenders. The author also wishes to thank: the GLAD staff; Sarah Wunsch, Esq., of the Civil Liberties Union of Massachusetts; former GLAD intern Margaret Brightman; Kevin Jennings for his editing; and particularly Jennifer Wriggins, Esq., for invaluable assistance and support.

2. This essay does not provide a comprehensive analysis of each state's law, nor does it in any way substitute for a particularized assessment of an actual problem by an attorney familiar with the governing local laws. Do not rely on this article as specific legal advice because the law constantly changes and is different in different places.

3. This section omits discussion of other important constitutional rights, such as the Fourth Amendment right to be free from unreasonable search and seizure. Moreover, it omits discussion of state constitutional guarantees, which in some cases are broader than federal guarantees, and similarly prevent arbitrary and capricious action by state and local governments.

4. Although rare, a private school may be considered governmental in character so that constitutional principles do apply.

5. The prohibitions on arbitrary and capricious action as applied to the state and local governments are found in the Fourteenth Amendment to the United States Constitution which states in part: "[N]or shall any State deprive any person of life, liberty, or property, without due process of law; nor deny to any person within its jurisdiction the equal protection of the laws" (U.S. Constitution, Amend. XIV).

Equal protection of the laws is not discussed here at any length because thus far it has not been a successful litigation tool for gay teachers. The equal protection clause essentially guarantees that all persons similarly situated will be treated similarly. Stated differently, it provides that any governmental classifications or distinctions must be grounded in a rational basis.

As more gay men, lesbians, and bisexuals come out, judges and courts will become more familiar with gay issues and anti-gay prejudice. Since prejudice is never a rational basis for a governmental decision, equal protection looms as a potent litigation tool for teachers and all governmental employees.

6. There is a pecking order of sorts in determining the scope of a court's decision. Cases decided by the United States Supreme Court (noted as "U.S." and "S.Ct." in these notes) are binding in every state across the country. Cases decided by

federal courts of appeal (noted as "F.2d") are binding in the federal courts within their jurisdiction. Cases decided by federal district courts (noted as "F.Supp.") are binding only in their own districts. Cases decided by a state supreme court (noted variously depending on the state) are binding only within that state. However, note that courts routinely refer to the decisions of other courts for guidance and may be persuaded by their reasoning.

7. *Norton v. Macy*, 417 F.2d 1161 (D.C. Cir. 1969).

8. *Morrison v. State Board of Education*, 82 Cal. Rptr. 175, 461 P. 2d 375 (Cal. 1969). A secondary school teacher, Mr. Morrison's teaching qualifications were revoked because of "moral unfitness" arising from limited noncriminal same-sex conduct.

9. The *Morrison* court set out the following factors to determine "unfitness to teach":

> [T]he likelihood that the conduct may have adversely affected students or fellow teachers, the degree of such adversity anticipated, the proximity or remoteness in time of the conduct, the type of teaching certificate held by the party involved, the extenuating or aggravating circumstances, if any, surrounding the conduct, the praiseworthiness or blameworthiness of the motives resulting in the conduct, and the extent to which disciplinary action may inflict an adverse impact or chilling effect upon constitutional rights of the teacher involved or other teachers. (461 P.2d at 386)

10. *Gaylord v. Tacoma School Dist. No. 10*, 559 P. 2d 1340 (Wa. 1977), *cert. denied* 434 U.S. 879 (1977).

11. Not every court is as eager as the *Gaylord* court to equate homosexuality *per se* with immorality. In *Ross v. Springfield School District*, 716 P.2d 724 (Or. 1986), the Supreme Court of Oregon rejected a teacher's discharge for immorality where the determination of immorality was based solely on a bald assertion of "community moral standards."

See also, Rowland v. Mad River Local School Dist., 730 F.2d 444 (6th Cir. 1984), *cert. denied*, 470 U.S. 1099 (1985), upholding the termination of an Ohio school guidance counselor who told school personnel she was a bisexual (discussed in section II, F).

Moreover, in 1983, the West Virginia attorney general issued a formal written opinion that a school board may dismiss lesbians and gay teachers for "immorality" (Opinions of the Attorney General of West Virginia, February 24, 1983).

Of course, conviction of serious crimes, especially sexual crimes, is a basis for a teacher's discharge. In the same vein, engaging in sexual overtures at the school can justify a termination. *But see, Board of Education v. M.*, 139 Cal. Rptr. 700, 566 P.2d 602, 603 (Cal. 1977), in which the court held that mere arrest for public homosexual conduct did not render a tenured teacher unfit to teach elementary school students.

12. *Tinker v. Des Moines Independent Community School District*, 393 U.S. 503, 89 S.Ct. 733, 736 (1969).

13. *See, Bethel School District No. 403 v. Fraser,* 478 U.S. 675, 682, 106 S.Ct. 3159, 3164 (1986).

14. *Keyishian v. Board of Regents,* 385 U.S. 589, 603, 87 S.Ct. 675, 683 (1967).

15. *See, Tinker,* 393 U.S. at 513, 89 S.Ct. at 740. In this case, where students had been suspended for wearing armbands to protest the Vietnam War, the Court ruled that students may express opinions, even controversial opinions, as long as they do not materially and substantially interfere with the discipline in or operation of the school, and do not collide with the rights of others. *Pickering v. Board of Education,* 391 U.S. 563, 88 S.Ct. 1731 (1969)(discussed in section II, D).

16. *NAACP v. Alabama ex rel. Patterson,* 357 U.S. 449, 462-63 (1958) (right of associational privacy); *Barenblatt v. United States,* 360 U.S. 109, 127, 79 S.Ct. 1081, 1093 (1959)(in HUAC-era case, individual may be forced to disclose her private associations, i.e., membership in the Communist party, when there is a compelling state interest).

17. *Shelton v. Tucker,* 364 U.S. 479, 81 S.Ct. 247, 251 (1960).

18. *Ancafora v. Board of Education,* 491 F.2d 498 (4th Cir. 1974).

19. *Pickering v. Board of Education,* 391 U.S. 563, 88 S.Ct. 1731, 1738 (1969).

20. *Ancafora,* 491 F.2d at 500-501.

21. *National Gay Task Force v. Board of Education of City of Oklahoma City,* 729 F.2d 1270 (10th Cir. 1984), *aff'd by an equally divided court,* 470 U.S. 903 (1985). This case has the distinction of being upheld by the United States Supreme Court in a 4–4 vote.

22. *National Gay Task Force,* 729 F.2d at 1274–1275. Another part of the law that provided for suspension or dismissal of teachers who engaged in public homosexual conduct (as opposed to advocacy) was upheld as valid.

23. *Keyishian,* 385 U.S. at 603, 87 S.Ct. at 683.

24. Several courts have determined that classroom activity is protected by the First Amendment, even when the activity stirs strong parental opposition: *Kingsville Independent School District v. Cooper,* 611 F.2d 1109, 1113 (5th Cir. 1980), in which a teacher's use of re-enactments to teach about post–Civil War United States history that sparked numerous student and parental protests was declared a protected activity for which the teacher could not be discharged unless "the classroom discussions 'clearly ... overbalance (his) usefulness as an instructor'"; *Keefe v. Geanakos,* 418 F.2d 359 (1st Cir. 1969), in which a teacher's discussion of the word "motherf——" in class and in the context of discussion of an *Atlantic Monthly* article on protest did not justify dismissal, despite parental protest.

 Compare, United States v. Coffeeville Consolidated School District, 513 F.2d 244, 251 (5th Cir. 1975), in which the Court found that a "single instance of bad judgment" in which a teacher allowed herself to discuss "her personal encounters with queers with her eighth grade class" was not just cause for her dismissal.

25. *Zykan v. Warsaw Community School Corp.,* 631 F.2d 1300, 1305–1306 (7th Cir. 1980)(nor can a school board fire a teacher for every random comment in the classroom).

26. *Solmitz v. Maine Administrative School District No. 59*, 495 A.2d 812, 817–818 (Me. 1985). A postscript exemplifies how court cases do not necessarily mirror the times. The same lesbian whose scheduled presence sparked such controversy in *Solmitz* was elected to the Maine state legislature in 1990, and spoke at another high school in Maine in 1992.

27. *Solmitz*, 495 A.2d at 818.

28. *Hazelwood School District v. Kuhlmeier*, 484 U.S. 260, 108 S.Ct. 562 (1988).

29. *Bethel School District No. 403 v. Fraser*, 478 U.S. 675, 106 S.Ct. 3159 (1986).

30. *Hazelwood*, 484 U.S. at 273, 108 S.Ct at 571.

31. *Bethel School District No. 403*, 478 U.S. at 685, 106 S.Ct. at 3165.

32. *Keyishian*, 385 U.S. at 603, 87 S.Ct at 683.

33. *Bethel School District No. 403*, 478 U.S. at 683, 106 S.Ct. at 3164.

34. The California State Labor Code, which protects against state interference with political activities of employees, has been interpreted to include within its reach coming out at work as gay, lesbian, or bisexual. *Gay Law Students Ass'n v. Pacific Telephone and Telegraph Co.*, 156 Cal. Rptr. 14, 595 P.2d 592, 610 (Cal. 1979). *See also*, No. 85-404, 69 Ops. Atty. Gen. Cal. 80 (1986).

35. This rule was articulated in *Connick v. Myers*, 461 U.S. 138, 103 S.Ct 1684, 1690 (1983), where, in the case of an employee who was dismissed for circulating a questionnaire soliciting complaints against her employer, no First Amendment violation was found.

36. *Van Ootegehm v. Gray*, 628 F.2d 488, 493 (5th Cir. 1980), *aff'd en banc*, 654 F.2d 304 (1981), *cert. denied*, 455 U.S.909 (1982).

37. *Van Ootegehm*, 628 F.2d at 492-493.

38. *Ancafora*, 491 F.2d at 501.

39. *Rowland*, 730 F.2d at 449.
     Although the United States Supreme Court decided not to hear this case on appeal, Justice Brennan, who did vote to hear the case, wrote,

> [D]iscrimination against homosexuals or bisexuals based solely on their sexual preference raises significant constitutional questions under both prongs of our settled equal protection analysis.... [H]omosexuals have historically been the object of pernicious and sustained hostility, and it is fair to say that discrimination against homosexuals is "likely ... to reflect deep-seated prejudice rather than ... rationality. (470 U.S. at 1014)

40. *Rowland* represents the ultimate double standard. It is unimaginable that a school would discharge an employee for stating his or her intentions to marry, for example, or disclosing a heterosexual dating relationship.

41. Bear in mind that employment at will does not apply to governmental employers.

42. Title VII of the 1964 Act governs employment. 42 United States Code, sec. 2000e et seq.

43. The Age Discrimination in Employment Act is found at 29 United States Code sec. 621.

44. The employment provisions of the Americans with Disabilities Act are found at 42 United States Code sec. 12111. The Rehabilitation Act of 1973, which applies to programs that receive federal funding, is found at 29 United States Code section 791.

45. The federal civil service guidelines have been interpreted to prohibit sexual orientation discrimination. Several federal executive agencies, including the Departments of Justice and Health and Human Services, have issued executive orders forbidding sexual orientation discrimination in employment.

46. An invaluable publication entitled *Gay and Lesbian Rights in the U.S.* lists the jurisdictions with anti-discrimination laws. It is available free of charge from the National Gay & Lesbian Task Force Policy Institute, 1734 14th Street, N.W., Washington, D.C. 20009, or by calling (202) 332-6483.

47. Massachusetts General Laws, chapter 151B, section 4(1).

48. It is doubtful that a court interpreting a gay civil rights law would permit an employer to pay a heterosexual employee a greater *salary* than a gay, lesbian, or bisexual employee who was otherwise equal to the heterosexual employee. However, in the area of employee *benefits*, which are technically part of an employee's compensation, such discrimination is rampant. Typically, this discrimination arises with health insurance, where an employer may pay for or otherwise provide a "family" health plan to married heterosexual employees but not to the families of gay, lesbian, and bisexual employees. Since lesbians and gay men are not permitted to marry, this is sexual orientation and/or marital status discrimination. For an analysis of the discriminatory impact of public retirement systems, *see* J. Wriggins, "Kinship and Marriage in the Massachusetts Public Employee Retirement Law: An Analysis of the Beneficiary Provisions and Proposals for Change," to be published in 28 *New England Law Review* (May, 1994). *See also* the federal law known as ERISA, 29 U.S.C. sec. 1132.

While a full discussion of domestic partnership is beyond the scope of this article, many public and private employers alike are beginning to extend benefits to the partners of gay and lesbian employees. *See, e.g.,* "Gay Employees Win Benefits for Partners at More Corporations," *Wall Street Journal*, March 18, 1994, at 1, col. 5.

Some of the most prominent litigation of this issue involves teachers. A case against a public employer using a city human rights ordinance was *Gay Teachers v. City of New York*, No. 46094, handled by Lambda Legal Defense and Education Fund. The case was successfully settled to allow health benefits for partners of gay and lesbian teachers. A case against a private employer using a state law (Massachusetts) to obtain equal terms and conditions of employment, is *Christine Huff v. Chapel Hill/Chauncy Hall*, MCAD No. 93-BEM-1041, pending at the Massachusetts Commission Against Discrimination. This case, handled by Gay & Lesbian Advocates & Defenders, asserts that Ms. Huff, a teacher, coach, and house parent required to live in dorm housing as part of her job, was forced to leave her job when her employer would not permit her to live with her same-sex partner in dorm housing.

Numerous resources exist on domestic partnership.

See, e.g.: Recognizing Lesbian and Gay Families: Strategies for Obtaining Domestic Partnership Benefits, available from the National Center for Lesbian Rights, 870 Market Street, Suite 570, San Francisco, CA 94102; *Domestic Partnership: Issues and Legislation,* available from Lambda at 666 Broadway, New York, NY 10012; *Legislative Briefing Series: Domestic Partnership,* available from the ACLU Lesbian and Gay Rights Project, 132 W. 43rd Street, New York, NY 10036; and M. Frank and D. Holcomb, *Pride at Work: Organizing for Lesbian and Gay Rights in Unions,* available from the Lesbian and Gay Labor Network, P.O. Box 1159, Peter Stuyvesant Station, New York, NY 10009.

49. For example, Massachusetts has an anti-retaliation provision that extends both to the individual who invokes the law and to any other person who "aided or encouraged" the complaining individual (Massachusetts General Laws chapter 151B, sec. 4A).

50. *See, e.g., Madsen v. Erwin,* 395 Mass. 715, 481 N.E.2d 1160 (1985), in which a lesbian reporter for the *Christian Science Monitor,* deemed to be an organ of the Church, could not maintain wrongful-discharge- and civil-rights-related claims in part because of the First Amendment rights of an employer to free exercise of religion).

51. The federal law governing organized labor relations for teachers (among others) is the National Labor Relations Act, as amended by the Labor Management Relations Act, and the Labor-Management Reporting and Disclosure Act. *See* 29 United States Code sec. 151–168 (1982).

52. The National Education Association is a leader in promoting teachers' civil rights and encourages its affiliates to bargain for contracts with comprehensive nondiscrimination clauses. See, e.g., NEA Resolution F-22 (July, 1990). The NEA Gay & Lesbian Caucus may be reached through the national office at 1201 Sixteenth Street, NW, Washington, D.C. 20036.

ADDITIONAL RESOURCES

Rubin and Greenhouse. *The Rights of Teachers: A Comprehensive Guide to Teachers' Rights under Today's Laws* (rev. ed.). New York: Bantam, 1984.

Editors of the Harvard Law Review. *Sexual Orientation and the Law.* Cambridge: Harvard University Press, 1990.

Hunter, N., Michaelson, S., and Stoddard, T. *The Rights of Lesbians and Gay Men: The Basic ACLU Guide to a Gay Person's Rights* (3d. ed.). Carbondale: Southern Illinois University Press, 1992.

Leonard, A. *Sexuality and the Law: An Encyclopedia of Major Legal Cases.* New York: Garland Publishing, 1993.

Rubenstein, W., ed. *Lesbians, Gay Men and the Law.* New York: New Press, 1993.

Appendix B
Gay and Lesbian Teacher Organizations

The information in this appendix is by no means complete, but is instead the result of a mail survey of groups known to the author and referrals made by those who received the initial mailing. Organizations interested in being listed in future editions of this book should write to the author in care of Alyson Publications.

National

American Federation of Teachers/National Gay and Lesbian Caucus
P.O. Box 19856
Cincinnati, OH 45219
Phone: 513-242-2491
Contact: Jan Smith, co-chair
•AFT/NGLC tries to influence local AFT affiliates to become more aware of lesbian and gay issues in schools, for both students and teachers. It also publishes a biannual newsletter.

Gay, Lesbian, and Straight Teachers Network (GLSTN)
P.O. Box 390526
Cambridge, MA 02139
Contact: Kevin Jennings, executive director
•Created in 1990, GLSTN is a national nonprofit organization that brings together gay and straight teachers from both public and private K–12 schools to accomplish two goals: first, to build support for gay and lesbian teachers; and second, to fight homophobia in schools. Its activities include: retreats for gay and lesbian educators; annual conferences on homophobia issues in schools, open to all educators; a

quarterly newsletter; and, beginning in 1995, week-long summer institutes for both students and teachers working on homophobia issues in their schools.

National Education Association Gay and Lesbian Caucus
    (NEA/GLC)
P.O. Box 3559
York, PA 17402-0559
Phone: 717-840-0903
Contact: Jim Testerman, co-chair
•As the caucus of the National Education Association, NEA/GLC serves all fifty states; Washington, D.C.; Puerto Rico; and the overseas NEA affiliate, which has members in a number of countries around the globe.

The NEA/GLC is established for the purpose of: protecting the rights and interests of gay, lesbian, and bisexual members of the Association and their supporters; promoting recognition of the rights and special needs of gay, lesbian, and bisexual students; and advancing the understanding and acceptance of gay, lesbian, and bisexual people in all areas of society.

Teachers Group: Gays and Lesbians Working in Education
P.O. Box 280346
Lakewood, CO 80228-0346
Phone: 303-232-3789
•The Teachers Group is a multiservice national organization based in Colorado offering free tutoring to youth in conjunction with a Drop-In Center sponsored by the Youth Services of the Gay and Lesbian Community Center of Colorado; training programs on gay and lesbian youth issues for professionals; monthly meetings for gays and lesbians who work in the educational system; and an informative newsletter that includes local, state, and national news pertinent to gay and lesbian educators and those who work with gay and lesbian youth as well as a comprehensive bibliography on homosexuality, homophobia, and gay and lesbian youth issues.

California

United Teachers of Los Angeles
Gay and Lesbian Issues Committee
2511 W. Third Street
Los Angeles, CA 90057
Phone: 213-368-6216
Fax: 213-487-1618
Contact: Gary Campbell, staff liaison; Carl Engelbrecht, chair
•As a standing committee of the UTLA, the bargaining unit of more than 30,000 teachers in the Los Angeles United School District, the committee recommends policy on gay and lesbian issues.

Bay Area Network of Gay and Lesbian Educators (BANGLE)
P.O. Box 460545
San Francisco, CA 94146
Phone: 415-648-8488
Fax: 415-824-3944
•BANGLE fosters support for gay and lesbian teachers through monthly meetings and social events, as well as working to make the educational system a more enriching environment for gays and lesbians. Local chapters are found in San Francisco, East Bay, South Bay, Contra Costa, and Sonoma.

Gay, Lesbian, and Bisexual Independent School Caucus
232-A Hartford St.
San Francisco, CA 94114
Phone: 415-552-4281
Contact: Paul Goetz
•A gay, lesbian, and bisexual parent and teacher group serving to support members and promote equity.

Colorado

See Teachers Group under "National" listings.

Iowa

Iowa Gay/Lesbian Educators (ILGE)
1534 Forty-seventh St.
Des Moines, IA 50311
Phone: 515-255-1684
Contact: John Lynch
•Primarily a support group, ILGE meets the third Friday of each month.

Massachusetts

GALE Network
P.O. Box 930
Amherst, MA 01004-0930
Phone: 413-253-3054
•A support group for gay, lesbian, and bisexual educators from pre-K through adult.

Gay, Lesbian, and Straight Teachers Network (GLSTN)
See "National" listings.

Michigan

Gay/Lesbian Educators Association of Michigan (GLEAM)
Box 271
Royal Oak, MI 48068
Phone: 810-755-7445
•A social and support group with monthly meetings.

New York

Lesbian and Gay Teachers Association of New York (LGTA)
P.O. Box 021052
Brooklyn, NY 11202-0023
Phone: 718-596-1864
Contact: Ronald Madson
•LGTA offers support and advocacy for lesbian, gay, and bisexual educators and students. It advocates for complete inclusion in the curriculum as well as for full benefits at the Board of Education and the

United Federation of Teachers levels, having successfully sued the city of New York for partner benefits for its members in 1993. Meetings are the first Wednesday of each month at the Lesbian and Gay Community Center.

Gay and Lesbian Educators (GALE)
Phone: 212-932-0178
Contact: Robert Schaecher
●GALE is a support group primarily for independent school personnel. It meets four to six times a year to discuss issues related to personnel policies. curriculum, youth support groups, and networking.

Ohio

Gays and Lesbians United for Education (GLUE)
P.O. Box 19856
Cincinnati, OH 45219
Phone: 513-242-2491
Contact: Jan Smith
●GLUE meets monthly, publishes a newsletter, and provides speakers for groups and classes. It also provides mutual support for gays and lesbians in education. GLUE works to raise the consciousness of educators and the general public concerning gay and lesbian issues.

About the Contributors

KIRK BELL is a high school teacher of the humanities at the Northwest School in Seattle, Washington. Kirk is also an abstract cartographic artist. Several nights per week he can be found two-steppin' across the floor of the Timberline, a gay and lesbian country-western dance bar in Seattle. On weekends, Kirk often hikes in the mountains or on the coast.

WARREN J. BLUMENFELD is coauthor (with Diane Raymond) of *Looking at Gay and Lesbian Life* (Beacon, 1988, 1993); editor of *Homophobia: How We All Pay the Price* (Beacon, 1992); author of *AIDS and Your Religious Community* (Unitarian Universalist Association Press, 1991); principal author of *Making Colleges and Universities Safe for Gay and Lesbian Students* (a report of the Massachusetts Governor's Commission on Gay and Lesbian Youth); coproducer of the documentary film *Pink Triangles*, a film study of prejudice against lesbians and gay males (Cambridge Documentary Films, 1982); and associate editor of *Empathy*, a biannual journal for people working to end oppression on the basis of sexual identities. In addition, he facilitates diversity workshops for educational, business, religious, and community organizations. In 1971, he founded the National Gay Students Center of the National Student Association, Washington, D.C. Today, this organization exists as the Lesbian, Gay, and Bisexual Student Caucus of the United States Student Association.

JIM BRIDGMAN grew up in Northampton, Massachusetts, and graduated from the public high school there. He attended the University of Massachusetts at Amherst, where he received his B.A. and M.A. in Latin and Greek. For several years he taught at Quaker schools in Pennsylvania and Long Island, before returning to his hometown. Currently, he teaches Latin at Northampton High School. He also writes a daily history column for the local newspaper.

LESLIE BRTEK teaches economics and history at a high school in Santa Barbara, California. She serves on a youth planning committee and the speakers bureau for the local gay and lesbian resource center. She loves the ocean, the gym, her cats, and, most especially, her incomparable friends.

DAVID A. BRUTON is a native of North Carolina. He received his undergraduate and graduate degrees at the University of North Carolina at Chapel Hill and teaches English at Chapel Hill High School.

HOPE E. BURWELL continues to live on a farm with her lover in northeast Iowa. An original mother of the Lesbian Teachers Network, she teaches composition and literature at Kirkwood Community College in Cedar Rapids, where she is the founder and advisor to the only gay, lesbian, and bisexual student organization in any Iowa community college.

GARY CAMPBELL is currently a full-time staff member of United Teachers Los Angeles, the union that represents more than 32,000 Los Angeles teachers. He received his B.A. *magna cum laude* from Inter-American University of Puerto Rico while stationed there in the U.S. Air Force. He also holds two M.A. degrees (in Elementary Education and Administration) from California State University at Los Angeles. He is a graduate of the Los Angeles Unified School District, where he also taught as a bilingual mentor teacher at the elementary school level for thirteen years. He has been involved in a number of gay and lesbian education issues, cofounded the National Education Association's Gay and Lesbian Caucus, is a past chair of Gay and Lesbian Educators of Southern California, is a past chair of United Teachers Los Angeles's Stonewall Scholarship Fund, and is a commissioner on the Los Angeles Unified School District's Gay and Lesbian Commission. He and his partner of fourteen years live down the street from the same elementary school where he was once taunted as a sissy.

DAVID ELLISON is an eighth-grade teacher. Born in Ohio, he taught in Texas and Spain before moving to California. He also coaches basketball and is a "mentor teacher" for first-year teachers in his system.

SARA FORD has been an educator for twenty-one years, both as a teacher and as an administrator. Many of those years were spent in New York City, where she taught in progressive schools. She has a thirteen-year-old son, who lives in New York with his father. She is a struggling writer, trying to change her life in such a way that she can have the time for her own work.

JACQUI GRIFFIN has taught school for twelve years and was coconvener of the Gay and Lesbian Teachers and Students Association (GaLTaS) in

1992–93. She has coordinated their federally funded Youth Hotline as well.

TERI GRUENWALD teaches reading, language arts, and social studies to eighth-grade students and runs an after-school writing group for a small group of eighth-grade writers. She writes poetry and prose and has been published in *SF Poetry*, *Across the Generations*, *Connections*, and *Lesbian Connections*. Originally from New Jersey, she now lives in Oakland.

JOHN HEINEMAN graduated from the University of Nebraska with teaching endorsements in speech, theatre, and physical education. He has taught junior high and high school for over ten years. He is currently completing his master's degree from the University of Northern Iowa in communication education.

B.MICHAEL HUNTER, a.k.a. Bert Hunter, is an educator, cultural activist, and managing editor of *Sojourner: Black Gay Voices in the Age of AIDS*, published by Other Countries Press.

"RUTH IRWIN" is a Euro-American lesbian who has been teaching reading and English in public secondary schools for eighteen years. She has lived in the Midwest all her life, the last four years with her partner, Donna, and their menagerie of dogs and cats. Ruth has been active in local feminist and lesbian communities for fifteen years, and is working on a master's degree in curriculum and instruction with an emphasis on multicultural education.

KAREN KEOUGH works at Milton Academy, where she is a physical education teacher and coach for grades seven through twelve. She also teaches a Human Sexuality and Relationships course and is a faculty advisor to GASP (Gay and Straight People), Milton's Gay-Straight Alliance. In addition, Karen is also on the steering committee of GLSTN (the Gay, Lesbian, and Straight Teachers' Network) and has served as vice-president of the Division of Girls' and Women's Sports in Massachusetts in 1993 and 1994.

ARTHUR LIPKIN, Ed.D., is an instructor, and head of the Gay and Lesbian Curriculum and Staff Development Project at the Harvard Graduate School of Education. It is a center for curriculum writing and teacher training in lesbian and gay studies for grades K through twelve and a clearinghouse for anti-homophobia work in schools. Prior to coming to Harvard, he taught for twenty years at the public high school in Cambridge, Massachusetts. His course, Staff and Curriculum Development for Anti-Homophobia Education, is the first gay-themed course to be offered at the School of Education. His address is 210 Longfellow Hall, Cambridge, MA 02138.

TODD MORMAN holds a B.A. in zoology and anthropology from the University of Miami (Ohio) and studied medical anthropology at the University of North Carolina. He is taking a break from teaching while exploring other career paths. Currently, he is an openly gay cohost of a community radio talk show and works for the National AIDS Hotline.

ANNE OSBALDESTON lives and writes in Seattle, Washington. Her poem "The Question" tells a true story. She is the only openly gay or lesbian teacher at the Bertschi School.

ROBERT PARLIN lives in Cambridge, Massachusetts, and teaches history at Newton South High School in Newton, Massachusetts. He graduated from Grafton High School in 1981, received his B.A. from Harvard College in 1985, and received his M.Ed. from the Harvard Graduate School of Education in 1987. He is currently the cochair of GLSTN, the Gay, Lesbian, and Straight Teachers Network. He is also regional workshop coordinator for the Massachusetts Department of Education's Safe Schools for Gay and Lesbian Students Program. He hates to write and is amazed that he finally wrote this story.

JOHN PIKALA is in his twenty-seventh year as an educator. He has worked with seventh- through twelfth-graders as well as adult learners, from "basic skills" to "talented," in English language arts, English as a second language, and Latin. Pikala was a Fulbright Scholar at the American Academy in Rome and a student at the American School of Classical Studies at Athens; he has been named a 1994–95 Fellow in the Bush Foundation Educational Leaders' Program. Currently a teacher on special assignment, Pikala is a writing specialist for the Saint Paul Public Schools. He was born in Albany, Georgia, grew up in Minnesota, has traveled extensively, and now shares a downtown loft in the Minneapolis Warehouse District with his nine-year-old cocker spaniel, Dashiell.

TONY PRINCE is a native of Jeffersonville, Indiana. He received a B.A. in theater and drama from Indiana University in 1984 and an M.A.T. in English from the University of Louisville in 1991. He continues to teach English and drama at Waggener High School in Louisville, Kentucky, and is a part-time lecturer in gay and lesbian studies at the University of Louisville. He is the chair of the Jefferson County Teachers Association's Gay and Lesbian Caucus and is also a member of GLSTN (the Gay,

Lesbian, and Straight Teachers Network). He plans to continue his union work and to fight ever harder for the rights of gay students.

RON RITCHART has taught second grade in New Zealand as well as third and fourth grade in the United States. He has been an elementary math specialist and middle school math teacher at Graland Country Day in Denver, where he currently works half-time and consults with schools around the country to develop meaningful math programs. In 1993 he received the Presidential Award for Excellence in Mathematics Teaching at the secondary level for the state of Colorado, which allowed him to meet President Clinton in April 1994. He is the author of *Making Numbers Make Sense* (Addison-Wesley) as well as numerous other book chapters and articles.

RAYMOND SAINT PIERRE lives in New York City, where he has taught high school for eight years. He is a poet and an HIV educator who also volunteers with the Neutral Zone, a gay youth support program in the city.

REGGIE SELLARS currently teaches Spanish for middle and high schoolers at Noble and Greenough School in Dedham, Massachusetts. He received his B.A. in Spanish from Yale University and enjoys leading trips to Spanish-speaking cultures with his students. In his first two years, along with teaching, Reggie started and coached a snowboarding team at Brewster Academy in New Hampshire, and for the last two years, he has coached football and wrestling at Nobles. Reggie is on the board of the Gay, Lesbian, and Straight Teachers Network (GLSTN). In his "spare time," he conducts workshops, gives presentations on homophobia issues and works with the Massachusetts Governor's Commission on Gay and Lesbian Youth.

JAN SMITH has taught for twenty-four years. She has two grown children and coparents her partner's fourteen-year-old daughter (but no cats) in a quiet neighborhood of Cincinnati. She sings in MUSE, the Cincinnati Women's Choir, a diverse group of women who sing for peace, justice, and human rights for all people. She is the cochair of GLUE, Gays and Lesbians United for Education, and also cochair of AFT-NGLC, the American Federation of Teachers National Gay and Lesbian Caucus.

PATTY SMITH teaches French at the Pike School in Andover, Massachusetts. She lives in Cambridge with her lover, Cindy Lewis, and their two cats, Ricky and Lucy.

ERIC TEMPLE teaches English at Crystal Springs Uplands School in Hillsborough, California. He also runs workshops helping institutions to dismantle homophobia. He is currently developing a Holocaust curriculum for high school students.

STEVE WARREN is from the Mid-Hudson Valley of New York State. He received a B.A. and an M.A. from Albany State, where he was selected "Student Teacher of the Year" for 1987. He currently teaches Spanish at Horace Greeley High School in Chappaqua, New York.

BOB ZIMMERMAN is a biology teacher, currently at R.A. Taft High School in Cincinnati, Ohio. He began his teaching career as a Peace Corps volunteer in Malaysia after graduating from Cornell in 1967. He and his partner Bill share their house with two golden retrievers and an assortment of exotic birds and reptiles.

Alyson Publications publishes a wide variety of books with gay and lesbian themes. For a free catalog or to be placed on our mailing list, please write to:
Alyson Publications
40 Plympton Street
Boston, MA 02118
Indicate whether you are interested in books for gay men, lesbians, or both.